ACCLAIM FOR *REWILDING & THE ART*

"Rachel writes with a grounded integrity plant whispers and wild awakening that beckon us all. Her words are a persistent, persuasive and urgent call to action for us to act differently and embrace the spirit in all things in our animate and sentient world. This book is a poignant reminder that the time to help our planet is now and rewilding ourselves is an essential place to begin."

— FAY JOHNSTONE, author of *Plants That Speak, Spirits That Sing*

"*Rewilding & The Art Of Plant Whispering* is a fascinating and practical invitation to open yourself up to the intelligence and wisdom of nature. It provides a life-affirming exploration into our relationships with non-human beings and how we belong amongst them as a relative and an equal. An important book at this time when, more than ever, we need consciousness to evolve and a new paradigm to emerge."

— LAURA STORM, founder of Regenerators and co-author of *Regenerative Leadership*

"A book fluent with insights and personal practices that enable us to reconnect deeply with our wild essence, the essence that is the wild Soul of Gaia and of all things, through the powerful portal of plants. An inspiring and empowering pathway for us in these troubled times."

— MADDY HARLAND, co-founder and editor of *Permaculture Magazine*

"Rachel's passion and experience blaze through her writing with a determination that healing our relationship with the wild is not just a niche interest but a fundamental need of our times."

— NATHANIEL HUGHES, author of *Intuitive Herbalism* and *Weeds in the Heart*

"This is an invaluable self-help guide as we move from our conditioned separation from the natural world and re-find our path of reconnection. Rachel opens our awareness to the process of personal rewilding - the ecological restoration of the self, helping to change us from the inside, as we become aware of the sentience of plants and our interrelationship with all of life."
— GLENNIE KINDRED, author of *Walking with Trees* and many other books on Earth wisdom.

"My stomach is fluttering, my heart is opening and once again Rachel Corby, you have taken me even deeper into the wildness of my soul, reminding me that I am not separate from nature, I am a part of Gaia. It is in reading this book a wonderful sense of wonder and excitement bubbles up in me, like an old friend has just walked into the room and we have so much to share and learn from each other! I have a huge sense of hope... could it be, that as every human begins to rediscover that they are nature, that we could make powerful changes on our planet?"
— LOUISE CARRON HARRIS, author of *Awakening Of The Western Woman*, Shaman, Medicine Woman, Radio Presenter.

"We live in challenging times, and the problems we humans have caused cannot be fixed with the same mind-sets that created them. We need to '*unlearn our behaviour*', says Rachel Corby, to peel back the layers of domestication, taming, and civilisation - and begin the process of rewilding ourselves. This is a call back home, an invitation to immerse ourselves bravely and wholly, to take the plunge and 'deep dive to the wild heart of the world'.

Rewilding & the Art of Plant Whispering fills me with hope. It makes me want to take the road less travelled, to use more considerate and inclusive language when talking about (or to) non-human beings, to slow down, to 'listen', to trust my feelings, and, more than anything, to learn how to communicate with our plant relatives. Already, because of the teachings in this book, my relationships with Oak, Crab Apple, and a few other plant beings in my neighbourhood, are changing. I look forward to these relationships deepening further, and to widening my circle of more-than-human friends."
— BRIGIT STRAWBRIDGE HOWARD, bee advocate and author of *Dancing With Bees.*

Rewilding
& the art of
Plant Whispering

Rachel Corby

AMANITA FORREST PRESS

Published by Amanita Forrest Press, Stroud, UK. 2019.
Copyright © 2019 Rachel Corby

All Rights Reserved.
No part of this publication, including text or illustrations, may be reproduced, stored in a retrieval system, or transmitted, in any form or by any means, electronic, mechanical, photocopying or otherwise, without prior permission of the author, Rachel Corby, www.wildgaiansoul.com

ISBN - 9781695077065

Production of print version by Raúl López Cabello
www.itsasunnyday.com

Cover and illustrations by Wendy Milner
www.wendymilner.co.uk

Disclaimer
Any personal rewilding or plant whispering work is always deeply healing. If you are currently taking prescribed medication for depression or mental health proceed with caution. If this describes you do not attempt to work deeply, or with shamanic journey work, or with entheogens without a guide. Such medication is designed to get in the way of what you are truly feeling, and thus of the communication. As such it will be very hard to fulfil the prerequisite of allowing yourself to be vulnerable and who you truly are in that moment, as the medication is protecting you from that. However, personal rewilding and plant whispering can both be of great value to you, in fact they may be what you need most. So, if you are using the aforementioned medication it would be prudent to be guided by an experienced plant whisperer with a clinical practice. If this is something you wish for, contact me using the details given on the About The Author page and I will recommend practitioners or other possibilities.

When undertaking the exercises outlined in these pages, your wildness, your connection to the more-than-human, and the feelings and physical manifestations that arise as a result may not happen exactly as I describe them to you. We are each wired differently, living in different circumstances and faced with different opportunities.

Do not imbibe a plant that you have not positively identified first. Certain plants have the potential to be fatal.

I have written with safety in mind, but when following any exercise, or in any work with diet or entheogens, the reader should proceed with due care and caution. I in no way encourage any reader to participate in any illegal activity, and will not be held accountable for any action taken by a reader based on information presented in this book.

This book is dedicated to all the species that have been lost forever during the years it has taken me to write these words. Species lost due to the unconscious and selfish actions of humankind. May humankind come together and halt this, the sixth mass extinction event, in peace and love.

Acknowledgements

This book would never have come about if it were not for the spirits that reside alongside us and largely go unacknowledged. It is you that reached out to me, I heard your call, I have seen your world, and now I too live there. And so with deepest gratitude I thank those that initiated this: *Sphagnum spp., Psilocybe semilanceata, Passiflora incarnata, Peganum harmala, Artemisia vulgaris, Brugmansia spp. and Urtica dioica* most especially. And all those thousands and thousands that have followed with contact, many on a daily basis. I also extend much gratitude to the other rooted ones, the stone people, the water people, the creepers, crawlers, swimmers, flyers and the four leggeds. To those that have gone before, and those that are yet to come. Without you I am nothing but dust. To you this book is my love song and my prayer of gratitude.

To human friends also I extend much gratitude. Teachers and writers who have worked tirelessly to spread their similar truths – access to the other parallel waking realms. Especially those whom I have had the great opportunity to learn directly from including Eliot Cowan and Stephen Harrod Buhner.

To all the people who practice this original way of being I also extend my gratitude. And to those whom I have come across in recent times who are breathing life back into this art. I know so many beautiful souls across this planet who heard the wild call and are now reaching out with this work. I thank all of you. Equally I extend gratitude to all of those who had the faith to study with me, and those whom have returned again and again to take it deeper, take it further.

I offer many thanks to my fellow wild women, Mandy Griffiths, Josie Bailey and Kelda White, for reading through early drafts and giving your honest feedback. To my dear friends Emma Morgan and Kamaldeep Sidhu for reading and helping correct the final version. To the team at Amanita Forrest Press; to Wendy Milner for the beautiful cover art, and internal artwork; to Raúl López Cabello for designing the interior and getting the files print ready. And finally to my husband Stephen, for reminding me to eat well through the gift of your delicious food, on the numerous occasions I stayed late in my office.

Contents

I *Seed*   13
Before I Begin   14
    A Little Word About Language...   14

1. Beginnings...   16
    Wild Lineage   18
    This Journey   19
    For You   22
    The Question Of Hope   22

II *Germination*   29
2. Rewilding And Why We Need It   30
    The Degradation Of Our Wild Spaces   31
    Our Interior Wildscapes   33
    How Did We Get Here?   35
    Rewilding Land, Habitats And Ecosystems   36

3. Personal Rewilding   39
    Fall In Love   42
    Ecological Restoration Of The Self   45
    The Three Key Elements Of Personal Rewilding   50
    Knowing Self As Gaia   54
    Attention To Detail   57
    Personal Responsibility   60
    Willingness To Be Seen & To Be Vulnerable   63
    Ability To Feel   69

III *Growth*   73
4. Interspecies Communication   74
    What Is Communication?   80
    Address The Other Directly   86
    Time   88
    Trust & Agreements   91
    Clarity Of Your Question & Knowledge Of Self   93
    The Body & Its Wisdom   95

Sensory Acuity 98
The Brain 101
The Heart 102
Direct Perception 106
Intuition 107
Listening & Common Blocks To Hearing 107
Changes In You 110

IV *Flower* 115

5. The Art Of Plant Whispering 116
Why Plants? 119
So What Is Plant Whispering? 122
Plants As Medicines 125
Foraging & Nurturing 127
Motivation 130
Medicine For Others 131
Your Sacred Contract 132
Why I Don't Tell You Which Plant Is For What 132

6. Practical Ways Of Opening Up To The Wisdom Of Plants ... 139
Initiating Contact 140
Sound & Movement 141
The Value Of Comparison 143
Dedicated Plant Study 145
Dropping Deeper – Sensory Noticing 150
Plant Allies 153
Dream Work 155
Sacred Elixirs 157
Preparing The Soil 162
   The Alkaline State 163
   Cleansing & Fasting 165
Shamanic Journey 167
   How To Journey 168
   The Journey Experience 170
Plant Diets 172
   Microdosing 174
Single Plant Immersion 177
Oscillation 180
Entheogens 181
   Exotics 184

Closer To Home	185
Doorways To The Inner Realms	186
Cautions	188
Gifts & Challenges	189
Another Way Of Working With Entheogens	191
Tying It Together – The Next Level	191
Make It Your Own	193
The Possibility Of Overwhelm	196
Our Natural Way Of Being	197

v Fruit 201

7. Interpretation 202
- Benefits Of Group Work — 205
- Layers Of Meaning — 206
- Humility — 207
- Specialism — 208

8. Plant Whisperer 214
- Life As Plant Whisperer — 215
- Everything Sacred — 216
- Personal Rebalance — 217
- Empathy For All Life — 219

9. A Collaborative Future 221
- Joining The Dots — 222
- Consciousness Revolution — 226
- Live It — 226
- Wider Implications — 228
- In A Nutshell — 235
- Epilogue — 237

Notes — 238
Recommended Reading — 242
About The Author — 243
  Other Books By Rachel Corby — 243

I
Seed

*Within a seed lies everything that plant,
and all it's descendants,
will ever be.*

Before I Begin

This book is about rewilding the self, through the ancient, and largely forgotten, art of plant whispering. In a wider sense it is also about rewilding the planet.

We live on a beautiful, rich and diverse planet. It is through my wish to keep it that way, that I am inspired to share my experiences. However, we are living through a time of climate emergency. A time of extreme degradation of our valuable and unique wild spaces. Of unprecedented levels of species extinction. And of both mental and physical health crises among the human populations. I cannot separate these facts because they are intrinsically connected.

I have been guided by my plant allies to include discussion of the perilous position we as a collective have found ourselves in, because the plants find themselves in danger too. We are losing plant species alongside animal species every single day. Their future is also in the balance.

However small my slither of the bigger picture is, if I keep it to myself I am complicit. If I hold back my truth, if I water it down to allow people to feel more comfortable, then I am doing nothing more than contributing to the current consensus reality and all the extreme failings it contains. In fact I would be giving my blessing. And so you see, I have no choice.

If the words in this book upset or anger you, then please, put it down. But if you *know* there is more to life than what we are being sold, if you have glimpsed it in dreams or daydreams. If you have been drawn into other realms and are fully aware of their existence. Or if you are willing to respect the possibility and keep an open mind, then perhaps you may just want to read on...

This is the point where, in the 1999 film *The Matrix,* Orpheus offers Neo a choice: the red pill or the blue pill ~ which is it that you will take?

Remember, all I am offering is the truth, nothing more.
Orpheus to Neo in The Matrix

A Little Word About Language...

Our current language is totally inept, totally inadequate, when discussing our wild animate world. We are not linguistically equipped to deal with not calling plants (or stones, or rivers) "it".

There is no respectful pronoun that is not gender specific. "It" objectifies and separates. We need a new word that we can use to speak of a being in the natural world that engenders respect and that reflects our relatedness to them.

The solution for some may be to assign sex to the more-than-human. A plant may have an overriding feminine or masculine *feel*, but allocating a sex to a plant rarely works for me. I don't tend to experience them as he/she and even when I do they can readily shape shift from feeling like a masculine to a feminine energy or vice versa. Animals of course are different as they are distinctly he/she whereas most plants (kiwi, avocado and various others aside) are simply not, they hold both sexes within them; commonly expressing both male and female reproductive parts in a single flower. For the most part I also tend to experience a stone, a river, a mountain as either both or neither sex, sometimes again shape shifting between the two.

Let's face it, there are a growing number of humans who would prefer not to be referred to as him or her. People who would describe themselves perhaps as "non binary" or "gender non-specific" despite having been born with the sex organs that relate to one or other sex. So, imagine a plant constantly being referred to as him or her, when in actual fact it is both and neither. We need a sexless word for the third person, one that does not imply an inanimate thing, or something that is "less than".

In the meantime I try to avoid the use of "it" (or he/she) where I can. Instead, where possible, will use "the plant" or "the bird". If I am referring to a specific individual plant or animal such as Daisy or Robin I will use capitals at the beginning of the name, as you would for Lillian or Dave. When I am speaking more generally I will stick to lower case, as is commonly accepted and also the way we use the word "human". Very occasionally you will find me talking of her or she when referring to a specific plant; it will be rarely and only when I am speaking of a plant whom everyone seems to assign the same specific sex to. It is however so difficult to totally avoid the use of it/he/she; as it becomes overly repetitive using "the plant" again and again, so in places I will use these pronouns due to lack of suitable alternatives.

You will notice I use the phrase "more-than-human" widely, throughout the book. By this I simply mean any being other than human. That can refer to a mountain or a pebble as much as it can mean a kingfisher or a rose. Any life beyond humanity.

These subtle changes in use of language have been huge for me and it's still very much an ongoing process. It is a retraining and very important. I will return to language and use of words and their meaning several times in this book. Language needs to change, to evolve, to catch up with the mental jump we are making back to an animate, inclusive, reciprocal world...

1. Beginnings...

> *Under the pavement the dirt is dreaming of grass.*
> **Wendell Berry**

It is impossible to talk of rewilding without plant whispering, or plant whispering without rewilding. One without the other is simply half the story. Personal rewilding involves adopting traditional ways of being in relation with the more-than-human, while plant whispering allows the unlocking of the sacred knowledge of the plants, without grandiose ritual. The combination leads to a life lived in gratitude and grace.

We all know deep in our bones that we live as part of an animate Earth, that we are not the only living, sentient ones. We know this because we communicate with other species; our mum's cat or neighbour's dog, perhaps our rambling rose. It may be that with every step we take we are greeting someone; every leaf we forage we ask and thank perhaps.

We each have many deep relationships with other life forms; with plants, soil, stone, bird and bee. Most of them I can safely assume are lacking a great degree of consciousness for the majority of us, most of the time. We drink tea and eat spinach, we may say grace and extend gratitude to the plants (and animals) we consume, but how about all the others involved in that relationship? The bacteria in the soil, the creatures that spread the seed, the butterfly that pollinates? Our lives are fuelled, from dawn to dusk, and on through the night, with millions of such relationships. Everything we do relies on relationship, however, most of those relationships, most of the time, go unacknowledged.

This book is about bringing those relationships to consciousness and how that changes everything. Changes how we are and who we are, where we fit in the world. Changes our lonely lives into sacred acts of communion in everything we think, say and do. Changes each relationship into a co-creation. Brings awareness to the vast, constantly interweaving, relationship network that is Gaia* which means us, and all life; right here, right now.

> *Learn how to see. Realize that everything connects to everything else.*
> **Leonardo DaVinci**

---

* *My use of the term Gaia throughout this book relates to this planet and all the life on it as a self-regulating mega organism, every piece of which is connected to every other, each a part of the whole. For more information on the Gaia hypothesis I direct you to Gaia, A New Look At Life On Earth by James Lovelock, first published in 1979.*

In rediscovering these forgotten connections and their invisible presence all around at all times, you naturally shed much of your social conditioning. Wild is then reinstated as sacred mentor. Where "wild" is not menacing, not out of control with a need to be tamed, but instead an original and sacred way with the rest of the natural world. A world of innate integrity, of intuitive insight, of deep knowing and deep loving, in line with the natural universal laws and cycles of life, love, health and death.

Wild is the intrinsic, indigenous, nature of all beings.

Within contemporary culture we were not raised with this deep sense of connection instilled within us, despite being born with it. It is therefore something which we have to re-learn. Through the process of opening yourself to the wisdom of plants, it becomes inevitable that the rest will fall into place.

I am under no illusion that I am the originator of plant whispering, it is within us all. Nor do I think I am the only person who knows wild and understands what it needs to grow, what it takes to "rewild", as again we all have it within us. However, what I do have is the benefit of more than 20 years personal experience of consciously reaching out to, and communicating with, plant spirits. In addition I have been working to rewild myself throughout the whole of my adult life.

> *I was gently lulled awake. Lulled into consciousness from my fitful sleep, by the soft, moist, delicate, voice of Sphagnum, back in August, 1994. Until that point I had struggled to settle into being human in this world, it just wasn't my thing.*
>
> *The plants had always been calling to me since my earliest rememberings, only this time I didn't just stir. My attention was fully captured and I fell into an enchanted state, never to return to my restless slumbering. As I wiped the sleep from my eyes, with Sphagnum as my guide, I was directed to the wild corners of this world and I never left. Since then I have been guided this way and that but always with a plant by my side and in my heart.*
>
> *How is it that I remember when so precisely? Because you never forget the first summer that you fall in love, do you?*

I have had the privilege of being mentored by humans born to cultures where connections with the invisible realms are strong and true. People from Africa, Asia and South America whose lineages have never been broken. I have also had the honour of learning from some of the most well known contemporary teachers.

My tribal teachers did not unequivocally tell me *how* to whisper with plants. Instead they shared their personal methods and then encouraged me to seek my own, led by direct relationships with the plants themselves. To become skilled in the art of plant whispering, and to feed our wild Gaian souls, we must go to the more-than-human, we must seek teaching directly from the source, that much has become clear to me. As I revealed how I worked to an elderly Borana medicine man in Northern Kenya, he took my hands in his, looked directly in my eyes and *saw* me for the first time since we had met a week before.

Within UK culture, certainly at present, there is no real place for this work, despite the great need. You are not encouraged to keep your fae connections as you settle into your human form. In fact, you are drawn away from them, from your imagination, from your invisible "imaginary" friends. The schools in my land do not include rocks and rivers as teachers or wise elders. Modern schools, despite the great work of initiatives such as forest schooling, on the whole prepare you for the modern work place, nothing more. You are encouraged to think like a computer, so that you can sit with one as your companion all day, all night, throughout your life. This is functional but unfortunate, as it completely misses the richness of being. Rewilding yourself and living the life of plant whisperer, will redress that.

Wild Lineage

My grandmother once told me that my blood comes in part from Roma genes, a people who lived close to and roamed the land. Ate the local terroir* and medicated with it. Had animals as companions and lived by the warmth of an outdoor fire. Sheltered under wagons and blankets crafted from natural materials. But I do not know them, that kin; all I have is a romantic memory stored in my DNA.

Your blood line may be all mixed up, your ancestors moving from continent to continent, your culture a mishmash. No matter where and how far your traceable roots go, for each of us, somewhere in our family

---

* *Terroir relates to the whole of the immediate locale, incorporating soil, topography and climate. It is usually used in relation to the production of wine, however aforementioned factors contribute to the lives of all the flora and fauna present. I like to use this word because it brings the living landscape together as a whole, as of course in reality no one thing that exists within it is separate.*

line, in our blood, is a culture of animism and foraging, of living close to the land and of reciprocity with all our relations. We *all* have it. Some in more recent generations, that still live to tell stories of the old days perhaps, some in distant ones where dreams and imaginings are our connection. But we are all of Gaia, all of star dust. We are all indigenous to this planet, every one of us. So, no matter how far you are, or feel you are, from being part of an indigenous culture, once you drop your learned culture and dig deep, looking to Gaia for wild guidance and mentorship, indigenous membership of the Gaian community is open to you, to each one of us. We can all call on that ancient cellular memory to remind us of this lost art and our forgotten connection through our every act; breathing, eating, drinking; everything that keeps us alive. We all have the capacity to reignite the sacred in how we live our lives and how we relate to the other sentient beings within this energetic network that is Gaia.

This Journey

For those who are wondering why embark upon this adventure, learn this art, I will do my best to explain. The art of plant whispering has encoded within it the art of living well. Once you hear the whispers and hear them clearly you will hear wild whisperings everywhere you go, in everything you do. You will become more deeply woven into the living fabric of Gaia. The golden threads that run through you will knit you in ever more tightly with your closest wild kin. You may have Oak and Stinging Nettle as your beloveds. Perhaps you will look Badger in the eye and know you are home. You may travel through rainbows in the heart of Quartz and discover your life purpose. We each have different threads that run through us. We connect at different points with different things; and that is what makes the whole such a complex and multifaceted thing of beauty.

The work I share in this book is at the level I consider to be true plant whispering; something that can be incorporated into the very weave of you as a busy living being. You will not need to stop, just slightly alter your rhythm to open up to a whole new magical realm and for it to inhabit your all day, every day. It is not difficult, it just requires conscious attention, persistence and a desire to know. The rewards far outweigh the effort taken to receive them. There is no right way, there are no special magic words. You are doing it already without realising it. Indeed many of you are already consciously doing it and want to take it deeper.

This book is mainly a lesson in communication. We can all talk. Anyone can talk to a plant, in fact many people do. But it is refining the art of listening and being entirely clear about what it is that you're asking. It is also about developing a sense of kindredness with everything out there, everything. To be alone no longer, we have to recognise the intelligence that is all around us; we must re-enter the conversation with all beings. And for that we need to start recognising all lifeforms as being *like us*, as being people in their own right, as being our relatives.

This book is not "just" for urban dwellers or people who have never communicated with plants. Neither is it "just" for experts, they simply do not exist within our culture (although of course some humans have a much greater degree of experience in the art than others). It is for people who are as I once was, still am; inquisitive about how to deepen one's connection with the more-than-human, and how to live in more than one dimension. How to live well and with meaning.

Part of the reason I am writing this is in response to the emerging demand. More and more people are hearing the plants calling, but are unsure how to respond. Many people have approached me directly after completing a training or ceremonies with plant spirits, work that has opened something up in them, and yet left them lacking confidence in how to subsequently proceed. The fluid exchange between themselves and the plants stalled. So, this book is here to dispel some of the myth that there is only one way, or a right way.

This book can be used as a practical guide, designed to encourage you to experientially explore and develop *your* personal connection and relationship with individual plant spirits. What I have written in these pages are the ways I have learned directly from wild felt observation. And also, those I have gleaned from my human teachers and students; both of whom have gifted me with multiple lessons in how to, and how not to, communicate. We *all* learn from each other. Everyone in the end will develop their unique way as they become more fluent. For each of us, as we become more skilled, these methods will diverge and then meet again, because we are all individuals of a common species.

The methods I outline, range from those that can be relatively quick and very simple, to the more in depth, requiring a greater investment of time and persistence. Some of my methods will speak to you personally, whereas others will not. But once you have begun, once you have overcome your initial inertia, you will find your own way with wild language. The intricacies of your communication skills will develop and mature into a thing of beauty and more than that, an essential way of being, of being wild.

This book is not so much about learning techniques but instead about unlearning social conditioning and shedding layers of domestication and all the insulation from wild that they provide. As you peel back the layers of domestication you will reveal your wild vibrant living core and all its abilities. Your wise body and feeling heart, your sensory prowess, your ability to *just know*. This is what you are working to reveal and re-enliven, as you work through the pages of this book. Giving your inner world permission to stand at the front, inform and direct you. Like picking away at a scab, where this culture, this tame and domestic society, is the ugly scab and when removed the fresh raw juices of a wild abundant life will flow once again.

It is my intention to take you on a spiralling deep dive right into the wild heart of the world. To a place where you find yourself so far beyond the point where you can just take the blue pill and wake up back in consensus reality as if none of this ever happened. I hope to take you to the place where every breath becomes sacred; not just your first and your last. Every single breath all day, every day, is imbued with significance, with life, with exchange with this animate Earth. A place where every breath is a prayer. A place where your pulse is wild and erratic, where you feel, and feel, and feel some more. Where tears wear tracks on your beautiful soft smooth skin, and smiles and laughter, wear lines on that very same face. Where you breathe out and relax on a bed of Lesser Celandine and Violets and talk to the Nettles all day long. Where every moment of every day counts. Where you are driven by compassion and where your thoughts are formed by felt experience and wild Gaian wisdom.

> *You take the blue pill, the story ends. You wake up in your bed and believe whatever you want to believe. You take the red pill, you stay in wonderland, and I show you how deep the rabbit hole goes.*
> **Morpheus to Neo in The Matrix**

I don't doubt that there are many things that you know that I do not; methods and techniques you use daily with great effect that have passed me by. So this book is not a closed list, not a complete compendium of how to rewild yourself through plant whispering. There are no doubt as many access points, ways in, connections, as there are stars in the sky. This is a collection of what has worked for me.

Personally I know that I am just at the beginning of this journey, despite being decades in already, because I know there is so, so, much more to learn. As time accelerates those things that took me years to understand will no doubt pop into mass consciousness. In the meantime this book is about what I know, what the plants, stones, and waters have told me, and guided me to share. It is my hope that you will find a use for this information on your own rewilding journey.

For You
The art of plant whispering is here for everybody. It is for you, if on workshops and retreats you participated in ceremony and ritual that opened the doors to this other world, but you currently lack the skills to draw it consciously into your every day. It is for you if you have read books and are captivated and curious. It is for you if you can hear the wild whispers but don't quite know how to respond. It is also for you if you are completely new to the concept. This is for you whoever you are, wherever you stand; to embolden and empower you. So that you may find your own path to the wildness that runs through you, through us all, back to source, to Gaia, to your connection with all that is. It is time to get this information out there, it belongs to everybody. You don't need to be involved in shamanic studies or be an herbalist; this information, the ways in which we can connect and communicate with other species, are part of our intrinsic nature.

The combination of our culture, associated acceptable behaviours and isolated lifestyles have helped us allow our inter-species communication skills to atrophy. But it *is* our nature and so we can *all* do it. The more time you invest the more accomplished you become, the more immersed you become, the more you understand without having to work to interpret it, the more it becomes first nature. It becomes a way of being. And when that occurs, you will realise that the wild has begun to reclaim you.

You are an incredible being living in a very important time. Everything you think, say, and do, matters. The plants are calling to you in the breeze and in your dreams. It is time to wake up and remember yourself as one of them and stand awakened amongst all your relations. And for the now, to help to be their voice – until all of our human relations can hear them again. Time is short, our journey ahead long. We must begin...

> *Nature is not mute; it is man who is deaf.*
> **Terence McKenna**

The Question Of Hope
Before I proceed, there is one subject that I wish to address, hope. This is because the beginning of the next chapter, the degradation of our wild spaces, is pretty heavy going by its nature. It is also because, as even our governments are beginning to acknowledge, we are in the midst of a climate emergency. In the light of which, when discussing rewilding either of oneself, or the landscape, hope has become a question that cannot be ignored.

My peer group is not unique. Within it I have known quite a few struggle with addiction. Sadly a small handful of them lost their struggle along the way. I also know of people that consciously have taken their own life, both those that were my age or older and from younger generations, people who were in their teens or early twenties.

Then there are the secret sufferers. Those on medication for anxiety and depression. You don't necessarily know who these ones are because unless you are very close it is not something that is often openly shared. But again I do know a handful of my peers on such medication, some have been on them for the long haul; a decade or more. I also know a few in the younger generations that are on such medication, the teenage offspring of my friends. They are still children but they are suffering so badly that it is deemed the best option for them, a desperate attempt to prevent them from following their peers who chose to put themselves in the grave.

This is deadly serious, quite literally. There is such deep, deep dissociation and unhappiness, and that is exactly what this work, what personal rewilding and the art of plant whispering, can address. I know first hand because it has done so in me.

It is no secret that humanity is currently committing mass suicide and has been for decades. Anyone who was at school in the UK during the 1980's, or since, will have been taught of the effects that our collective lifestyles are having on the wider natural world. I was taught of acid rain, the hole in the ozone layer, and the "greenhouse effect" more than thirty years ago. But it is only now that we are really beginning to absolutely understand the extent of the degradation our collective actions have caused. Each day it seems there is another deeply worrying report of devastation and loss, circulating around the world's media. This reporting has accelerated hugely since I began writing this book, to the extent that it seems to be on everybody's lips all of the time. This, strange as it seems, is a wonderful thing, because until the extent of the damage is accepted, and we claim full responsibility for it, we cannot hope to redress it.

As information is drip feeding in, the need for change is becoming apparent. Small changes in the way we consume, what we consume and how we choose to live our lives are already slowly beginning to happen, but this is still fringe. Despite all the access to information that anyone who grew up with the kind of Northern European privileges I did, has had lifelong access to. Even so, when the tipping point is reached change can occur very, very quickly. But our main issues as a collective, and their solutions, are still far from hitting mainstream.

Perhaps because of this, at some point my mantra became *there is no hope*. I felt overwhelmed by the extent of general dissociation from our wild roots and the consequential exploitation of this wild planet, humanity has wrought. I cannot pinpoint where or when it snuck in for me, but at some point everything changed, forever. I know that it does so with each passing moment, that is the nature of life. And yet something more, something overriding, an invisible change occurred after which hope seemed to leach from the very fabric of feeling. A barrier was breached that perhaps had never been breached before and a subtle shift took place in my hopes and dreams.

It was not just me. A wave of hopelessness started to draw the solidity of life on the planet from under our feet, grain by grain as if we were all standing on a shoreline and an incoming tsunami was drawing all the water and wet sand inwards to feed its voracious appetite. Eventually, and inevitably, it will release all that it has absorbed in an explosive few moments after which the world will be reeling. Life will never be as it was. As time passes the new lives will never know what went before, that will be the stuff of story and legend; as the misty swirls of Avalon and Arthur and watery wisps of Atlantis and Lemuria are to us.

The remoulded Earth will take new form and with every passing moment life will continue to change. But still, at this moment, while standing side by side, with the grains of sand being dragged backwards into the black hole of unknown consequences most people have chosen to look elsewhere. Some hide from humanity and live the low impact life of a hermit in the mountains or jungle. Others attempt to ignore the obvious by filling their lives with distractions.

> *When a person can't find a deep sense of meaning, they distract themselves with pleasure.*
>
> **Viktor Frankl**

Distractions take many forms and include watching TV, engaging with endless social media, eating heavily processed foods and taking drugs that numb, that free from this uneasy feeling that something is not right.

> *Isn't there supposed to be more to life than this? If not, what exactly is the point?*

Each time a sleepy head stirs and raises a question they are cunningly distracted by a new model car, a new shopping mall, another 24 channels. Or simply drugged to a new level with higher quantities of food additives, and chemicals from agriculture and industry infiltrating the drinking water. Many people try to turn their back on this feeling, this intuition.

Something is not right, it's not right.

To help bury it, they numbly graze onwards through the vast array of life's tranquillizers.

Forget you are an animal. Don't trust what you feel. If you can't buy it it has no value.

And all the time there is a part of me screaming...

Despite what we know, the current paradigm still maintains that we are the only ones truly living and feeling in an otherwise dead, or at least spirit and soul-less, world. The lonely, empty, hopeless, helpless, feelings this paradigm generates are what people gorge on distractions specifically not to feel. So they can trudge on regardless, despite the nagging, worrying, deep loneliness; the empty stranded hopeless feeling we have created for ourselves. People busy themselves, overstuffing their bodies and souls with distractions and medications, to mask the emptiness.

Once you pay attention, once you really notice and *feel* into what we have done, it is so painful – who wouldn't want to take that away? Why not tranquillize yourself? However, the only effective way of removing the pain is to treat the cause, not the symptoms. And that requires changing our attitude, our behaviour and way of life, nothing less than a complete paradigm change. Anything else can only deliver temporary relief – which is why the next distraction is always required and embraced, no matter what form it is presented in. Seeing the full extent of the mess we have created and how we hold ourselves separate from that, is the first step in connecting the dots and subsequently doing something positive about it.

Of course, I acknowledge that we are all at different stages and I respect that. But for those of us who can hear the screams of the hedgerow, or are concerned by the melting ice caps, or Pacific floating plastic island, we have to act. To turn the tide of hope we must share what we know and trust that, in so doing, we will turn a few more on to this beautiful animate planet, to Gaian intelligence and the call of the wild.

If you hear a call, feel uneasy in your skin, know there is more to life than this. And if you are ready to leave behind how you are currently living, the way you always thought was right. And if that uneasy feeling is more than a niggle, but a pull, an unstoppable urge, an itch that just needs to be scratched. Then you are ready, you are ready to open to the overwhelming flow that is interspecies communication. It is not just the learning of a new skill, something to add to your résumé, something you can feel good in the knowledge that you have "done". As you immerse yourself in the art of interspecies communication you will slowly find yourself losing control over your domesticated ways as the fabric of the life you have known begins to become unstitched at the edges. Until one day you look around and no longer see your old life at all, the veil has been rent and real life in all its multisensory dimensions has begun.

So is there hope? I know that saying "there is no hope" is disempowering. It stops us trying to change or seeing the point in change, especially if it may be uncomfortable. It is as if someone somewhere has an agenda to keep things that way, keep the masses disempowered and lacking a positive vision for the future. Only we can change that. Even then it may not be enough, or happen fast enough, to halt planetary shifts that will cause unimaginable happenings. But we do not know the power that we individually, or as a collective, are party to unless we try to access it. We are all just energy after all and no matter what the history books say I find it rather incredulous to believe that it took one thousand men with ropes and rollers one thousand years to build the Giza pyramids (or whatever fantastical numbers are claimed) with such precise alignment to celestial bodies. I believe it was because perhaps we had access to the unknown abilities that lie buried within...

The "no hope" option is not for Gaia as a whole, anyway. It is for humanity, specifically. And, of course, the many other species that get swept along in our appetite for destruction. Gaia will do what it takes to maintain dynamic balance, even if that means ejecting the odd species here or there along the way; that is the painful truth.

We need a complete redesign of how we live for there to be significant hope for the continuation of human life within the Gaian matrix. Our behaviour proves that we have fallen out of love with life. Even with our children, with *all* future generations. Otherwise we simply could not behave the way that we do. The way we fill children's lives with throw away plastic (except of course we all know that there is no "away"). And drive them the half mile to school, pumping toxic fumes into the air (that they breathe) as we go. These actions, alongside many others, destroy any chance that those children have of a happy, healthy future. And yet all the while we claim that we love them...

This is not about powerlessness. *This is about having power.* Having the power of choice in everything that you think, say and do. Everything. *You have the choice.* And when you have allies in the non-human world, they help guide you to making the right choices. Choices that benefit life, not quash it, not diminish it, but encourage, nurture and grow it.

We have to be able to let go of hopes for self and humanity, because change will come, and it will be huge. The direction and ends of that change, of course no one knows. No one knows what we will be left with. So we each have to go forward with love as the driving force, with no attachment to the end point.

If I truly felt there was no hope whatsoever, I would retreat somewhere wild and lay back in my hammock and relax through the end of days, hiding away from the mess of humanity. But something is changing, something is turning; it could be that we are entering an era of hope. So this is my contribution towards what I believe we need, to allow for a more sustainable, inclusive future. For the love of Gaia.

> *There is such a thing as being too late. This is no time for apathy or complacency. This is a time for vigorous and positive action.*
> **Martin Luther King, Jr.**

II
Germination

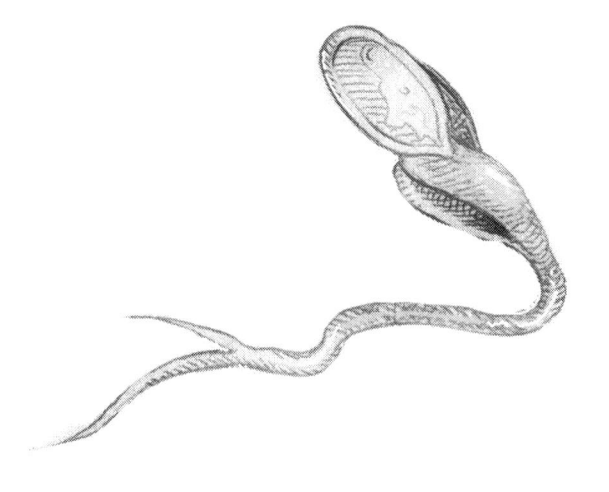

*When the conditions are right, the seed
transmutes from dormant to active.
Roots are sent deep into the earth seeking
nutrition and a firm anchor, a base
of operations from which to grow.*

2. Rewilding And Why We Need It

Wildness is the state of complete awareness
                                                Gary Snyder

Wildness exists in the tiniest pockets. Although often heavily disguised, it in fact exists everywhere, certainly within each one of us and within each and every living being. *Wilderness* is what happens when that wildness is unrestrained, when that wildness has the opportunity to run free and live to its potential. Wilderness is more than scarce here in the UK, whereas wildness is everywhere if you know where to look. This book is about finding wild in the most domesticated and unlikely of places, and allowing it the opportunity to run free, to meet its potential.

I grew up in a small commuter belt town, just 10 minutes from London Luton airport. I could have come from an even more wilderness deprived inner city, so this is not about poor me. But even so, I think it is fair to say that I have come from a wilderness-poor environment. I currently live in a small town surrounded by green, rolling hills. The wild here exists as tiny unkempt pockets, areas that have been forgotten or overlooked, as more or less everywhere is managed, farmed, inhabited. There are riverside walks and nature reserves, lakes and woodlands but each of these tantalising wildnesses are so limited in size and scope they become nothing more than a tease. And so very often when visiting to seek personal wild connection, to seek solace from the modern world, it is most likely that you will find these sanctuaries overwhelmed with other humans seeking the very same thing.

As it stands, even the pockets of wild we *do* have are floundering. As such, sometimes the little wild around us is just not enough, sometimes we hunger for deep, unrestrained wild. Too long without it and I personally begin to feel caged and the ragged, doubt-filled edges of my mind take hold. Then I know I need a wilderness top up.

To reach deeper and wilder, to find true wilderness, I must go further than legs or pedals alone allow me. I do not have the opportunity for a frequent deep dive to draw upon as I would if I lived in a country where great expanses of wilderness still exist. But historically, I have visited, and so I know that there are such places. I have roamed and wild camped in the forests of Transylvania amongst wolves and bears, in the high altitude desert of New Mexico amongst coyote and javelina, and in the dripping jungles of Guatemala where the screeches of howler monkey and shadow of jaguar kept me from sleep.

If you ever find yourself in a place where there is barely any particulate pollution, light pollution, humidity, dust or cloud, look to the point where the land meets the sky. Watch the stars set one by one as the Earth turns and they disappear below the far horizon. Lay down on the Earth and watch as it unfolds. This is pretty epic stuff. This is the kind of wilderness I yearn for. The question is how do we bring it home? How do we draw such moments of wildness and awe into our day to day?

Really the only way to remedy this situation is to support and protect and expand any patch of wild you have access to, even the most tiny ones. It is a necessity to find wildness where you live, in your garden or the local park, along the canal side or hedgerows that line the farmer's fields. Perhaps our lack of wilderness is exactly why we English love our gardens so (those of us fortunate enough to have them). Because within our gardens we find our connect with the more-than-human, and with the spirit of place. Our gardens become our wild sanctuary. Encourage the wildness to thrive around you, because that is exactly what you have access to every day. By encouraging our local wild to thrive it will grow and strengthen. As our lives change and we invite the wild back in, who knows what possibilities lie before us.

The Degradation Of Our Wild Spaces

> *By taking away one plant you take away a whole world view.*
> **Linda Black Elk**

More and more I feel suffocated, like I can't quite get enough air. It is not getting better, it is getting worse. Places I know and love where little undisturbed pockets of wild paradise once existed are being discovered, depleted, developed and in turn are becoming barren and tame. Wild places are disappearing[1]. Of course there are secret pockets. Streams and leafy valleys, cliffy crags and shingle strewn beaches. There are still places where the wild flows unabated; but such places are pretty rare, and becoming more so.

In the UK around 70% of land is farmed[2], a further 10.6% is built upon[3]. That leaves a little under 20%. Woodland accounts for 13% of this remaining land[4] some of which is coniferous monoculture plantations, only around 3% being wild ancient woodland. So we do have non urban, non agricultural spaces; but most of our land is managed, manicured and domesticated to some degree or another.

But what are the implications of losing our wild spaces? Let's not kid ourselves with the extent of this loss; human activities are driving what is becoming recognised as the sixth mass extinction event in the Earth's history. A mass extinction event is exactly how it sounds, a catastrophic decline in wild species across the board. Since 1989 a German study has noted a 76% fall in insects. This has not happened in isolation and has led to a drop in those that feed on said insects, which amongst other creatures of course includes birds. The number of birds populating Britain's farmlands have dropped by more than 50% since the 1970s, a separate UK based report found. Everything is connected, every loss and decline will have an impact on some other population somewhere along the line[5].

To get things in perspective here, consider for a moment the number of species we are losing globally on an annual basis, not just a lowering in the populations of species that remain, but those we are losing for good. No, let's back track here; let's look at how many plant, animal, bird and insect species we are losing worldwide on a *daily* basis. It is estimated that this figure lies somewhere between 150-200 *every 24 hours*[6]. Think more closely still; that means that in the last hour between six and eight species have gone, ended, vanished, will be no more. Yeah, that's like a punch in the stomach right?

What does it mean losing all of those species? All of those unique traits and characteristics that each species evolved to possess before it was snuffed out? Each species with its distinct behaviours and physique. All of the relationships each of those species shared with the other lives they came in to contact with. The reciprocity. And so, with each loss, a direct impact on the other lives that benefited from their presence. All of these elements that make up the individual, combine to be its unique experience and contribution to life. Each of which hold a teaching about life, from that one unique perspective. With each species that we lose, and the loss of everything it was to be that unique being, as Linda Black Elk so eloquently stated, "we lose a whole world view". Gone.

This goes beyond the simple thoughts that are now tumbling through my mind of reduced diversity, and loss of species we never even knew. Something much greater; if you can entertain the possibility of each species as sentient, as intelligent, does that not then equate to losing global, planetary, Gaian intelligence?[7] The consequences of which, with no doubt, lead to a less diverse, less resilient and less intelligent whole. A form of brain death, loss of personality, creativity and capability. With every species we lose, the damage to the collective Gaian brain deepens. Really heavy stuff, I'm sure you'll agree.

Any decline in plant, animal or insect species is not just a reflection of declining wild spaces, but also of the way in which we are treating the lands we have tamed and how we live on them. I don't need to go any further; there are many places where you can read depressing statistics about our dwindling planetary wild and desecration of that which remains.

Our Interior Wildscapes

The personal implications for each of us, of the loss of species and wild spaces, are clearly immense. One of which is that, the more urban and sanitised our lifestyles become, the more "civilised", the greater the chances of becoming allergic to the world within which we live. We are becoming allergic to our sanitised world. In the 1950s only 1% or less of people suffered from allergies. By the 1980s this had increased tenfold to around 10%. Currently in the UK Between 25-30% of adults suffer from at least one allergy. This huge change in such a short time cannot be down to genetics and so it must, at least in part, be environmental, and evidence seems to show that this is specific to "developed" countries only. The evidence is such that if a family moved from the "developing" world to the "developed" the risk of developing an allergy increases threefold after living in the new country for just 10 years[8].

An allergic reaction is similar to an inappropriate response by the immune system, in that it is a reaction that *should* be reserved for protecting us from germs and viruses. Instead we are reacting in this heightened defensive way to pollen for example, that should by all rights be harmless. However, modern industrial agriculture grows huge quantities of the same crop at the same time in a small area releasing unnaturally large quantities of a single pollen type into the air at the same time. In addition to this scenario there are genetically altered crops. Not just what we describe as GM (genetically modified), but selectively bred plants, where various mutations or characteristics have been encouraged through generations of cross pollinating to achieve results that may have never come about had the plants just been left to their own devices. At this point I must say that the plants themselves may well have been silently directing us in this genetic transformation, so hold that thought. I will come back to that later.

An allergic reaction can be the release of histamine, which can cause itching, redness and swelling to skin. If you suffer from anaphylaxis this can also generate wheezyness and a severe drop in blood pressure. Asthma, which can be triggered by allergies, kills around three people in the UK every day[9]. People were always exposed to allergens so this great increase in numbers of people suffering allergic responses and asthma is not simply due to exposure to allergens. Something else has changed.

In our sanitised world we have fought a war against bacteria for a long time. By cleaning up our act we now have the opportunity to live a little longer perhaps, and are much less likely to die from infectious wounds and diseases than people of the industrialised nations at the beginning of the last century. The quantity and variety of bacteria we are exposed to on a daily basis has been drastically reduced since that period in time when epidemics swept through the urban slums killing the weak and vulnerable as they passed through. However it is becoming increasingly apparent that the outcome of this war on bacteria is not all good.

Bacterial diversity in the gut is key to allergies, it now seems. If your gut has a low diversity of bacteria you will have a greater chance of developing an allergy. At the same time, absence of bacteria in the lungs leads to greater mucous production in the airways, again making one more prone to allergies. Without everyday exposure to bacteria, our immune systems can overreact on contact with new bacteria.

Antibiotics destroy bacteria. Antibiotics are used to halt the proliferation of "bad" bacteria and thus, in theory, arrest infections. The problem is that they don't just target the bad bacteria, they also damage the beneficial ones, leaving us vulnerable to attack by other infections and also to long term compromised microbial health. Exposure to antibiotics early in life leads to greater chances of developing allergies later. So, if for example a baby under the age of one has received a course of antibiotics their overall chance of developing eczema is raised by 40%, while every further course of antibiotics at that crucial age will increase their risk of developing eczema by an additional 7%[10].

I truly believe bacteria are the most misunderstood life form on the planet and that the attitude that they must be annihilated, upheld towards them until recently, has almost killed us. We have historically overlooked the delicate balance necessary for good health that our symbiotic hitch-hikers are deeply involved in. Bacteria are part of our wildlife. They contribute to a healthy wild population and, although for the most part invisible, are essential to the healthy balance and flow of all life.

Habitat and species loss, our lack of access to unrestrained wild places, pollutants in the atmosphere and an unbalanced bacterial profile are together adding up. One by one we are becoming overwhelmed and, in some instances, choosing death over life. Although these reasons are not the only cause, they cannot be overlooked as a contributory factor, in the extreme choice some are making. By 2016 suicide was the eighteenth largest cause of death worldwide, accounting for 1.4% of all human deaths in that year; in other terms suicide is occurring at a rate of approximately one every 40 seconds globally[11].

We have lost our wild context. We live within urban blandscapes surrounded by rolling fields of agriculturally maintained lands. Even our "wild" uplands are sheep trimmed grasslands, present only because of animal husbandry. A wild context would make a very different people. As it is, we are removed from the cycles of day and night, sun and moon, of the contact with plants and animals. Without the morning breeze ruffling our hair, rousing us from sleepfulness, without the birdsong and babbling brook as our background music, without the tickle of the ant and caterpillar on naked flesh, we have lost multiple dimensions. No wonder we feel so unhappy and no wonder we try and find something to fill the void that the absence of wild has left within each and every one of us.

As it stands we are a threat to ourselves; we need to shape shift into something that can live well. Humanity is facing a huge mountain of problems, that much is clear. We are in danger of overwhelm. The lack of belief that anything, or enough, can change is paralysing, so let's concentrate on a solutions-based approach. What can we do to work towards a solution? Well, first we need to dig just a little deeper, to see if we can find where all of this stemmed from...

How Did We Get Here?
As Chellis Glendinning argues in her masterpiece *My Name Is Chellis And I'm In Recovery From Western Civilization*; following the change from hunter gatherer to animal husbandry and agriculture "...the human psyche came to develop and maintain itself in a state of chronic traumatic stress.".

Our condition is chronic. It has crept up on us slowly and insidiously, but it is all enveloping. And although some of us now turn to find relief, a cure even, the vast majority don't yet recognise the basic nature of what ails them. That our culture and society is so dislocated in our domesticated, tame and civilised lives that we have lost all connection with the further parts of ourselves. Our leaf covered brothers and scaly cousins, our winged relations and the very Earth itself.

It all goes back much further and deeper than Descartes it seems, and I have held him accountable for so very long! That which ails us as a species (or at least a good 90% of humanity) goes all the way back to our first efforts to shield ourselves from the world. From the winter storms and summer droughts. That time when we enclosed ourselves in sealed little boxes from which we looked out onto the land that we had tamed and begun to cultivate, and from which we now find ourselves physically separate. And so, our separation and subsequent desecration of the wild all goes back to the birth of modern agriculture. It set things in motion.

For now, we find ourselves longing for a sense of belonging, not even just among all other species but with humankind too, so effective have been our protective shields and the isolation they have caused. In the action of domesticating plants and animals for our benefit, to support our own domestication, an essential change in the relationships and bonds we had always shared with other species occurred. Agriculture, on the surface at least, is essentially enslaving wider nature for our own gain. To tame an animal, or a plant, so that you can exploit them means you simply cannot respect them as equals. Our relationships changed and eventually we stopped communicating as a matter of course with the more-than-human world.

The breakdown in communication was also a breakdown in empathy. The dissociation from the wild and natural world, the more-than-human, led to a total disconnect; which we still suffer the consequences of today, in fact never more so. It is this dissociation that allows us to wreak damage and destruction on the life support system that we rely on, the other living beings that we live alongside. This dissociation is a symptom of the chronic traumatic stress that Chellis Glendinnning was talking about. It has become a self perpetuating negative cycle - we protect ourselves with dissociation from exactly how destructive this disconnect is. This is in fact self-harm.

> *You are another me. If I do harm to you, I harm myself. If I love and respect you, I love and respect myself.*
> **Luis Valdez**

Unless a total collapse of our culture occurs, and 90% of the human population is wiped out, this land will never again be cloaked in its climatic climax community of mixed leaf woodland. To believe otherwise is pure fantasy. There are too many people here to revert to being simple woodland dwelling folk. So what then is rewilding and what is the point?

Rewilding Land, Habitats And Ecosystems

Rewilding, as it is now widely understood, refers to retuning an area of land, or habitat, to a natural, uncultivated state. Probably the most often cited example of successful rewilding comes from Yellowstone Park in the USA, and what happened as a consequence of reintroducing wolves in 1995 after a 70 year absence. Bear with me if you have heard of this miraculous transformation before, I promise it has great relevance to what needs to occur within each and every one of us.

So, as I said, wolves were re-introduced to this national park in 1995, and with plenty of monitoring over the subsequent years the widely felt impact has been accurately measured and recorded. As soon as wolves were back on the scene, the elk in the park, who until this point had been enjoying a relatively free reign of the land with few effective predators, immediately changed their behaviour. Instead of roaming widely in great herds, nibbling whatever took their fancy, they began to graze more carefully in smaller groups and in places from which they could escape with relative ease were a wolf to show up.

Within just six years the trees in those more risky grazing sites, without the nibbling elk stunting their growth, began to record heights up to four times greater than before the wolves had returned[12]. This created more habitat for small birds which began to return. It also encouraged beavers to recolonise as there were trees to fell and with which to damn up sections of river and create their lodges. In turn, this created the conditions necessary for water loving mammals, amphibians and fish to thrive. At the same time the wolves were eating some of the coyotes which meant that small mammals, rabbits and fox populations expanded. Carrion left by the wolf kills enticed birds of prey, such as eagles, to return to eat their spoils. Bears also joined in eating the left overs and in addition also benefited from the increase in berries on un-nibbled shrubs, an essential part of their diet. The banks of the river became more stable as willow grew, which duly changed the behaviour of the rivers. Another unforeseen consequence of the wolf reintroduction was that soil erosion decreased. This is the abridged version of what occurred, but you get the general picture.

> *The reintroduction of wolves to Yellowstone shows that a single species, allowed to pursue its natural behaviour, transforms almost every aspect of the ecosystem...*
> **George Monbiot**

Wolves are considered a keystone species. At the top of the food chain if you like and that is why the impact was so huge. What they set in motion was a trophic cascade, a change in all the relationships within the food chain and the associated ecology.

> *Top predators and keystone species unwittingly re-engineer the environment, even down to the composition of the soil.*
> **George Monbiot**

The behaviour of humanity has caused the taming (or un-wilding) of the landscape and ecosystem in the first place. So for any rewilding to work there has to be an agreement in place, a desire for change, and an understanding as to how it will benefit the whole. Unfortunately without these things in place comes "illegal" rewilding, where a species is reintroduced without permission or legislation in place to protect it. In the Tayside region of Scotland this happened. Beavers were reintroduced illegally, with the consequence that at least 21 beavers were shot and killed within just three years[13]. It was claimed that the beavers were causing damage to agricultural land as their behaviour caused flooding of areas that were being used for grazing. You see, unless it is a protected area, a park or a reserve, any reintroduction of species has to be understood by the humans they will impact beforehand, otherwise the humans will just do their damnedest to get them removed all over again.

It is also true that when an element is reintroduced into an unbalanced ecosystem it has the potential to do more damage to the frail and failing ecology, especially if it has no predator to keep the new population behaving as it would in a healthy ecosystem. Rewilding is a complex thing and, it seems, is most effective and beneficial if that keystone species can be identified and focussed upon as the one thing to reintroduce; as with the wolves of Yellowstone. In addition, such reintroductions preferably need to occur away from any human activities, at least initially. Changes which occur in direct relation to the reintroduced species can then be carefully monitored so that all change they bring about can be assessed. This allows for a full understanding of both the benefits and potential sacrifices human populations are subsequently likely to encounter were the reintroduction of that species to be widened to areas populated by humans and human activities.

Humanity has become a species so separate from the rest of nature that we barely venture outside, and yet that is where our relatives are. And so we have forgotten them. If you rarely visit your elderly aunt, although you know she's there and you think about her from time to time, you kind of forget about her. Then you visit, and you remember everything that she is to you. Everything that she is to the world. And you notice things about her, that she is ailing, she's not doing as well as she once was. The same is happening outside your door.

For widespread rewilding of the land, habitats and ecosystems, and for the consequential revivifying of our wild spaces, there needs to be a change in human behaviour and attitude. We need to remember our elderly aunt, we need to want her to be well. Without that we will just continue to build golf courses and pipelines; it's that simple.

3. Personal Rewilding

To merge with your destiny, you must locate, liberate, and live what is truly wild.

Bill Plotkin

Many years ago, my days used to begin with my morning mantra. On hearing my alarm clock I would repeat "fuck, fuck, fuck." One morning my boyfriend, curled up next to me, casually said "If you don't feel happy when you wake up, then perhaps you're in the wrong job." I think perhaps I was actually in the wrong life. I have returned to his casually cast words of wisdom many times in my life. Remembered, treasured and let the wisdom of his words guide me. If this rings true at all for you, it is time for a radical overhaul.

The soul is your essence and in reality it is wild, but it is cocooned, insulated, by layer upon layer of domestication, taming, "civilisation". That wild core has become hidden to us as we have become more and more disconnected. Rewilding yourself requires breaking through, layer by layer, all of the conditioning modern life has wrapped us up in; until eventually we find the wild core of ourselves – our raw, wild, naked core.

The whole of (domesticated) humanity is still dealing with the shock and trauma of being separated from our wild and natural world. Because for one it is ongoing. Modern life by its nature is traumatic. There is very little within daily routines that connects us with wild, with natural cycles, so we simply continue to reassert the separation with every activity, every action, every day.

The physical separation narrows if you live in a back-country cabin and your TV is the sky and the trees, the lake and the birds. Your transport cross country skis, kayak, bicycle, foot, barefoot. If you are outside all day every day, cook in a lean-to, and sleep in a yurt. If you go on a week long wilderness immersion each month, or go to the mountains to wild swim and wild camp every weekend. *Then* you will have the wild connection. You will know the voice of the Stream and the Kite, the Fox and the Toad, you will nibble on Bramble and Wild Rose. But, unless you were born into that lifestyle it is probable you began somewhere in a house on a street and are still peeling back layers of domestication and detoxing from this disconnected start to life.

Our separation from wild is not just physical, caused by living in brick houses in urban areas. There is also the separation caused by our relationship with technology. Technology is not inherently a bad thing, not at all. However it can, and often does, create a further separation from the wild in the world and our natural way of being. Artificial lighting and heating control, for a start, cuts us off from the natural diurnal rhythms and annual cycles. Then of course there is personal computing in its many forms, some of which are increasingly being recognised as addictive. Social media especially can flood the mind, taking over and suffocating out all else. For better or worse, technology has become more than just something we use, it has become very much a part of who we are and what we do. It has infiltrated our lives so deeply that we would be lost without it. Some will argue here, but even without the daily use of a laptop or smartphone, unless you live completely isolated, without even solar power, simply existing solely off the land upon which you live, then your life has indeed been infiltrated by technology.

> *The technological reality that now threatens to determine every aspect of our lives, infiltrate our very genes and molecules and encase the entire planet is like an addiction, completely out of control.*
> **Chellis Glendinning**

The antidote, at least on a surface level, can be simple. It is unequivocal that time spent outdoors and away from technology helps reduce our stress levels, improve our mental health and increases feelings of being part of something greater than just oneself, there is no argument. Even looking out of a window upon a natural scene, or at an image of green, of trees, mountains and vegetation, can help calm people, improve morale, speed healing, even act as pain relief. Hundreds and hundreds of studies undertaken over the last twenty years or so demonstrate this[14].

While we are sleeping each night we, at least in part, reset to our wild animal selves. We unplug from our over-thinking, waking minds. We are fed with fresh energy. We connect directly with the universal flow, no dissociation, no barriers. Yet each morning as we wipe the sleep from our eyes and open them to our domesticated surroundings, we soon forget the new lessons bestowed by Gaia during the wee dark hours. To keep this wild energy flow alive during the waking hours, there are many activities you can engage in, many of which I discussed in my previous book *Rewild Yourself: Becoming Nature*.

It can be simple and brief. Standing outside barefoot each morning for a few moments can help your body realign and help you hold on to the wild that flowed through you as you were sleeping. Taking time to notice and remember this beautiful wild world we live in, to acknowledge it, can have a profound effect on your day. Let your feet make contact with dew and moss rich grass. Wiggle out and stretch your toes as they hold the earth beneath them. And what is that earth anyway? A selection of different grasses and plants with which you are in direct contact. Below them, millions of microscopic soil organisms, tiny insects, earthworms, broken down plant matter and bedrock, pebbles and stones, all the way to the molten core. Pause to notice it all, the beauty of it. The breeze on your skin. And what is that breeze anyway? Laden with moisture from far off oceans and lakes, rivers and glaciers. Dust particles from distant deserts and mountains. And chemicals given off by the plants that you are standing by, signals and messages infused in with the gases we exhale and those we inhale. And so you step into the multifaceted world with all its possibilities as you open up to all of this life before you sip your morning tea. Give yourself even just these few precious moments each morning to become re-enchanted with the magical mystery, depth and diversity of it all.

Beginning your day with this simple five minute practice makes you ready for your sacred work – the thing you came here to do. The alternative we all know is to sling on your coat and shoes whilst eating your toast and walk on concrete to your car or the train. You never really arrive awakened into the day if this is how you begin, not fully, not enough to recognise and carry out sacred work. Just enough to continue the monotonous job of being a cog in the machine. This, the way you begin your day, is language. It is a communication between your wild body and the wild animate Earth.

Certain activities, such as collecting spring water, foraging food and medicines, and gathering firewood help to keep you awake and aware of the wild and all its beauty in your every day. Whether you have the chance to undertake such activities or not, there is always the option of a short period of time undertaking some form of deep wilderness immersion. This may be in the form of a 24 hour stretch in a nearby wild place. Where you are unlikely to be disturbed by other humans, and where you choose not to distract your body from the experience with food, or any of the encumbrances of modern life (such as a tent!). It could also take the form of a full four day, four night, vision quest style immersion; or of course anything in between.

If you venture into a deep wilderness immersion experience you will find that even after just 24 hours the impact can be quite incredible, potentially life changing. You don't have to be in a particularly remote or exotic location for this, a tiny copse, or forgotten corner of a field on a local farm, will do just fine. You may have great insights or experience a complete rearrangement of priorities. Full 96 hour vision quest style immersions, typically become turning points or wake up calls. Such is the power of time spent away from other humans and usual human engineered distractions, in a wild, or at least wildish, place.

Wilderness immersion absolutely touches your core and makes you look at yourself and your relationship with everything in a new way. But when the impact of 24 hours wild is so beneficial, what is the effect of being so cut off the rest of the time? The other 24/7/365, or proportion of that, in which we find ourselves immersed in deep domestication. Think about that for a moment...

Do you feel it inside you? How much are we weakened on a daily basis by our domestic blandscapes? It has to be the equal and opposite of a wilderness immersion. We are breaking ourselves down. I think this is where my restricted, suffocated feeling comes from. I'm not in the ideal location and conditions to thrive (like a sickly pot plant in a dark and forgotten, dingy corner).

If 24 hours spent immersed in wider nature can fill you, inspire you, grow you, change you; all of that is happening in reverse with every hour and every day we sit inside. That beautiful inspiration, flowing feeling, sense of freedom, expansion, growth, clarity that you experience during an immersion, is to a large degree shut down within our urban, domestic lives. Even if you live in a country cottage in the middle of nowhere, for every moment you spend indoors, the same is true for you. This is where the sense of being cut off and separate comes from – or should I say how it is perpetuated, as the origins of our separation, as we now know, are historic and cultural.

So, we must at least attempt to punctuate our daily lives with outdoor visits as much as possible. Whenever you get the chance, walk within wild surroundings, and let it impress itself upon you. Spend time away from other humans. Visit alone and take time to notice. And in the moments where that is not possible find other ways to feed the wildness that grows hungry inside; eat wild food, invite plants to grow inside your house and on your desk, there are many, many, ways.

But there needs to be something more than this; a deeper level...

Fall In Love

It may be a bit, or even very, controversial, but I have to say I'm getting sick of talking about "Mother Earth". *We are Earth.* We have to grow up. We have to stop acting carelessly while trusting that "mother" will protect us and rectify our mistakes. We need to step into that time of life when the roles reverse, when we turn to care for source. The paradox is that ultimately this is self-love, self-care. If you are not treating yourself to the best love, best care, you can muster, then you are not treating the Earth to it either. To truly love and care for the planet we must first start with ourselves. Love yourself like you would an ancient forest or a newborn.

One evening, several years ago, I sat alone in the slightly chilled air of late summer. I closed my eyes and slowly, slowly, began to trace the lines on my face with my fingers. The contours, the wrinkles, the rough and the smooth. I touched the places where tears had worn tracks and smiles carved deep reminders. It was like being touched tenderly by a lover for the first time.

Tears sprang up as I touched the soft sensitivity of my lips and smooth roundness of my chin. I realised *myself* as lover. For so long I had looked outside of myself for that role to be filled and yet here I was realising my gentle beauty for the first time. As I did so, I remembered the warm soft Earth, the gentle whispering breeze, the fat kiss of summer rain. It all suddenly flooded in, the connection to Gaia, myself as Gaia, and through my newly found self-love, a deeper love of Gaia.

In falling in love with myself a healing was initiated. Realisations set off a chain reaction in my being, without loving my own sweet piece of it how could I truly love Gaia? Through returning the love, and healing the broken parts of myself, I realised I was also returning the love and healing some broken and disjointed parts of Gaia ~ *there is no separation.*

Rewilding yourself, at the bottom line, is remembering self as nature, made of stardust. That is what we are, an animated piece of Earth made from stardust. It is everything we can be. Everything that all life on this planet is. Thus we are all connected, all family, all the same. The same as Daisy and Stone and Lake. Something pure and perfect. Every moment we look outside of ourselves to find that perfection we step away from our wild beauty and cause our own destruction. Every time we reject our own beauty, it is a rejection of nature, of wild.

While our societies are broken that is a reflection of Gaia, Earth, being broken. While we as individuals are damaged and broken, so is the Earth. So, the first step back to repairing our damaged Earth is to repair ourselves. The first step in rewilding our Earth is rewilding ourselves. The first step on the path of rewilding yourself is to understand the relevance and absolute importance of starting with yourself. And the first step in that is to fall in love. To fall in love with yourself over and over and over again. To accept the wounds, scars, inconsistencies and imperfections and love yourself anyway. And as you begin to do so, you will change, your behaviour will change. And as you realise you deserve the best love and care at all times, everything you do will reflect that and the Earth will heal as you do. As you use only organic and natural, the Earth will benefit.

Really, truly, there is no separation. You cannot heal Earth without starting with yourself. You cannot heal yourself without accepting and forgiving and loving what you have already got, period.

As you explore and find ways to immerse yourself in wild, even if you have no direct access to wilderness, but the wildness of a tree sheltered compost heap, a little urban wasteland, a cheeky naked midnight swim in the local fishing lake; it becomes an opportunity to learn about yourself. You will notice in these moments of wild dalliance a doorway to your soul, to the soul of Gaia, to your shadowy depths and all of your unclaimed gifts. The wild reflects your innermost self and in that is the opportunity to discover what is most unique within you and what is universal, what is shared amongst the whole of Gaia. And thus begins the homecoming, the return to the true essence of you, what you came here to do, your purpose, your healing skills, your place in service to life.

A wasteland is a land without meaning, without love. But it can also be a wild oasis where wild plants and creatures grow strong, where, with love, it can become an enchanted wilderness. Being part of it, tending it with your attention and love will help it blossom and thrive. Sit amongst that wilderness and learn from it, about it and in so doing learn something about yourself, about the wasteland civilisation has created within you and within your heart. If you tend the wasteland that you find inside with attention and love, you will thrive. It's a love affair, a life affair, a life affirming affair. Loving a scrappy waste patch will bring it back to life and bring a bit of you back to life.

In rewilding ourselves we inevitably influence our locale and that, alongside ourselves, is where we need greater resilience, diversity, richness and wildness. We each have to create our own wild sanctuary internally to compliment our external rewilding efforts. It will become a positive feedback loop if you do the work, if you let it. But how do we set it up in the first place?

Personal Rewilding is taking human back to its original form. To do that we must unlearn and let go of many behaviours that make us modern human, so that we may return, as best we can, to the original way of being. To the point where there was no separation between ourselves and other species. The separation we now perceive is what we have created and fed with our behaviours. To remove that sense of separation we have to remember other species as equals, it is that simple.

Bearing in mind the way in which we have been introduced to the world, it is no surprise that there is a fear of wild in most of us. I have felt it definitely. When you suddenly become aware of other presences that are aware of your presence, watching you even. I can be scared of tiny insects that don't even bite. These irrational fears are in part symptoms of the domesticated lifestyle; we are just so unused to sharing our space with other lifeforms that when we do, at the beginning at least, they freak us out. The question is, is it just their unfamiliarity that generates fear, or could it be that they are reflecting aspects of our own unfamiliar wild interior, and that is what is generating the fear? There is only one way to find out and that is to explore them both. Communication, integrity and honesty with self, and reaching out with communication, integrity and honesty to other.

Ecological Restoration Of The Self

Ecological, in most contexts, refers to the relations of living organisms both to each other and also to their physical surroundings. Restoration is the action of returning something to its original condition. And so, ecological restoration is the practice of renewing and repairing degraded, damaged, or destroyed ecosystems and habitats by active intervention. Ecological restoration *of the self* is the practice of returning yourself to your full potential, to everything that you can be, enjoying fully functioning relationships to other living organisms and your physical surroundings. This will require taking a journey to the depths of yourself to draw your wild out of its shadowy corners to stand restored at the centre of your being.

While we live in a world cut off from more-than-human nature we find ourselves living in a degraded state. Intuition, capacity to listen, ability to commune with other lifeforms, sensory acuity, visceral wakefulness, body wisdom and many more facets of the wild human remain undeveloped. It is our overriding intellect, consensus reality and the culture within which we find ourselves embedded, that have contributed the most to this degraded condition. Inadvertently we have turned our backs on both the wildness in the world and our own inner wildness.

Restoring your personal ecology to all that it can be, requires searching for the parts of self that you either disowned or repressed. These are collectively known as the shadow parts. To be the person you thought the world wanted to see, to behave in a socially acceptable manner, at some point you turned your back on those parts. They may at the time perhaps have seemed greedy and uncouth, or made your mum shout at you. This partial self-rejection happens to all of us during childhood and youth, even into early adulthood. We each in our own way did it to allow us to fit, as best we could, into this tame and domestic world.

Looking into the shadows can help you discover the reasons behind your reactions and behaviours. Not necessarily to solve them, to "fix" them, but to understand them and know why they are there. Once you know, you can pre-empt them, and avoid or disarm the triggers before you react. You can know more parts of yourself and understand the inner workings and thus be in control. Rigorous self-examination like this allows you to spot any games you may play – even on yourself, how you always feel guilty, or that you are always right. It requires unfolding who you are, so that rather than being in a runaway car fuelled by your own behaviour and emotions, you can see the bend in the road before you reach it and thus manage to safely navigate without yourself or anyone else getting hurt.

You may have been protecting yourself for a very long time by hiding these parts of your personality from yourself. But while those parts are still there in the shadows they are not truly hidden. They cannot be banished entirely. Unless stared in the eye and acknowledged, they will slowly eat you from the inside. Your shadow will eat you, until you look into the dark and see who's there.

Wildness is one of those parts that for all of us became shadow for purposes of societal acceptance during later childhood and adolescence. Of course it follows that to reconnect with wild, with your wild and natural skills and communication abilities, even if you leave all the rest of your forgotten parts languishing in the shadows, you will need to retrieve your wildness. But to thoroughly restore your personal ecology it will become necessary to seek out *all* of those lost pieces of yourself. The aim being to become whole, to become a person of integrity. The more whole you become, the easier it is to reconnect with your wild counterparts, with the more-than-human.

Building bridges to these lost parts will help fill you out, will improve your capacity to feel. Drawing those parts back into your being will give you more perspectives to work from, will make you more resilient and resourceful. It will help you become more honest, more authentic, really true to yourself, with nothing to hide.

You may have hidden these parts of yourself very well, for a very long time. It may require not just persistence but also an element of bravery to retrieve those parts from the forgotten dark corners of yourself, where they may have grown hungry, or angry, and most certainly have been unloved. Perhaps you will need to coax them out. Just as a heads up, standing barefoot, howling at the moon and swimming naked in wild waters, are fabulous and very enticing invitations to those wild parts of yourself, to re-emerge from the shadows.

Be vigilant for your civilized part, that it does not start bringing in safe and domesticated parameters to help keep things acceptable. Give in to the urge to crawl and roll, to explore like a child again. That was the last time your wildness flowed unrestrained through everything you thought, felt and said. Tap back in. Invite that part back. You need her/him now. We all need her/him now; more than ever.

Make space and time to explore the shadow and invite those that are lurking there back into your personalty. This may also be your first step into deep listening, not yet to beings outside of yourself, but to your innermost self. When you find the unloved shadow parts of yourself, give them energy and life. Talk to them, really work to remember why you banished them, ask them. Communicate. And when you are ready, invite them to become visible, integral, parts of your personality once more. Invite them to stay. Let them know exactly how much you need them for you to be whole, and how the world needs you to be whole - you cannot do it without them.

An example of who may be in the shadows, could be the excitable part of you. The part who at age four ran into the kitchen super hyped and excited after seeing butterflies in the garden. You tugged on your mums skirt, jumping up and down, shouting, spilling over with excitement, awe and wonder. Your mother, tired from a long and stressful day, currently occupied with cooking the family dinner, brusquely brushed your sticky fingers away and shouted at you to be quiet, to perhaps, not be so silly. Your mother was not being mean on purpose, it is just that she was busy, her head was elsewhere. But once that part of you had been told to be quiet, two, three, four, times, eventually they got it and closed down. The thing was, as they retreated into your shadows, taking their sense of awe, wonder and excitement with them, they believed that by expressing those things, love would be taken away from them (that they would be shouted at). So it may take some convincing for them to believe it is safe to re-emerge. Communicate with them. Work through the stages I suggested in the paragraph above. Eventually, once they feel safe, needed and loved, they will come back out, bringing their sense of excitement, awe and wonder with them. Their reintegration into your personality will restore you with their qualities (in this example excitement, awe and wonder).

Parts of yourself can retreat into the shadows at any age, sometimes in response to disturbing and distressing conditions. So retrieving them can be deeply emotional and involve revisiting past traumas, some that you may have buried or forgotten, often those that you never resolved or found healing for. As you can imagine this work can be extremely powerful. If you are very afraid of what lurks in the shadows, find a human guide to help you work through this process. A psychologist, a shamanic practitioner, a healer, or a sympathetic ear. If you feel you can do this by yourself I recommend it. I like to consider this work, organic soul retrieval, bringing all those parts of yourself back together. This soul retrieval becomes all the more powerful when it is *you* initiating it, *you* doing the hard work – looking at the wounds, addressing them, inviting the parts back.

Your personal wildness, your own inherent wild aspect, is an essential part of you. You do not exist without it, but as I have just described it can be deeply suppressed. However it is just like Ground Elder root – you just need to have the most tiny bit present and as soon as conditions are suitable it will begin to grow, and given a chance it will spread and spread until it takes over all available space. The integration of your wild parts is essential if you are to complete your ecological restoration of the self.

As you welcome the wild back in, you welcome back personality traits, values and perspectives that had been lost. There may be some pieces that you find hard to accept - perhaps abrupt and antisocial parts. But you are strong enough and with the life experience you have had, you can discern how to reintegrate your wildness; when those parts need to be toned down and when they can run free. Perhaps you will find yourself making agreements with your wildness to smooth social interactions and necessities. But, beware of taming this resource, this deep and true essence of yourself, because wasn't that what you did all those years ago that pushed your wildness into the shadows in the first place? It is a delicate balance, but if you trust nature, Gaia, then know that you will achieve it. Ask for mentors, for allies to help you in this process and if you pay attention, if you know how to listen, then someone will always pop up with a lesson, with wisdom for you. Be they Ash or Tansy, Stream or Stone.

Your personality as it stands will of course undergo radical changes once you make space for your wild to return. This is a one way journey – once re-encountered it is very difficult, if not impossible, to ever go back. No more uncomfortable suffocation while head in the sand and bum on the sofa. It may still very well be uncomfortable though, but for a whole host of different reasons. It is particularly horrific when you look back and realise perhaps that your childhood wasn't as happy as you thought.

It may even at times be terrifying as we peel back layers of conditioning, of cherished blindnesses, to see who we truly are, where we truly exist and how alarming the state of relations between humankind and other lifeforms has become, how it has deteriorated. But, without the element of wildness we will remain unbalanced, somewhat dislocated, fragmented and essentially incomplete. We will never become mature elders in direct communication with Gaia without it. As you consciously welcome your wild back from banishment, be open and notice the elements that reintegrate with your personality as you do so. Don't be quick to judge them as negative or wrong (why they were banished in the first place) notice the positives; strength, resourcefulness, sensitivity, compassion, alternate perspectives, clear sight.

Through reclaiming your shadow parts, restoring yourself to a state of greater integrity, more of your sacred path in this life is inevitably revealed. There are side effects to all of this, you may find yourself regaining a sense of purpose if you perhaps lost yours somewhere along the way. You may also find yourself being fired up by that thing for which you have the strongest passion, and discovering what that thing is! Such is the importance of this work, this restoration of the self, this ecological restoration of the self. You may become an ambassador for the wild. You may dance non-stop. Or make music. Or write. Your individual passion will reignite and lead you. And suddenly sitting in that call centre dealing with angry clients becomes easier as you are living a more compassionate life. Or it could be that you give up your high flying career, as you suddenly wake up to how damaging and pointless it is. No matter how, you *will* change and it will not only be you, your spirit, that benefits; but Gaia, all your relations.

As your ecological restoration progresses it becomes clear that we are not static, isolated units independent of the local landscape; of the soil and wind, the rain and plants, the bacteria and insects, the mammals and the bedrock. They all flow through us with every breath and salty tear, every bite and every movement, they inform us and shape us without our conscious acknowledgement or consent. Imagine the elevation your existence would experience were you to bring all those entities to the table and ask them how you could live best, how you could honour all of their lives through the way that you live yours? Imagine, just for a moment, long enough to feel the world opening up around you, accepting you, calling you back in to the council of all beings, the one that you turned your back upon but never actually left. And then start working back towards it. Invite it back in to your life and make a concerted effort to take your seat at that table again and again and again until you remember that that is exactly where you came from and where you belong.

Everything is in relationship. We are a product of the landscape we live embedded within, our thoughts generated by the place where we live and those that we share it with. The closer you are to other humans the more you will be formed by their thoughts, the closer you are to wilder relatives, forests and cliff backed beaches, the more the words, sounds and thoughts of tree, stone and ocean will form you. Building your connections with more-than-human nature, is then really about spending time in the latter so that you too can start "thinking like a mountain"*. However, to really reform strong wild roots, to feed that achingly hungry part of our soul, we need to do better than an occasional jaunt into wider nature, we need to embed connections with more-than-human lifeforms into every moment of every day.

Ecological restoration of the self cannot be separated from the landscape. The landscape moves through us as we move through it. Some things passing gently while others make an impact that changes everything. We are not an object with an impervious coating moving through an inert landscape on a lifeless piece of rock hurtling around the sun. We are imbued with every element, with the touch of the rain and the oxygen rich breeze, the evening chill and the midday burn. The uneven ground, the water catchment. We are the living embodiment and a beautiful Gaian expression of all of those things. Inviting all of these elements back in with your newly restored wildness creates the richness of being, the restored self realising its full potential, everything it can be. Pay attention and you will notice as life somehow takes on more dimensions and becomes filled with meaning.

The more work you do to reclaim, to restore, your wild core, the more the wholeness of Gaia will be revealed to you. Layers upon layers that you have been blind to up until this point. Having well-developed connections with non-human relations and investigating your own wildness, knowing what helps it to grow and thrive within you, is a path of sacred discovery.

> ...we discover something astonishing: nature and soul not only depend on each other but long for each other and are, in the end, of the same substance, like twins or trees sharing the same roots.
>
> **Bill Plotkin**

The Three Key Elements Of Personal Rewilding

Personal rewilding, of course, goes much wider than shadow work, than working to reclaim lost parts of yourself. As by rewilding we are seeking to reconnect not just with the wild within but the wild in the world, and essentially to feed and grow both.

---

* *A phrase first coined by Aldo Leopold*

There are three elements to personal rewilding that I consider key. Firstly, *livingness*, which means understanding the animate nature of all our relations. It means recognising sentience and intelligence, the presence of soul or spirit – the characteristics that make us alive - in *all* beings. After all, how can a world that formed us with those things, not have them as inherent in all the lives? Livingness in a sense is animism. Animism comes from the Latin word *anima* which refers to soul or spirit.

The second is *communication*, and is in effect what the rest of this book is about, so I will refrain from discussing it at length here. Suffice to say that it is essential to your rewilding, because unless you communicate with other species as a matter of course, you will find yourself to be nothing more than a lonely and isolated human; which feeds into *the great illusion*, the third of my key elements. The great illusion being what consensus reality tells humanity; that we are separate from the rest of nature. Not just separate but superior to. That we are the only ones who possess livingness – feelings, intelligence, soul, spirit. Once you understand the concept of livingness and apply it to all beings and, in addition, communicate with them as equals, the illusion is already quashed, it is that fragile. Once you have managed to overcome the anthropocentric standpoint that we are encouraged to hold, and instead hold nothing as central, all as equal, you will discover yourself to be well and truly disillusioned.

Animistic beliefs were, and are, common among indigenous peoples the world over. Animism is the belief that every place, animal, plant and natural phenomenon has awareness and feelings and can communicate directly with humans. And that there is no hierarchy, nothing is all powerful, and the world does not revolve around humanity. To me, this is a basic truth. I don't imagine that anyone these days can look at a Meerkat or a Humming bird and not see a living being. I think we can safely say that we have passed that mechanistic phase where people once believed all life, other than human, to be simply performing function; haven't we? But collectively we have yet to arrive at the place where those living beings have intelligence, feelings and sentience. And so we are yet to arrive back at the place where our ancestors once resided, the place where we engage in conscious, two way interactions, with the more-than-human world. The place where we live in a fully animate universe.

In 2009, The Treaty of Lisbon recognised animals as sentient beings (what took them so long?)! In 2017, quite incredibly, a river in New Zealand was granted the same human rights as a human being, after the local Māori tribe fought in the courts for their relative, Te Awa Tupua, the river in question[15]. In fact "rights-of-nature" legislation has been gaining ground worldwide over the last decade or so, and even became woven into the Ecuadorian constitution in 2008[16]. Increasingly, alongside all of this, on the periphery of the mainstream, I am noticing comments, reports and documentaries about the intelligence of plants. At some point it will have to break through, that they too are sentient and need to be protected from maltreatment and exploitation, that they need to be treated as relatives. Each step in this direction is a step back towards our place amongst all beings as equal. I'm not holding my breath but we are progressing, the paradigm shift is coming.

There must be *no* hierarchy and yet currently hierarchy prevails. A hierarchy where we humans are most important. Next up are large animals, down through insects to trees, down to single celled slimes, eventually at the bottom of the bunch the, wrongfully assumed, inert soil and stones. This is so old fashioned, so wrong. A cow has no more value than a whale, a whale no more value than an oak, an oak no more value than moss, moss no more value than a pebble. If you believe otherwise, turning that all around is a vital starting point on your rewilding journey.

We are all equal, all of us. Unless and until we realise that, nothing much will change. Disrespect will perhaps shunt from one species to another as we cherry pick what deserves respect and what we can exploit without honouring its life. None of us are more or less valuable than another – not another human, not a blade of grass, not a water droplet, not a grain of sand. We are all part of the whole, part of each other.

We need to breach the learned barrier that separates our human lives and spiritual presence from that of plants. At which point, we will still have to accept the soil and the rocks, as equals among us. When that happens *everything* changes.

Once you accept the livingness of the more-than-human, nothing remains inert. It allows the more-than-human to have a role too. It presents the possibility that other beings are not just victims, being manipulated, ripped from the wild and bred, exploited by humans. That in some circumstances, at least, they have directed events.

Wheat, for example, had a sentient role in its evolution, its co-evolution alongside humanity. This is an idea that Yuval Noah Harari presented in his book *Sapiens: A Brief History Of Humankind* that had me on fire. Ten thousand years ago Wheat was a simple wild grass whose natural range was the Middle East. Within a few thousand years it had spread its range to being world wide, with its companions, humans, doing the leg work. To this date it has become one of the most successful plants in the history of Earth. Across certain stretches of the planet you can travel for literally hundreds of miles without seeing a single other plant. According to Harari, the land under Wheat worldwide amounts to ten times the area covered by Britain, roughly 2.25 million km^2 [17].

During the expansion of Wheat's range, its empire, it harnessed humans to cultivate it, to fall in love with it. So much so that we changed our hunter gathering nomadic ways to being static farmers, clearing fields of any competition, animal, insect or vegetal, even rocks and stones. We built fences to protect it from hungry animals and fed it water to ease its great thirst. Wheat has direction and made choices, it worked with us. And, as you notice it was there at the beginning of our choice to separate ourselves from the rest of nature – our rift from wild.

We did not domesticate wheat. It domesticated us.
Yuval Noah Harari

Many plants have grown up alongside humanity. There are plants that specifically benefit from humans harvesting them as our actions help spread their seed, or perhaps thin them and so they don't get overcrowded and stunt their own growth as a side effect of their own success. Such circumstances demonstrate mutually beneficial relationships, some of which go way back into history. Don't overlook the fact that plants *can* love us, and need us, too.

You will have, no doubt, met plants that have shouted out to you "put me in your garden, give me space to grow". No doubt there have been others that have called out "eat me!". Once you think about it, in both of these instances there is a communication coming from the plant; it's not all coming from us (how arrogant of humanity to think so). The plants are involved in their own destiny – they are directing us, their more mobile cousins, to help in some of their quests.

For effective personal rewilding we must meet all that is wild as an equal. When you touch the bark of a tree, it means to be meeting that tree skin to skin. You are no longer *doing* something to the tree, the tree being neither inert or unconscious. It becomes the meeting of two sentient beings that both hold the capacity to feel. This, in effect, is the adoption of animism. Allowing yourself to recognise that every stone, river, plant, has spirit. To live with the knowledge that all living beings have the ability to feel and to respond.

Look for it, for the thoughts and feelings you assumed were self-generated and begin to notice where you were guided in choices and decisions by the living intelligence of plants or other beings. Once you attribute livingness to the more-than-human it really does change everything. It changes our history and our relationship with the world. Living with acknowledgement and respect for livingness and in constant communication, fully disillusioned, will change E-V-E-R-Y-T-H-I-N-G!

I don't mean it lightly when I say everything. To demonstrate, I invite you to pause for a moment. Take a deep breath. Maybe even close your eyes. And imagine, imagine a world where everyone respected and paid attention to other species. Loved them as they do their human family. Gave them space, time, respect, love. Listened to them. Imagine that world. Stay there a moment longer and really *feel* into it, into every part of it. And now, now you really know what I mean when I say that *everything* changes.

Knowing Self As Gaia

> ...in the midst of this mass technological society we inhabit, making declarations about returning to the Earth to address our human pathologies can never succeed so long as they remain mere pleas to step outside and smell the grass. Our declarations must constitute radical acts with far-flung implications for the ways we live and how we perceive ourselves as living beings.
>
> **Chellis Glendinning**

When we begin to consciously reinvigorate our innate wildness, the starting place for most people is to take every opportunity to walk barefoot or forage for wild greens. Whichever rewilding style activities you undertake, your health, physical, mental and spiritual, will improve immeasurably, that is a given.

These activities most certainly reacquaint you with wild, both outside of and within, yourself. But looking back at the Yellowstone example, this would perhaps be like reintroducing species on trophic level one of the food chain. The position occupied by species that fix solar energy, that in essence, prepare food. Such rewilding activities act to provide food and nurture for our wild souls. Important and effective, but how long do the effects of a foraging walk last, and with what level of knock on effects? What we really need to focus on is to identify and reintroduce our "wolf", our internal keystone species. The one thing that through its reintroduction will set off a trophic cascade within our being and affect everything that we are, down to the soil itself, or at least our inner version of that.

Successful personal rewilding requires a total paradigm shift. For that we must examine how we experience ourselves in relation to the rest of nature. What must happen for each and every one of us is that we begin to experience, *to know*, ourselves as Gaia. One must accept oneself as nature, with an ongoing free flow of information and energy between all species at all times, nothing more, nothing less, no separation. This is our wolf.

If you do not experience the world and all its inhabitants as animate you will miss this truth. But to see the world in a participatory way, to see it as a further part of yourself there can be no separation, no species divide. Knowing and recognising the autonomous nature of another in a stone or a river, looking for meaning and communication there, that is what we have lost and what I propose returning to...

Experiencing, knowing, yourself as Gaia is knowing yourself as a sacred realm. A universe of energy flow and exchange. A realm of biota and bacteria, fed by wild water and sunlight. It is recognising yourself as a wild sacred ecosystem that you contribute to with everything you feel, think and do. This becomes increasingly expansive as you realise the life forms that live on the outside of your skin boundary, which includes the whole of your gastro-intestinal (GI) tract*, are being exchanged with everything you touch, taste, breathe upon. Where do you end and other begin? Suddenly there is no distinct boundary.

The basis of this new paradigm has to be that we are god(dess). We are Gaia. We are the hologram, we hold all within. All that has been, and all that is yet to come. There is no separation from any of it. Full deep connection with all energy, all movement, all thought. We are each the whole, the microcosm held within the macrocosm.

It may help to visualise the building blocks that we are actually made up of, atoms. A very simplistic description would have it that everything in the universe is created from atoms (and subdivisions thereof). I have heard it described that if an atom is the size of a football stadium, the nucleus is like a fine grain of sand inside that stadium and the electrons surrounding the nucleus are like motes of dust floating in the remaining space. That structure (mainly space) we share with all other beings on the planet, with the planet itself.

Matter as such then is largely an illusion. In fact matter is really an energy interference pattern. The form of matter is created by the frequency of light/energy flowing through it. What the eye sees is an energy frequency interference pattern. Where photons (light clusters) activate photoreception in the eyes, which in turn create electrical impulses in the retinal ganglion cells which are then decoded by the neurons in the

---

* *The whole of the GI tract, from mouth to anus, is considered as being outside of the body. The reason being that it is open to the external environment at both ends, the mouth and the anus.*

brain. Smell, like sight, is based on recognising frequencies. Sound, like light, is vibration. In fact there is no matter, only vibrations. A vibration is information. Information is communicated through frequencies – higher frequencies have more energy and carry more information.

The "space" that fills the atoms, is not empty, but filled with those vibrations. Filled with a field through which billions of waves move and connect. This energetic or so called quantum field, makes it possible to be connected with everyone and everything, consciously or unconsciously and simultaneously[18]. When we interact with another, quantum entanglement occurs, and in that moment the other becomes a part of us and we become a part of them. No matter what degree of physical separation subsequently occurs, we will always remain connected within that quantum field, which means communication can be ongoing despite not being in each others presence.

To experience yourself as an individual is in fact a fallacy of the modern mind, there is really no such thing. We are all connected with our Gaia mind. Thoughts ripple through and reach all parts eventually (the hundredth monkey effect)*, one mind. Just as you can pick thoughts out of the minds of those closest to you – your mother or brother, your lover or child; you can with beings further out. It just takes a while to remind yourself how to tune back in. You are receiving messages, thoughts that just drop in from outside of yourself, all the time anyway. We are just not great at recognising them and subsequently extrapolating back from whence they originated. Thinking of yourself as separate and individual is drawing yourself back into the great illusion.

We are living within the electromagnetic field of Earth, which sits within the electromagnetic field of the galaxy, which sits within the electromagnetic field of the universe. An electromagnetic field not only affects the behaviour of that within the field, but each field extends outwards indefinitely; so everything about the universe, our galaxy and Earth is enfolded within us. I like to think of it is as if we are the villi within a GI tract, or the fingers on a hand; we each experience every encounter a little differently so that when added together all thought, all experience, all sensation, all angles are covered and the hologram is complete.

Isn't it time to acknowledge ourselves as embedded within this sentient matrix, this complex intertwining of energies, of felt sensation and thought? Can we continue to take seriously a paradigm that insists upon our separation? Upon the arrogant assumption that humankind sits separate atop the invisible hierarchy of worth?

---

* *The phenomena that a new idea or behaviour spreads rapidly once a critical mass adopts the new idea/behaviour.*

And so ask yourself, where does the plant you just ate end and you begin? Where do the mountaintops covered in snow that feed the spring that forms your water supply end and you begin? Where does the animal who breathed the same air as you just moments ago end and you begin? Where do your dust covered toes end and the Earth beneath them begin?

When you recognise yourself as Gaia, eating another for your survival is a merging of yourself and the other being. The rabbit becomes you, you become rabbit; the kale becomes you, you become kale. With this realisation each meal becomes sacred. It becomes a point of reconnection between yourself and your plant and animal relations as you combine, as you become each other. This is shape shifting in its finest form. Choose carefully what you shape shift into.

Attention To Detail

Our languaging patterns interfere with our ability to see the world for what it is. One example is the term "nature connection" which has subtly slipped into common parlance. When this happens in language we tend to accept it without thinking too deeply about what it actually means. But I invite you to do just that, to take a deeper look into what "nature connection" actually means. It implies that nature is something other than self that you need to connect with, something outside of yourself. But, remember the wolf? We *are* nature. And yet the phrase itself solidifies a separation between human and nature. Simply using the term nature connection, despite good and worthy intention, is subtly reinforcing the distance between us and "nature" and undermining self as nature. Reinforcing the great illusion.

This is a perfect case for *paying attention to detail* because if you do so, you instantly appreciate that this is a somewhat awkward phrase to use, one that does itself a disservice. I will talk about attention to detail a lot in the coming chapters because collectively we have become very bad at it. Our survival generally does not rely on it. You don't need to remember where that berry bush is lest you starve. You do not even need to remember when your next doctors appointment is as they will text you a reminder. No one pays much attention much of the time, head in the clouds, head in the phone. But it is simple; take time to notice, pay attention.

Personal rewilding has as its basis recognition of self as nature, there is no separation. With rewilding you understand your own wild truth, or are at least seeking to. Every living moment is one of nature connection, even if you are sat in solitary confinement. The connection is *already* there, it is just a matter of unlearning all the human social behaviours that have led us to believe that there is a separation. You are *always* carrying nature within you – you are nature. So to connect to nature means first and foremost to connect with your wild self.

Although I understand the well placed thoughts and thinking behind phrases such as nature connection or "take time to notice nature everyday", they actually highlight the dislocation and feeling of separation of the writer. It keeps the human as an observer. This may just seem to be a matter of semantics, but not really. It is the *meaning* in the phrase that is most important and we need to be really vigilant for turns of phrase that we are used to using, but that hold us as outsiders from the rest of the living world, a very Cartesian place to dwell. What it does sadly show, is that even people involved and encouraging others to reconnect need a radical shift in perspective, otherwise that reconnection can never be real. Even language holds us as separate, isolated from that "nature" out there. We have to breach that culturally imposed barrier between ourselves and wider nature. And yes awareness, noticing (wider nature), helps us to do that. But absolute attention to every detail includes the language we use to communicate with other humans and what the words we use actually mean.

I don't mean to denigrate those encouraging nature connection but to urge them to pay attention to every detail. Especially when the name of the activity itself undermines the intended outcome. It may sound small and petty but it is the small, the miniscule, the minutiae that make up the large, the giant, the gargantuan and the whole. Attention to the smallest detail is paramount. The smallest thing can be an imperative indicator of something; it can be a sign or a form of language that can easily be overlooked when not paying acute attention.

Simple words we habitually use to describe something in whatever area of life, can contribute to our disconnect. Think of log or beef. Now think of limb of tree, or muscle of cow. We use language to create a separation from what something actually is so that we can use it as a commodity, as opposed to realising it as the sacred body of our relation. Whether wood or meat, tree or animal, pay attention to your words and notice any that introduce that degree of separation. And how changing the words that you use would direct you to behave more respectfully with the recognition of the other sentient, animate being.

Of course, I am far from perfect, and no doubt I use words and phrases that also cause and reiterate a disconnect. I am vigilant but probably a phrase I use really gets to someone else, it happens. I have definitely made the mistake myself, prescribing spending "time alone in nature" for example, when saying "time amongst wider nature" would actually remove the separation the first phrase engenders. Notice how different this second phrase feels...

I am still working on my phraseology and the words I use, because words have power and energy, and lay invisible suggestions and meanings inside our heads. So really try to get inside a phrase to notice how it feels. Sometimes it may need to be a much longer sentence, but at least it will actually mean what you are intending to say.

In Martin Lee Mueller's book *Being Salmon Being Human*, he raises another use of language that has unintended consequences (or were they at one point intended?). The speaking of natural beings in sentences that are structured as subject – verb - object. He uses the example of "we (subject) catch (verb) fish (object)"[19]. There is only one animate being in that sentence and that is "we" doing something to the object, the clearly inanimate fish. In an animistic world, the kind of world inhabited by people who live in communion with more-than-human nature, the object becomes alive. As Mueller noted, among native North Americans, the Salmon "gift" themselves to the human. This has a very notably different feel about it. In fact it really changes the meaning altogether. The Salmon are no longer inert objects having something done to them but they are active, they have a will, and are exerting it by gifting themselves.

A Tomato gifts its fruit, so that the eater spreads the seed and the Tomato lives to the next generation. Unlike the Tomato example, you may wonder what benefit a Salmon would receive by gifting itself. *In a wild and balanced system*, where a Salmon gifts itself to Bear, the Bear then deposits waste in the woods. This waste feeds the trees with essential nutrients. Trees growing alongside streams containing Salmon grow three times faster than alongside streams that do not contain Salmon. In addition Sitka Spruce, along Salmon inhabited rivers, take only 86 years to reach a thickness of 50cm in comparison to three hundred years to reach the same diameter in areas without Salmon[20]. In return the trees feed the streams with nutrients from their fallen needles and leaves and hold the banks in place with their strong roots. It is reciprocal, each being having a role and *gifting* the others with their activity, which together keeps the whole ecosystem healthy and vibrant.

We are in such a habit of separating ourselves from more-than-human nature through expressions and language. It is going to take a lot of vigilance to start weeding these isolating habits out. It is early days for me and I apologise for any that I continue to use, it is a process and I am learning and correcting myself as I go. I encourage you to do the same. It is all part of maintaining our illusion of separation, it is a trick of language that we are playing on ourselves.

Personal Responsibility

With a wild awakening comes a sacred responsibility to live a wild life, to honour and feed your wild core. It is just like eating your five a day, at first perhaps you have to consciously think about it and set aside time for relationship building, for your own wild recovery. However, the more vegetables and fruits you eat, the more you realise that five a day just doesn't cut it, and so move up to ten. It becomes the same with your five minutes barefoot morning ritual, you will find that you need to expand it to feed that growing wild part of you.

When embarking on a personal rewilding journey it is essential to take full responsibility for all of your actions, including thoughts and, as we have just discovered, words. Resistance to personal responsibility can conceal itself, so be vigilant. Pay attention to detail!

When we wish to see a change within ourselves, in our habits and behaviours, we often turn to healers or therapists in the hope that they will do the hard work for us. Externally, in the wider world, it is even more common to look elsewhere for someone to implement the changes that we wish for. Look for areas where you may be waiting for change to come from somewhere else, or blaming the status quo on another (especially on government or multinational corporations). Real change can only come from you, no one else will do it for you.

If we wish for personal and wider, planetary, rewilding, we need to take action. It is impossible to rewild by understanding the concept alone, we each need to live the change for it to come about. In the wider context, it is often said that real change has to come from community, from grass roots groups. However, if you are waiting for a community group to emerge then you are waiting for something outside of yourself to come along and make that change. This is magical thinking and will never happen unless *you* are willing to stand up and start that movement, start that community group. *We are the ones we have been waiting for*[21], this cannot wait. Together we are of course stronger than one, that's a given. But one is stronger than none at all and every revolution has to start somewhere.

> *And yes we need a system change rather than individual change. But you cannot have one without the other.*
> **Greta Thunberg**

If you have a vision then you should action it, take steps towards it, otherwise how will it ever happen? We are *all* responsible for the current state of the world, so claim full responsibility for all of your actions and all of the outcomes, all of the time. One hundred percent responsibility is not enough, take two hundred percent responsibility! If you are not prepared to "be the change", then why should anyone else be? Examine your behaviours, do what feels right. Hoping our current situation will change, yet doing nothing to change it yourself, is tantamount to being complicit.

One fine example of taking personal responsibility, is a woman who in seeking to make a positive change in the world, begins to drink organic herbal tea to benefit a health condition, instead of taking pharmaceuticals. By purchasing the herb tea she took responsibility for her health, for the impact that the alternative, chemical medications, would have had in the world, and managed to avoid all of that. Her journey has begun. But to take the full two hundred percent responsibility would be for her to notice how much further she could take it.

The herb she is buying is grown in Africa, where water is perhaps more scarce than where she lives in England. In addition the field workers may not be fairly treated or paid, how could she know? The herbs are transported using oil; first by truck, then by boat, or air. Somewhere along the line they are packaged and wrapped in a single use plastic sleeve, before going back on a truck and out to the store. Having ample outdoor space which enjoys sunshine and rain, and plenty of free time in the evenings, the woman could choose to try growing the plant for herself.

After chatting with a friend the woman discovers the plant grows well and happily in England, and so when she is ready to take the plunge purchases a small plant and takes it home to her garden. There she waters it when it does not rain, gives it a bigger pot when it grows, or better still has the courage to plant in the earth. She begins to harvest the leaves and make fresh tea every day. Fresh leaves taste so much better and work on her ailment more strongly. She begins to fall in love with the plant, smiling as she brushes past it each morning on her way to work. In summer so much grows that she has excess, which she dries for the short winter days, to save her going out in the dark and cold to fetch some.

The plant grows so much that after a couple of years she takes a cutting for another friend, who also slowly begins the journey of falling in love with this green leafy cousin. Of course the plant originally came to the woman in a plastic pot, but that got reused for the friends cutting. There were also resources and transportation that surrounded getting that original single plant to market. But that is where it ended, no more resources, no more plastic or oil, just a little water here and there and the long deep experience of falling in love with plant, self and planet.

Always have another think, could you go further? Is there more that you personally could be doing? Never stop asking.

In pursuit of taking two hundred percent responsibility at all times, you may find it useful to apologise to Gaia (which of course inherently includes yourself) for anything and everything you have *ever* done to degrade and diminish it. Be specific. By acknowledging everything that you have done both consciously and unconsciously that has had a negative effect on either your individual health or that of another aspect of Gaia, is then owning it, for which you can then take two hundred percent responsibility. This is a starting place for change. Feeling the sorrow, feeling all the pain you have caused and letting it flow. Allowing those feelings to flow. Not attaching guilt (this is very important) but giving yourself permission to feel and acknowledge. Take your time. Write it as a list if it helps. Say sorry to Earth, to self, to Gaia. And mean it.

If you really work with this, feel into the pain of the things you have done, learn the lessons, then you can let them go for good. This is not about wallowing in misery, guilt or self pity; but claiming your mistakes, your actions. If you let each one run through you and feel it deeply, it becomes much more difficult to repeat those mistakes or damaging actions. If you have ever cheated on a lover or lied to a friend, and then come clean, in the moment of admission it is terrible as you are faced with the pain that you caused. But once you have acknowledged what you did was wrong, said sorry (and meant it), you will most certainly think twice about doing the same again, right?

Owning your actions is an essential stage if you are ever to take two hundred percent responsibility and rend the veil of illusion that exists between who you tell yourself you are, and who you really are.

With each new extinction, each new polluted watershed, each new pristine landscape turned industrial wasteland we become more deeply impoverished, and for what? A new outfit? Car? Device? Handbag? Each consumed to supposedly enrich and improve our lives and sense of well-being. Instead actually undermining our health, wealth and happiness, and chances of having it in the future in innumerable ways. We can do better than this. We deserve better. Our children and our children's children deserve better. Our relatives, all of them no matter what species they belong to, deserve conditions in which they can thrive.

We are the destruction in the world, each one of us. And yes some more than others, but we have *all* contributed. I recognise that I am the problem *and* the solution.

With regards to this modern world, our "separation", our condition, it is simple; we did it to ourselves. We do it to ourselves every day with the choices we make about how we live our lives. Thus we can extricate ourselves, and work to make ourselves whole again. We can reconnect with our inner wild and the wildness in the world. We just have to want that enough to begin to make subtle changes that invite the wild back in.

As I noted before, so many of my wild sanctuaries, once pristine and rich, are gradually eroding away to make more space for people; our planets ever growing human population. We all need to be somewhere and so the wilder ones tame another bit of wild edge for their cabin, while the others have woodlands and meadows bulldozed for their cul-de-sacs and high rises. We all want space around us, large rooms, big gardens. But we can't have it all. We are *all* responsible. If the world population continues to grow, it is simple maths; there will be more people, which leads to a greater pinch on wild spaces, leading to less chance of wild well-being not just for humanity, but for all species. It is more than controversial to say it, but if you are at child bearing age especially, contemplate that for a minute. It certainly influenced my personal choices.

So, in summary, take full responsibility for everything and then some more, two hundred percent. Why two hundred percent? Because there really is no getting away with it, no more room for that. No more excuses, no more "just this once". That is what has got us into this mess. "It is only one plastic straw" said 8 billion people[22]...

Willingness To Be Seen & To Be Vulnerable

Authenticity is the true ecstasy.

Lene Rose

If you don't show who you are to the world – if you are not willing to be seen, shields down naked and vulnerable, can you really expect to learn anything of depth about the world in which you are embedded? Can you expect anyone to give up their secrets, show you themself in the raw, if you are so defended you do not show your true face?

If it is hard for me to get close to a person, to find out how they tick, for them to share something genuinely intimate with me, I will back away with a big red warning flag aloft and think to myself *what are they hiding?* It pushes me away. I most certainly would not share intimacies with someone who is putting on a show; nor would I trust them. The plants, the rivers, the stones, the four-leggeds will feel the same. Only with those in front of whom you allow your mask to slip, will you enjoy true intimacy. The better you become at unmasking, the more connected and richer your life will become; until suddenly you find yourself wondering what you were protecting yourself from in the first place.

To be seen and to be vulnerable means having the ability to look another in the eye and speak your truth. To stand up for what you believe – not to make others uncomfortable – but to be true and genuine. It can be done in a non-threatening way, that would not be construed as judgemental or confrontational. You can do it with softness and vulnerability – that is in fact a very brave and strong way. Don't allow the truths you know to be swept under the carpet for the comfort (or avoidance of discomfort) of others. You owe yourself, the wild, Gaia, that much. If you don't stand up for your truth who will? Just keep clear and speak from your heart. This requires courage and deepens your authenticity. Constraint, timidity, holding back, will get you and your cause nowhere – this is not your wild, but your tamed part speaking. You can still be humble but you must be straight. This is how to truly honour people, to let them really see you and to speak to them from your heart.

Don't be frightened to embrace all of your qualities, wear them, allow others to see them. Exposing your own vulnerability is an invitation for others to open up. Being meek and hiding does not serve you or anyone else, believe me, I know. Allow yourself to be seen as your authentic self.

In our earliest days we were truly wild; our communication and relationship with the world around us was unfettered. It is that untamed version of ourselves that we seek to reinstate with rewilding the self. It is stepping back into a sensual and magical relationship with all that is, with no self imposed limits, no holding back for the sake of politeness. You will never gain full access to your wildness and all the gifts therein if you suppress your wisdom, strengths, insights, agility and avoid speaking your truth. If these potent aspects of your wild self remain hidden and subdued so as to be accepted and behave respectably, you will remain a tame and disempowered version of your full potential. Illuminate your shadow!

True wildness requires authenticity over social acceptance; in so doing you give others permission to do the same. Your rewilding becomes instrumental in the rewilding of others in your family, your peers, your community. And thus in the wider rewilding of society. Authenticity and integrity will need to become your baseline, your go to point and the place from which you operate. But for that (again) you need to know yourself. You must stop pleasing others at the expense of your own integrity. For this you need to connect with your heart so that you really know what it is saying.

To rewild you have to relinquish your former domesticated self, give up all the things that have limited you, that defined you in your tame and inauthentic way of being. If you can do this you will be able to live your wild life more fully. With true integrity you will be able to feel the world more clearly, what is truly there, rather than skewed through your own distortions created by projections, protections, and misunderstandings. You will the have the capacity to experience more fully, feel what is true and feel it deeply, know it. And with time know what it means. You will regain greater passion, awe, sense of wonder, vitality and resilience.

A prerequisite to being vulnerable is to overcome the artificial limits we place upon ourselves, then, the barriers we use to protect ourselves. If you are protecting yourself you have to ask yourself what from? But first you have to be able to spot those limits or barriers that you are imposing on yourself. They can come in so many forms, only you will be able to see them all.

Returning to the woman who grew the medicinal herb a few pages back, she will now kindly demonstrate the limits that we can potentially impose upon ourselves. The herb she was drinking as tea was to help her manage extreme and paralysing anxiety. Before she ever could buy the living plant, she would first have to overcome some of her inner demons.

Purchasing the plant would be the first step of release for her and start to pave the way out of debilitating inertia. She gave herself so many reasons why that plant could not be purchased or planted in the ground. In multiple ways the actions of spending time outside, gardening, nurturing, growing, harvesting and making her own remedy would have been her medicine. But her demons had defined her for so very long she was terrified to begin her long walk to freedom, how would she be, who would she be, without them? Almost as if she had Stockholm syndrome, where her condition was her captor, she clung on to what that condition meant to her as if she was clinging on to a life raft in a tropical storm. It took her a long time to break through all of her doubts, fears and inertia, to overcome the feeling that she "couldn't", to finally take the plunge and buy the plant.

No one can make you break through the limits you have imposed upon yourself, although outsiders may help you to see where you have placed those limits. Be vigilant for times where you find yourself coming out with a string of excuses (either internal or external) as to why you cannot do that thing. So for the woman with the herb tea, facing the thought of being whole and well would mean to totally redefine who she was, as she had hidden behind and been defined by her condition for so long. The unknown, despite its promise of freedom and happiness, was incredibly scary; better to cling to the miserable known.

It is certainly much easier at times to stick where you are than to trust and move forward. It takes great courage and sometimes a huge shunt from outside of yourself such as an accident, a death or an illness. Sometimes even these are not enough. Change really has to come from a deep desire within, otherwise within days, weeks or months you will find yourself back at your default position, the comfortable (even though unsatisfactory) known. The problem is that it becomes just that bit less comfortable as you have opened your awareness, even just a little, to the something more that is out there beyond your comfortable reach. And so, although more uncomfortable and misery filled than before, you find ways to reinforce you limitations, to justify your position – you fight to keep yourself in that unsatisfactory place.

A true dedication, a soul longing, needs to be in place to break down your self-imposed limitations. The *only* way is with rigorous self-examination. You will need to ask the questions; why are those barriers there? What am I protecting? Then you can begin to look at them closely and realise that they no longer serve you. They had a purpose once but you have outgrown that now. You will need to tell those parts of yourself who cling to those limits (parts whom perhaps have been in the shadow for a long time) that more is possible, better is possible, wilder, happier, stronger is possible.

> *And the day came when the risk to remain tight in a bud*
> *was more painful than the risk it took to blossom.*
> **Anaïs Nin**

The limitations we set in an attempt to protect ourselves most often, if not always, are sitting over a fear. Fear of failure? Of not fitting in? Of being ridiculed? Of being better than anything in your wildest dreams? I have placed limits upon myself due to a disproportionate fear of success, failure and any number of other things. Working to disable those fears takes time and a deep honest look at oneself.

Fear has to be faced if you are to present the true unmasked version of yourself to other beings. Faced so that you can understand it and when appropriate override it. Fear arises when you don't feel equipped to deal with a situation. When a bear is on the path ahead of you, fear is an appropriate response. Your fight/ flight mechanism is necessarily activated, your sympathetic nervous system prepares the body for intense physical activity so that you can navigate the danger. When the physical responses are in place ready for evasive action (running through the woods to escape the bear) your heart rate is raised, your adrenal glands pump out epinephrine and norepinephrine, your liver releases glucose and your digestion is suppressed. These responses are all necessary when fear is appropriate. When it is inappropriate we succumb to stress, the sympathetic nervous system goes into overdrive, placing your body in perpetual fight/ flight mode.

With rigorous self-examination, time and patience, you can discover what underlies your fear. If it is out of proportion to the situation or indeed an inappropriate response entirely, you can work to find a solution.

Many years ago, I undertook a vision quest in the high desert of New Mexico. It was not fear of Rattle Snake, Javelina, Coyote or Tarantula that I needed to overcome; I knew the likelihood of coming to harm from one of those beings was possible, but unlikely. Instead I had an irrational fear of unknown insects. Not ones that bite or sting necessarily, simply the unknown. And so despite the much reduced danger posed by them, it was this fear that I first needed to overcome to sit comfortably on my mountain ridge.

When in a new location, with unknown residents, it is healthy to feel a little fear, until you know who you are sharing that space with and the potential threat that they pose. The greatest personal challenge potentially is the internal fears that you hold that paralyse you, limiting your experience of life, holding you back from being all that you can be. It is those that need exploring and overcoming.

Fear can also work the other way, lack of fear, this is the condition that most adrenaline junkies inhabit. This is another potential symptom of a life lived dislocated from wild. It presents as an overwhelming urge to feel something real. If this describes you more accurately, it is also worth some rigorous self-examination to see what lies beneath and to strive for a more balanced relationship with fear.

While some in this dislocated domesticated world feel too much all of the time, at the other extreme there are those that experience their lives almost devoid of feeling. We have created a reality that I could liken to a desert, but instead of lacking water it lacks the overt presence of wild. Only we can remedy that, by seeking and nurturing wild in every moment. Allowing our fears to be balanced.

Do you even know how many layers of armour you wear? Are you even aware of the real you underneath it all? You may have done so much work that you feel fresh and naked and yet after a while you start to notice something, it is gossamer fine, thin as the finest silk but another layer nonetheless. So subtle it fits you so well, you have been wearing it so long, and yet it is there. Never stop checking.

A lot of the work I do with my long term clients and my apprentices, is to identify and pick away at these defences. This in itself can be a long process but you won't get very far in deciphering the meanings of the world around you if you are not prepared to drop your defences and see yourself for who you truly are, and let the world see you too. It is an absolutely essential part of rewilding - you cannot proceed without standing naked, mad eyes bulging, rivers of snot – for all the world to see. There is nothing stronger or more brave than being true, with all of your vulnerabilities visible. There is nothing I find more beautiful. It is a sight that I cannot help but fall in love with over and over again.

Don't run away from feeling. Explore it. Explore the fruitful darkness and emerge unafraid, because you met it, you knew it and it did not defeat you. That gives you freedom. Freedom from your fears, knowing that you can look them in the face, examine them, and survive intact.

I mention shadow work a lot, but often it is the things we choose not to see, the things we choose to ignore or deny, that have the strongest hold over us. This is on a cultural, not just a personal level. Once as a society we begin to look at the dark underbelly of our culture, the wrongs, the recklessness, the damage wrought – only then can we address it. And yes, more and more people are beginning to look, beginning to poke around in the dark and expose what they have found, and thank goodness, maybe as more people do so we will find it is not too late to change things.

With regards to you and your personal shadow; it is just as essential that you examine it closely. Shadow work will only ever strengthen your rewilding quest, never undermine it. In your bid to become a wilder, more whole version of yourself, there is no longer a place for shadow, just integrity and truth.

If you can identify and disarm your protective barriers and shields, any layers of self-limitation then you can be fully present. Then you will be able to feel in all dimensions. Your communication with the more-than-human will be unfettered once more, and your interactions will flow. The paradox is that even if initially approaching with protective shields the more-than-human can help you become more visible and vulnerable. Working with wild allies, can help you strip away the lies you tell yourself, your defences, show you who you truly are, what you need to change, and how your life could be if you make that change. The change would still need to come from you, but certainly in the right circumstances wild allies can be the perfect medicine to facilitate this.

Ability To Feel

When we use a smartphone, or any other computer, the average person does not appreciate all of the things it can do, its full potential, perhaps just using 10% of its capacity. You can travel through life like that unfolding only the surface 10% of experience and never really understand what is going on around and within you; all the beautiful meaning filled layers of complexity. To get there, to the deeper layers of your wild soul, and thus experience all the realms we coexist in simultaneously, you have to be willing to look deep within yourself each time something touches you.

At this point in time a large proportion of our DNA is termed "junk" as we have yet to discover its function. This doesn't mean that the greater proportion of our DNA has no purpose, just that scientists have yet to discover what that is. There are so many unknown, unexplored depths, so much capacity that we do not yet know we have. Rewilding opens the doors, how far through you are willing to go is up to you.

All of the feelings that we have are important and should be honoured. Following on from our discussion of fear, we need to look at anger. Humankind has vilified anger to the extent that it has become an undesirable feeling to have, people shy away from it, look down on it, disapprove of it. Humankind has vilified the Opium Poppy and the Coca plant too. Both of these plants however offer incredible medicine. Most people will be treated with an opiate at some point in their life for the analgesic properties, essential pain relief in dire circumstances. The people of the Andes region rely on Coca for its ability to help the body adjust to high altitudes, whilst also providing essential nutrients and vitamins in an environment where many edibles find it hard to grow. But through our twisted manipulation of the medicines those plants offer in this unbalanced world, we have created monsters – disruptive, addictive, unhealthy.

Anger is an essential feeling but when we are out of balance with our natural way of being, our relationship with anger can fall out of balance too. In right relationship anger is just an energy. The energy to get things done. The short sharp burst of energy that makes you shove someone who is standing on your toe; that is where in right relationship this energy ends. When out of balance some people find themselves in perpetual rage (just as others find themselves in perpetual fear), angry at the smallest thing; holding on to that anger and carrying it forward into future interactions.

My anger, in equal measure with joy, is what drives me to do this work. Anger at what humanity is doing to this planet and its residents. Anger at the ignorance and arrogance of humankind. In equal measure is my joy at feeling the wild run through me, wild connections with other life, my love of that. Anger has given me the energy; joy and love the direction. They are both necessary and equal in relevance.

Don't hide from your anger, explore it. What feeds it? What does it give you the energy to do? If something makes you angry take that energy and use it to help you change the thing that made you angry in the first place. When working with anger, it is essential to, once again, be engaged in extensive and rigorous self-examination at all times. So that you understand what is pushing your buttons, making you so angry. You must ask whether your anger stems from your unresolved issues, or whether it is justified? Unfold it, look at it. Maybe that energy needs to work through you, to assist you in changing something internally, even though it may initially seem to be caused by external stimuli.

Anger is OK as long as it relates to current events and situations only. As soon as archaic stuff is brought in it stops being useful energy, as suddenly it transmutes into being a release of rage stored up from the past.

Why does this discussion even have a place in a book like this? Because to be whole, to be wild, you need to be able to feel. And not just to feel the pleasant sensations, while ignoring or filtering out those society, or you, deem to be wrong or bad. But to feel *everything* you encounter, so that you can unravel the meaning underneath it and allow that to tell you something about you, about the world, about the nature of the being you have encountered.

Sadness is also a natural feeling state, one that we all experience from time to time, part of the wild world. It is natural and healthy to feel sadness when it arises, as long as you do not hold on to it. Depression on the other hand is where that sadness has got stuck and is not able to flow through, to be felt and released. Depression is a message from the deep self to say there is something you need to look at, something that is wrong. Medications for depression are taken to help one avoid feeling, without the feeling you don't have to face the fact that something needs to change (possibly on a very fundamental level). Such medication can never be anything but a temporary solution used for emergency treatment of psychosis, and other acute episodes. When medication for depression is prescribed long term, the opportunity to make the changes you need to feel well again, are taken from you. In such circumstances you become disempowered. It may seem controversial to say this, but you also, on some level, become a slave to giant pharma. It requires bravery to face your inner demons and look at what is wrong in your life and work to change that.

We, through necessity for the last remnants of sanity, have become experts at dissociation. Like playing dead, leaving our bodies so that we don't feel the trauma of our current situation. The purpose of this behaviour is self-preservation. It allows us to survive through something we are otherwise not equipped to handle. Something overwhelming (sound familiar?). It allows us to keep trauma locked away and is an avoidance technique, designed to allow us to continue without having to assimilate it.

Well, to become effective at communication with any more-than-human life, the final key element of personal rewilding, you are going to have to bust through that. You have to be able to feel. Once you do, and you let it all in, and let it all pass through, you will become an effective change-maker in this world. You cannot witness all the pain, feel it all, and not turn yourself around to doing something to remedy it.

Personal rewilding, as you have read, goes beyond physical activities, beyond rolling naked on the grass and sleeping under the stars. Of course *do those things*, they are essential. But so too is the paradigm shift, to where we are living in an animate world and communication is free flowing between all life, across the perceived species divide. Once you know all species as your relations, you will find yourself on a deep dive to the wild heart of the world.

III
Growth

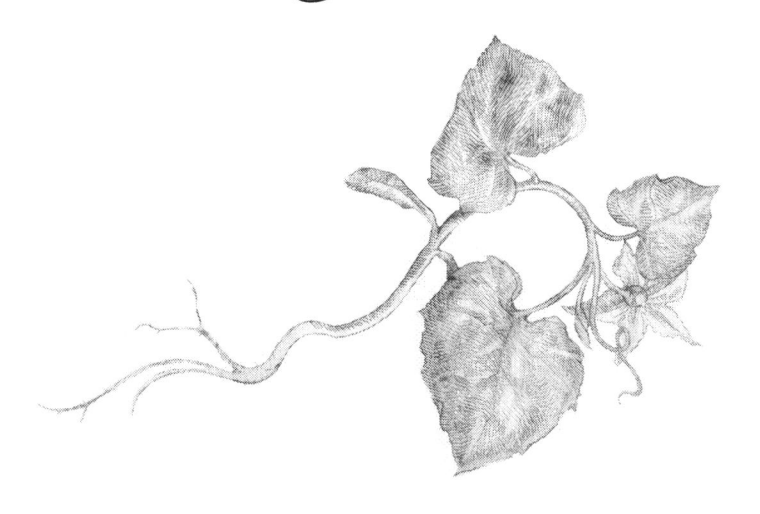

*The first leaves poke above the cool moist
earth, kissed with warming sunlight they
reach up to the sky, expanding
and spreading in response.*

4. Interspecies Communication

To honour a wild thing, converse with it on its own terms, in its language, on its territory. Its gift might be to make you wilder.

Bill Plotkin

Communing with the inhabitants of the natural world is essential if we are going to reclaim our psychological wellbeing and regain the ecological understanding we need to create a sustainable culture.

Chellis Glendinning.

Sense of connection with all beings is politically subversive in the extreme.

Joanna Macy

The question "how do I rewild, connect with wild, if I don't live in a wild setting?" is a really pertinent one for the majority of people, and one that I have been asked on numerous occasions. The answer is to learn how to talk as the wild ones do. And learn how to listen. Our ancestors left the non-human community when they sought work and comfort in villages and towns further and further from wilderness. However, albeit a little beleaguered, the wild is still here around us, everywhere.

Interestingly urban areas are increasingly becoming richer in species diversity. It has been known for some time that urban bee keepers can be more successful than rural bee keepers surrounded by conventionally farmed countryside. In Amsterdam alone, bee populations have increased by 45% since 2000[23], albeit it due to positive intervention. It is also true that about 50% of regional and national plant species in the Northern Hemisphere can be found in cities, while in the city of Warsaw, 65% of the bird species present in the entirety of Poland, can be found[24]. And so even when you live far from a great wilderness, there are opportunities for making wild connections all around you. The more you pay attention, the more you see. Just step outside and notice who is there; listen to bird song, smell the approaching rain on a summers day, touch the soft cool moss, taste a wild leaf fresh from the lawn.

Our wilderness is damaged, constrained and all but gone. However, despite our domesticated lifestyles, where we drink, breathe and eat toxins; where we are separated from the wild outdoors by plastic, MDF and chemicals; we survive. Wild plants, animals and birds, in the shadowy, plastic littered, back alleys and paved yards of the industrialised world, do so too. We have all adapted to survive in these less than ideal circumstances. So the wild is there, just as it is in every one of us – we just have to learn to treasure every Dandelion and ask it what should we do? Everything is *still* communicating.

All of the work in the personal rewilding chapter was recommended to help you prepare for the most important element; communication. Probably the first thing to say is that each of us has a natural capacity to engage with more-than-human nature, no intermediary required. If you are willing to put in the work and time it takes to slow down, then more-than-human nature will speak for itself, it already is, you just need to unlearn what our culture has led you to believe, and remember how to listen.

When you know yourself as equal then you can work in partnership with more-than-human beings. It becomes collaborative. It is the next step in human evolution, to remember ourselves as Gaia. In fact it could be thought of as de-evolution, as it is essentially going back to what we once knew, how we once operated as equals with all beings, collaborating with no species or alternate realm divide. Essentially this book is intended to be your guide through this process.

The only thing that will stop you being able to freely communicate with more-than-human nature is you. If you believe that you can't do it, that you are not good enough perhaps, that will stop you. If you recognise this in yourself and are having difficulty with any of the suggestions that I make in the following chapters I recommend coming back to this sticking point and changing your mind. Reset your prefixed perceptions to ones that not only say that you can do it, but that you are a natural, that the plants (and other beings) have been waiting *all of your life* to communicate freely with you. They wish to speak through you in everything you do, every action you take, all of the time. You are sacred, you are blessed, you can do this, you were born to do this.

I spoke of self-limitation in the personal rewilding chapter and of the importance of rigorous self-examination so that you spot it when it crops up. This, telling yourself you cannot, that you are not good enough, denigrating the self, is self-sorcery. It is one of the strongest forms of sorcery, only you can break it, only you can overcome it, just as only you can hold yourself under its spell. If you tell yourself you can't do something, you will be right, until you tell yourself that you can. So remain vigilant, if you find yourself slipping into beliefs such as these weed them out, tell yourself something else and believe it.

The sea speaks in an ancient language that all our coast dwelling ancestors and human cousins once knew. Some, such as the Southeast Asian Moken, are still fluent in the swells and breaks, the rips, the richness, the treasures and depths of our deep blue neighbour. The same salty broth that swims in our joints and bones, our cells, our tears, our sweat. We are, at the most fundamental level, still one. Where does your boundary end and that of the sea begin? When you dip in her shallows your waterproof skin holds all of your body mechanics in and yet somehow you exchange. Maybe it is the flow, the motion, an ancient memory stirred; if not of salty ocean dwelling ancestors, perhaps as recent as our journey within the salty pool of our very own mothers amniotic fluid filled womb. Either way, the sea enters you as you enter it. You become more sea. The more you spend time with sea, the deeper your communication goes, the more fluent you become. The more this occurs, the more at home you are and the louder the song of the wild swells and sings in your waters. When I have been far from the sea for a long time I forget her language and yet as soon as my hair becomes encrusted in salt from the onshore breeze, the voice of the Ocean infuses back into my blood, reminding me. Relationship with Ocean becomes visceral. As it does so, my body remembers that wild ancient salty tongue.

Becoming fluent in sea-speak, just as with plant or stone, we become more fluent in the language of the wild soul of Gaia. In order to fathom the wild sacred depths of Gaia, you must learn to communicate with them. You must remember the wild language that blows through the branches of trees and moves dried leaves across the ground. You must remember with all of you. Not just your overworked mind, but with your body, your gut, your skin, your heart. Existence is a language that we breathe in and out, that we taste and drink, that we smell and touch, that moves silently and deftly, that creeps up in the dark and jumps out, loud and shocking. It is all a language invisibly and visibly touching every facet of ourselves, weaving through every moment, every thought, instinct and dream. To learn this language, to whisper with plants, is to launch into a multidimensional, multisensory landscape of meaning. No longer blindly travelling on bland marked out paths deemed safe and known with no need to think or feel. In this new landscape, feeling, noticing, sensing, are everything...

That marked, well-trodden path, that signposted trackway, is the safest for those that lack fluency in wild communications, that lack self confidence, sucked out by domesticity. It is a way, but a way that will bypass the richness of being and as such can never be truly fulfilling; if it was why would you be looking for something more? Why would you feel that little nagging feeling, that whispering in your ear while you sleep, that there is something more; that you are missing something. Something big, something essential. That marked route is the one for those that have lost their innate instincts, their creative connection with wild, their inherent intuition or confidence in following it.

The wild path is the one that takes you into dark thickets, where unidentified creatures brush past your shins and wiggle between your toes; where silence lays heavy, where whistles and whispers engage your hackles. There is danger but you will be guided, and anyway we *need* danger to feel alive. After all it was the sanitised path that lulled us into this coma of unfeeling and inertia in the first place. It is time to take that step off the cultivated and safe road, into the wild unknown. It will awaken you on every level and resuscitate the wildness that is sleeping so restlessly within you.

It is a step into true livingness and a step away from perpetual anxiety, away from fear of your own energy, your own anger. It is time to engage, to use your ability to feel, to let the feelings flow, and begin to use them for the reasons you were endowed with them in the first place. People talk about waking up, this is more than that; it is coming alive to, and in, all dimensions.

The well-trodden, the *safe* path, is how society says we "should" be. It is living the 9-5, owning a house and a car, a flat screen TV, embarking on weekend shopping trips and an annual summer holiday. It is having a wardrobe filled with an outfit for every occasion, with shoes and handbags to match. It is not asking too many questions. If you recognise yourself walking this safe and sanitised path and you not just yearn for something more, but you feel it, you hear it whispering to your soul. Then it is time for you to step into the wild unknown and begin communicating once again in the tongue of the wild, the language of the wild Gaian soul. In so doing you step into your unequivocal integrity, into confidence and strength, into the fullness of your wild being and connection with the source; with the true wild core of all life.

The path less travelled, through the wilds of the world, slowly becomes your food. You would not be without it as you discover that this is the ecstatic path.

Two Roads diverged in a wood, and I – I took the one less travelled by. And that has made all the difference.
Robert Frost

Interspecies communication is the key to healing a life of fatigue, of depression, a feeling of being trapped or suffocated, of lacking creativity or a creative outlet, of lacking in self confidence and direction. Without free flowing interspecies communication you cannot be wild. A walk in the woods will help while you are there. Or a naked dip in a Northern hemisphere January sea will make you feel alive if just for a moment. But, for that vital life force to flow unabated, undammed and free, in all its ecstatic wanderings, the invisible barriers between human and more-than-human language and culture must be lifted, permanently. And to do that you must learn how to communicate. Not just how to pray; to put your desires, requests, pleas out into the universe. But, also, how to listen. How to feel and hear the response with all of your being.

How can we hope to really integrate, to settle among the wild ones, become one of them, if we cannot speak their language? You can fool yourself into thinking that you are fully wildly integrated, but if you are not speaking the same language and knowing your neighbours to be the same as you, then you will always be separate. This is why clear, two way communication is essential. Without it you will always remain an outsider looking in. Think of it like this. It doesn't matter how many times you visit a country, if you don't try to learn the language and communicate with the locals you will only ever be a tourist. The more you sit down and practise with one of the locals, the more fluent you become. And as you begin to learn the idiosyncrasies of that language then you begin to be able to see the world from their perspective. You break through and suddenly you are able to assimilate into that culture and participate as an equal. In addition you will be able to contribute wisdom from your perspective and culture, without imposing it or judging anyone.

I was once gifted the story of a tree. I dropped so deeply into the dreaming of the tree that I travelled through its body from the furthest root tip all the way up to the leaves, right up on the highest point of the crown. As the seasons passed I then dried and crumpled and fell. But as I lay there at the base of the tree in my autumn gold and brown colours I soon softened and, aided by the mycelium rich in the ground all around, I became soil particles once again. I entered back into the tree through the roots. I travelled up the trunk. This time I paid more attention to the details as each tiny leaf began to unfurl. Again time passed. Again I was shed and became food once more. Again I travelled through the trees annual cycle. This time paying more attention to the other lifeforms that shared the space on the branches of the tree, the insects, birds and tiny mammals. I repeated this journey, this annual cycle of the tree, again and again and again. I lived cycling through the tree for decades as I learned so many minute details, saw the tree from every angle inside and out. Until I knew what it was to be that tree.

Once the lines of communication are open and trust has been established through your perseverance and open hearted approach, once you are truly listening, you will be welcomed in by the other beings.

Without this ongoing conversation with the more-than-human world, we drift alone and isolated, with no context. We lose a vital part of ourselves and so instead concentrate more wholly on human and the affairs of human. We become obsessed with humans. It becomes our whole story. Think wider. Invite the other beings in and pay attention to how your life and all of it, your whole story, changes as they become woven back in. Having lived under the illusion of separation, we have lost fluency in interspecies communication. However, wild language is instinctual, free-flowing, fed by the very living Gaian interconnections themselves; we can regain the skills, it is in us.

The language between species is constantly evolving and unfolding as the conditions of life respond to the perturbations in the energetic field and in physical circumstances. After all, even our written languages change with the times. The addition of novel words that have gained a place in common parlance into dictionaries is evidence of this fluidity, while the words removed to make space for the new ones is further evidence. When it comes to the choices made by the editors of the Junior Oxford dictionary in 2007 one recognises some quite alarming reflections of what is slipping out of our world as the words culled included – herring, minnow and otter – all names of wild relations. The cull continued in the 2012 edition with the further removal of words that related to our wild relatives including catkin and chestnut, whilst new words added included blog and chatroom[25]. Ensuring that from a young age we are trained to remain tame, speaking and writing of our attachment to machines, over our dreams of the wild.

Where there is life there is change, transformation, readjustment. It doesn't matter so much where we left this interspecies discourse; what does matter is that if you choose to pick it back up, you must pay attention. That means attention, not only to the incoming, but to what you are putting out there; your thoughts and actions as well as actual gestures and vocalisations. We co-create Gaia. If you had the misfortune to spend your youth playing shoot-em-ups on huge screens in your living room every evening, breaking only to watch a film imbued with violence, disaster, cyber take over (the silicon revolution), then that is what you are drawing in to this reality.

Of course, interspecies communication is nothing new. Our ancient connection to other lifeforms has always been there since before life as we know it began, when we were all still joined as stardust. And because of that ancient beginning when we were all one, we are still connected through quantum entanglement, any perturbation anywhere, occurring for any life form, we can feel and pick up on. So this is an ancient art that modern peoples have largely forgotten. It's about accessing what is already there and allowing yourself to engage with it. This is about re-engaging, remembering, unlearning; that's it.

What Is Communication?

Communication (kəmjuːnɪkeɪʃən) *n*. **1.** *the imparting or exchange of information, ideas, or feelings*[26].

It has become such, that we often fail to pay attention to detail in communications with other humans. Wedding invites, retreat preparation notes, vacation equipment lists, are often quickly scanned over and in so doing we miss the finer details. Even in business emails, it is quite routine to have only half the questions acknowledged, or half of the instructions actioned, some of them differently to the detailed and specific directions. So, it is no wonder that we miss the subtle messages and communications we are surrounded by and bombarded with by more-than-human nature. Also no wonder that at the beginning of this journey, when we begin to take note, and attempt to pay attention, it can be so challenging.

If you fail to pay attention, whether it is your friend giving details of their birthday plans, or of a flower opening before your eyes, then you are communicating that the other doesn't matter to you, not enough to pay attention to them anyway. Be careful what you communicate to the world. If you communicate that you don't care persistently enough, sooner or later, the other party will pay attention and in return will stop caring about you.

Not paying attention to detail indicates a lack of respect. Respect for what is happening in the lives going on around you and the impact your behaviour is having on them. The other communicator having to send endless reminder emails for example, or you turning up at the wrong place or time and causing a delay or alteration in proceedings. If you don't pay attention to communications and turn up with everything wrong, it is disrespectful to both the other communicator, and yourself. It indicates that perhaps there is an unmet part of you playing out, a part who needs attention, who wants it to be all about them.

If you recognise yourself in this description, that you often lack attention to detail when sent instructions or invites, needing reminders, forgetting essential pieces of information or getting the details wrong, you have to ask yourself why. Rigorous self-examination is a phrase you will already have noticed me using a lot. I inherited the phrase, and more importantly the practice, from my time apprenticing with Stephen Buhner. Now is the perfect time to undertake some! Break it down. For example, you can ask yourself, where does it (lack of attention to detail) happen – at work or socially? Is there a certain person or group or activity where this happens uniquely, or is it across the board? What lies underneath your lack of attention to detail? Is it that you don't really want to be doing that thing? Is it that you don't like your job or that person or that activity? Is there something deeper? Are you nervous, afraid? Is it that a part of you wants to feel special, needs coaxing, needs special treatment? And if so why? There can be so many layers to something as simple as this, but if you can unpick it all and discover which part of you is causing this behaviour and why, then you can change things. If you can do that your chances for better, cleaner and clearer communications with all of your relations, both human and otherwise, will improve dramatically.

There is also a pattern I have observed, that some people, in their absolute avoidance of personal responsibility, request set limits. Lines drawn that define what is acceptable behaviour, rather than discerning for oneself what is appropriate. This is especially predominant in people who live very structured lives or who have a very disciplined personal practice. It indicates an immature state of being and in this circumstance the lack of respect is directed towards oneself; ones own needs. It is important to know and honour when one needs some quiet time, for example; this is basic self-care. To communicate effectively, you need to be very clear about your needs and wants.

One of the first steps in clear communication, then, is to take back responsibility for yourself, bring it all under your own control. We each have spent a lifetime of parents, school, society, friends, government, stepping in and setting limits, telling us what's what, without us having to discern for ourselves. To be wild, to be open to your deep wild interconnected yet independent soul, you need to pay attention, be clear, know what you want, listen (with all senses and in all ways), and be able to communicate in response.

Paying attention to detail includes not just our impact on the world but its impact on us. Notice how, as you explore the other, it in turn explores you back. As soon as I realised this truth, I really began to notice it. I began to notice how the buds of evening primrose brush their light dampness upon me. How the flowering grasses tickle so sweetly. How stones so often poke harshly if they wish for my attention, or for me to be more aware of where I am placing my clumsy bare feet. I have learnt that I love to be touched, just as much as I love to touch.

Perhaps consider it this way; instead of going somewhere new and seeing it, how about meeting the place? How about shaking hands by standing barefoot, eyes closed, smelling, touching, hearing, feeling. And in that moment allowing the land to meet you, to taste your spirit, and feel your intentions.

As your attention deepens you will begin to realise that not just with touch, but with each of your senses, noticing is two-way. You notice the smell of another, they notice your smell. You notice the sound of another, they notice the sound you make. You see another, and they see you. When you walk in the forest there are eyes upon you, the eyes of wild. Notice in the same way as if you walked into a room full of humans, some turn to look at you. Seek them out; the ones who watch. The more attention you give someone, the more alive they become; whether you are talking about a puppy, your own skin, or a giant redwood. Through paying attention and noticing with your senses, the more everything enlivens, including yourself; Gaia enlivens. Beyond that, as we awaken to this two-way noticing, something more happens. Fundamentally through noticing the other and their impact upon us, we are noticing ourselves and thus we become more self-aware. Self-awareness, not just of ourselves, but Gaia in its entirety, grows as of course, there is no separation.

Return to the five minute barefoot practice I described at the beginning of the Personal Rewilding Chapter. As you stand barefoot each morning, feet in contact with Earth, making your acknowledgements of the wild world of which you are a part, notice how your feet are not just standing on, but being *held* by the Earth below. Return to the breeze once more, and notice your interaction as it touches you while it passes. And how as you inhale, that breeze is breath shared with all the other mammals and birds, fed with oxygen by the plants. How it changes in composition with each of those breaths. The pollen, pheromones, and moisture it carries are all messages. It does not just touch you, but each plant and rock and animal it passes. And with each being it embraces on its journey, the messages carried by that breeze update. It becomes that a simple action, standing barefoot and breathing, becomes a taking in and release of information. It is an exchange - as you are given, you too give. That in its most basic form is communication.

As we notice and acknowledge breathing as an act of reciprocity, a mutually beneficial exchange, be aware that within an unbroken wild system, eating is also a mutually beneficial exchange. Our bodily waste products breaking down to provide food for plants. So the plants gift us their leaves and their fruit and when the cycle is unbroken we gift back our nitrogen rich urea; food in exchange for food[27]. Life outside of our domesticated reality is one of perpetual reciprocity, where each exchange is a communication.

Become conscious of your communications with the world. Let the energy, breath and messages flow. You will feel topped up with oxygen laden breath, Earth energy tingling through the awakened and dewy damp soles of your feet. Again and again, awareness. Not thinking, but *feeling*. You start to become aware of what your body yearns for (this daily contact perhaps). The more you notice, the more you tune into the wild whisperings of Gaia.

> *Some people conclude that what looks simple are practices for beginners. Many of us equate complex practices with advanced work. This is a misperception.*
>
> **Sandra Ingerman**

To allow the wild whisperings to meld into your very being, access *must* be simple; so that it can *always* be occurring. In return your whisperings become your interweaving with the wildness of the world, become messages and markers of your wild place, of your inherent wild core and connection with all that is.

Language is different to communication in that it is the *way* in which you make that communication. There are many forms of language; body language, the spoken word, the language of the heart.

I often feel limited with the spoken word, especially by my vocabulary, by my skill at eloquently expressing the depths that exist within and without me. There are so many more layers to feeling and experiencing something directly than I can accurately describe with the spoken or written word. I spent a large part of my early adulthood in countries where English was not the first language and so time and energy was invested in learning a spattering of basic conversational words in several other languages. At the same time my English languished and vocabulary became stunted through lack of practice with other fluent English speakers. What I lost in my own language I gained in appreciation for words in other tongues which have no English equivalent, words formed by poetic descriptions or observations of object, action, event, that my language has overlooked. Although unable to perhaps express concisely and elegantly in English, I learned much of the beauty and superior expression of many other tongues. *And* that there is so much more to communicating, to conversation, than the spoken word alone.

I have become pretty good at grasping a meaning, or a feeling, encoded within a communication, even if it is subtle and underlying. Even when something is expressed in a language I either don't understand or only have the vaguest comprehension of. In fact it can be easier to feel into the true essence of the communication when you do not share a common tongue, when all you have is gesture and feeling, as even tone can be misleading. So, although the spoken word is the most common form of communication between humans, there is a whole world of visible and invisible signals that are working alongside it. Feelings you are putting out and picking up, for example.

Your capacity for communication will evolve as the nuanced minutiae are noticed and become more relevant. You will move beyond the blundering limitations of the spoken word, no matter how articulate you are, as you begin to feel language not just in your physical body and its responses, but further and deeper in, right to your soul. To the very spark that is you as you were always meant to be, the essence of you.

Language, the medium through which you convey thoughts and feelings, is not entirely verbal then, in fact far from it. You will have to train your body to be an antenna, your heart to be a finely tuned receiver and sender of messages. Of course, both the body and heart are already compliant, it's the mind that has run away with itself, taken over to the extent that we have forgotten exactly how to tune back in to the dialogue the heart is having and the discourse the body is involved with...

Peter Wohlleben, in *The Hidden Life of Trees*, describes perfectly one way in which trees are communicating that we intuitively pick up on, most of us without consciously trying. Pine plantations are an obvious example, straight row upon straight row of the same variety of tree, a monoculture lacking in almost any species diversity, devoid of most all other life and the stability and resilience that a wide diversity of species is naturally characterised by. Added to this is the potential stress the trees will be under if the plantation is out of their natural geographic range, which activates chemical defences (against thirst for example). Such chemicals (phytoncides) are released into the air. As we walk through such a forest we will be inhaling those chemicals and in combination with the unnatural setting, devoid of diversity, many people will have a feeling of unease develop on the periphery of their awareness[28].

As you begin to pay more attention to how you *feel* you will notice how different forests have a different feel about them, make you feel more, or less, at ease for example. You will also notice how different areas within the same forest make you feel differently. Eventually your sensitivity will be such that you notice each separate tree as you are passing, distinct from the general feel of the micro-locale. This is all communication and all occurs without the spoken word. I will talk more of how to increase your sensitivity later in this chapter, but it is essentially the same as feeling different in the presence of different people.

Communication, can come in many forms then, and clearly, not all of them immediately obvious to the observer, or indeed visible. Trees respond when nibbled. They can discern from the saliva, who is nibbling and they choose how to respond (making a choice of course indicates intelligence). They can send chemicals that are toxic for that specific predator to their leaves. Or they can let off a gas that is detected by other nearby trees, who can prepare for potential attack by upping their levels of the specific chemical in their own leaves. In addition, or alternatively, they can send out chemicals that attract the predators of the one eating, as fabulously detailed by Peter Wohelleben, once again in *The Hidden Life of Trees*[29]. What I mean to demonstrate here is that this is a considered response based on choices and decisions. It is a communication from predator to tree of its presence, and a communication between trees of defence strategy. All happening invisibly and imperceptibly to a human observer, but happening nonetheless.

There is so much we don't know about communications, most certainly invisible ones. It is always on the edge of my consciousness to consider the role of DNA, predestined to work as a sender and receiver. DNA communicates within the body but also, and essentially, with DNA outside of us. In addition DNA also serves as an information recorder. There is so much that we currently don't know. And perhaps we don't need to know the how or the why, but just that somehow or other there are an endless quantity of communications going back and forth between all things, in all moments, to achieve dynamic balance within the great wild Gaian matrix.

> *Since the discovery of DNA, people have believed... that DNA is exclusively occupied, with the help of our genetic code, with making protein bodies in the upper portion of the cell. Surprisingly, however, almost 90% of our DNA is not needed for protein synthesis, but rather is essentially used for communication.*
>
> **Pierre Franckh**

Eloquence can come in many forms and mastery of communication involves not just having an astounding vocabulary and command of the verbal language you speak, but the ability to listen viscerally, to hear with your flesh the response to your touch upon the world.

Address The Other Directly

I have already mentioned how we must stop talking of "nature" as a separate thing. We must be vigilant with ourselves about how we speak of our relatives the rivers, the whales, the oaks. I cannot stress enough how the language we use can cause greater separation. You must address the being directly. If you fail to address the being directly, talking *about* it rather than *to* it, then that being, whether it is a child or a plant, an eagle or a beaver, will continue on regardless of you and will no longer attempt to capture your attention, as you are not reaching out to it. So don't be surprised if at first it feels difficult to capture the attention of that living being, especially if you have been side-lining them for a long time.

Notice the difference between addressing indirectly: "wow, what a beautiful set of trees" or "there is that gorgeous tree again", to directly: "oh wow, you are so beautiful, and you, and you, and you" or "oh my goodness it's you, how wonderful to see you again!". Feel into those different sentences, read them over, and notice how differently each one makes you feel. The difference is palpable. Once you engage in direct communication it is like stepping through a doorway into wonderland, it is actually opening Aldous Huxley's doors of perception; no mescaline necessary! *Everything* literally moves in to greet you. You may get overwhelm at first and have to close back up slightly, before re-opening your doors of perception just a slither at a time. But that simple change of phrase, different orientation, changes your relationship – makes it a direct relationship. And that *changes everything* else by opening up a whole new vibrant living world of possibilities.

Just as there is a difference between approaching directly versus indirectly, there is a difference between learning directly *from* something to learning *about* something. Say you wanted to learn of Bwiti and the forest peoples of Gabon. Perhaps you first read a little of this spiritual tradition and that is where your interest sparked. The next step, if you were to learn *about* it, perhaps would be going to a professor in the field, sitting for three years in a lecture theatre to become a learned academic on the subject.

However, to learn directly would require an entirely different approach. Having read the book you would then head straight out to Gabon. At first it would perhaps be really hard to locate one of the relevant forest dwelling tribes. Once you do, no one really wants to engage. Except perhaps the children who are quite intrigued by you. Then there are the women who quietly worry about you, who want to feed you. Slowly you begin to learn a few words of the local tribal language, over time you are able to string a few words into a sentence or two. All the while the old man has been observing you silently. When he is satisfied that you are dedicated, that you have fallen in love with his tribe, and that your intentions are pure, he beckons you over. And you sit on a stump of wood next to his for the next two years. Learning everything he has to share, and living in the richness of his community. You know the land, the weather, the food, the medicine, the laughter, the challenges, the triumphs. You don't just know it intellectually, you know it viscerally.

Each journey into the knowing of Bwiti – through intellectual enquiry at university or through living among the people – takes the same quantity of time. One comes with qualifications and certificates. But only one path will take you to the true heart and soul of Bwiti. If you chose the latter path (the wild path), it may be much more uncomfortable with interminable bouts of diarrhoea, no privacy or personal space, being so far from home with barely any contact perhaps. However the invisible connections that you have built and gained are worth so much more than the discomfort it took you to get them or any number of certificates and job offers that you would have gained with the former approach. This is real knowing. Direct knowledge. And it is multi-dimensional. It follows that it is not learning "about" other species, but directly "from" them where the real wisdom and knowing comes.

When you choose not to directly engage with something that is a communication in itself; one of value and worth. If you bypass the other person in the room and instead of asking them about themselves ask a third party, that would be disrespectful even if they appeared to be cognitively impaired. The polite behaviour would always be to direct your attention to that person whom you wish to learn of. It happens a lot with children, the elderly and disabled, they get ignored while questions and communication instead are directed at their carers. If you wish for a direct response you must ask a direct question to the person which you wish to learn of, whether they be human, animal, plant, mineral.

Direct communication goes beyond admiring, to engaging with someone. Think again about addressing the other directly versus indirectly, this is where it gets applied. You see some beautiful horses in a field and think to yourself "wow, they are really handsome horses" and then one turns and walks towards you, and you change in that moment from admiring to engaging. As suddenly you are speaking out loud, saying "Hello gorgeous, look at you, oh hello, hello..." as you reach out and pat it. So the point is to understand the difference between these two positions and when wishing to engage with a more-than-human being to learn how to adopt the second position – learn how to meet them eye to eye. It is not difficult at all and yet it changes *everything*. That is the most simple thing you can do that will make your world more alive, that will bring the wild to life. If you just want to be embedded in a more animate world it can be as simple as that, as simple as you want it to be.

Time

At this point it is pertinent to mention that this is going to take time. You *can* get a lot very quickly but to really get down there and root around amongst the bones of the thing, we are talking a mature and unhurried relationship; like a good marriage.

I am still learning new things about my husband after almost 20 years together; not because he has been hiding things but because as different circumstances come together, you learn to stand in a way you have not stood before. You draw on strength you never knew you had and thus different aspects of yourself emerge and can be witnessed by those around you. We all change in these ways through the ups and downs, stresses and joys of life. Nothing is static. And so as new layers of complexity and beauty emerge in *your* being another facet is added to your ever evolving eyeball and artist's palate. You can see from a slightly different angle, or perceive a slightly different hue. Your needs shift and change. As do your offerings to the world and thus your relationships; which includes your relationships with the more-than-human world.

There is a richness of knowing that comes with time – but never assume too much. Never just *think* you know and that you have nailed it. There are many perturbations in any local environment on a daily basis, let alone the whole of Gaia, or the entire universe. All of which will have their influence on each living being, each plant, and that influence will never be uniform across the board – as one species going extinct approximately every 8 minutes will testify.

We are living in a world where instant gratification is becoming more and more expected in almost everything. I am certainly guilty of it – sometimes working on two laptops I also pick up my phone as I wait for pages to load and buffer. But to be wild, to be connected, to be a wild flowing Gaian animal, you must train your senses and your intuition; skill sets that you can only build with practise.

I have had students totally frustrated that they do not immediately see the world in a grain of sand or heaven in a wild flower, as Blake once wrote of. But, do you expect to be able to compete in the Tour de France the day you learn to ride a bike? It takes time. Dedication. Perseverance.

Some people most certainly have an easier time. Those with more logical brains sometimes struggle at first, especially with trust. Sometimes it is the questioning deep inside whether the mythic truly exists that puts the breaks on. You may have to remove the barriers you have erected against felt experience and its value. Other people may find it slow going for other reasons. But this does not mean that someone else who seems to get it straight away is any better than you (and a bit like yoga it is not a competition, instead about you and your personal experience anyway). With persistence and practice, I am yet to find a person who cannot do this.

Don't be disheartened if you find communication with other species hard, some species are more difficult to connect with than others, plants for me are easiest hence the weighting of this book. Finding it hard is not a bad thing though, it just means that when you do finally get it you will have so much more value attached to it, because you know how long it took you to get to this place of open communion and two-way sharing.

You can never hold on to anything in this life. The turning of the seasons teaches us of letting go, you cannot hold on to the heat of midsummer, just as sure as the snow melts in spring. As I write this it is early morning on July 4th and I notice that this time two weeks ago there was so much more light in the sky. The longest day soon turns to shorter days, you cannot hold on to the light of solstice, just as you cannot hold on to the silver darkness of a total solar eclipse. Everything is changing all the time, that is the way things are. So relationships, people, plants – you must look at them as new each time you meet, as your eyes have changed, maybe only a titch, but they have changed as experience has changed your perception. Likewise, although their soul essence remains essentially unchanged, the minutiae, the tiny details *are* fluid, they change.

The trick to really developing your art into a mature one, is to experience the other as new each time you meet; to give them the opportunity to be different, to have changed. Not to assume, for example, that your partner, after a weekend away with friends, is the same person when they return Sunday evening that left the house on Friday morning. It follows, not to assume that what Nettle is offering to you and to the world next spring, is the same as last time its tender fresh top leaves emerged from the frozen ground. It is all so intertwined. You change, your needs change, your relationship changes. To truly honour the other you must take the time to notice what's new and give space and attention as you adjust to the subtle and miniscule changes in each other.

If you are not vigilant, if you do not practice noticing the new every day, if you allow the lazy to take over and make assumptions, you will miss out. Your relationships will be out of date. Weakened. Like those friends you knew best 15 years ago who still buy you a bottle of booze for your birthday even though drinking is largely a thing of your past. It is not a bad thing, they clearly still think of you. But it does show either that you haven't seen each other for a long time so they made an assumption based on who you used to be, or that the relationship is not important enough for them to have paid attention to the changes in you.

Give space for all your relationships to continually evolve. Be vigilant for even the most subtle differences. Life is a constant course of micro-adjustments to the micro-perturbations that each one of us is party to.

Once you have unlocked your ability to communicate with the more-than-human world things may begin to happen very quickly but you won't suddenly know the other being; it is like getting to know a human, it is a lifelong process. Initially it may take a while, take perseverance, to gain their trust – we have been ignoring them for so long you see?

Great enthusiasm, rushing from being to being, can be common when the world of interspecies communication first opens up. It is exciting, and the desire to deepen your knowledge of every being in the universe can be strong. So by all means make contact, acknowledge, fall in love. But look out for one where the connection is especially strong, and dedicate time to building that relationship, otherwise you will never go beyond the surface level. You can of course work with multiple beings concurrently, but with each new one you add to the mix, take time with them individually, or how will you know who is who?

It takes time for trust to build, for you to reveal your true self to each other. Dedication, perseverance, patience. Give time for the other being to infuse into you cell by cell, let it run through your veins, get right into your bones, truly inhabit your heart. Some will move faster than others, like any friendship or love affair. Some take years to reach maturity, deep trust and great value. Others will be like wild fire, exciting, fast and within a short time you will indeed see the universe in the others eyes, or unfurling leaves, just as you do within the eyes of your beloved. But don't stop, just as you shouldn't after the first exciting fireball of a new lover; keep working, stay present and never assume you know; as there is always something more, always a deeper level. That is one of the greatest secrets of a true plant whisperer; it is not how many plants you know, but how deeply you know them, how many layers you have peeled away to get there. A few strong, deep, relationships have a far greater value than a large number of relatively surface level ones – we all know that from human interactions after all.

Time is essential. Give yourself time to practise. You have to learn from the other species themselves. Create space for this kind of interaction to occur. Space that is uncluttered with schedule, with "shoulds" and agendas, any and all mind chatter. Make time to be alone with the wild ones, ask them, and honour them by giving your 100% clear attention, no distractions. If you don't set time aside for this it will only ever be a sideshow that you do at the weekend or when on a workshop. For it to become real and an essential part of the fabric of your being, intricately woven into everything you do, think and say, it will require your undiluted attention. Make intentional space in your routine, until it becomes who you are, until it becomes you and your whole life is spent whispering back and forth between species without a second thought.

Trust & Agreements

The current paradigm trusts information, science. It likes to be able to prove and test things so that it can be sure they are real. Feelings of course cannot be tested or proven. And so, we have been taught not to trust what we perceive, what we feel. But we need to learn to trust ourselves again, this is a vital step if we are to trust the incoming messages from the more-than human.

A great starting place is to keep all agreements that we make. Not just firm and spoken agreements, but also the implied, the assumed. So with regards to external relationships this means showing up when you say you will or, when as sometimes happens and circumstances change, to renegotiate at your earliest opportunity.

The assumed agreements are just as important as firm ones. So, for example, if you are always home at a certain time and your partner cooks for you, although you never agreed that you will arrive home at that time, your partner assumes through your regular routine that you will be there in time to eat. If one day you have to stay late in the office, or bump into a friend on the way home, it is very simple to send a quick message to say that you will be later than expected. Why is this so important when you never made a firm agreement that you would be back at a certain time? Because once you have broken this unspoken agreement, once, twice, three times, it starts to undermine the trust your partner has that you will be home at that time. And perhaps eventually it will lead to break down in trust elsewhere in the relationship. It is simple courtesy to let the other know the change in your plans, and then all trust will remain intact.

Internal agreements can be easy to overlook, but are hugely important in building trust in yourself. I can't count the times when I promised myself I would start a yoga class, or do a mini cleanse, or take a day off, and then without a second thought ignored that promise to myself. The thing is, if you habitually promise yourself things that never materialise, you will begin to know when you say them to yourself that they will never manifest. You have lost trust in yourself. Which makes it incredibly difficult to then trust that the insight you are gaining from Granite or from drinking a herbal tea is in fact a true communication, not just an imagining. So keep those promises to yourself, start that yoga class, or stop promising yourself that you will. Just like with external agreements, if circumstances change, your boss perhaps requires you in the office on the day you had promised you would take off, then renegotiate. Renegotiate not just with your boss about which day you can have, but with yourself, reassure yourself that you will still take that day for yourself, it will just be next week instead of this.

The more trustworthy you are, the more others will be inclined to share their secrets with you, that includes the more-than-human. If you trust yourself, you will be able to trust messages that your body is sending you. You will be able to trust what you are feeling. You will trust that Granite really was offering insight into how to cope with your grief, it didn't just come from your own mind wanderings. I cannot stress enough how much trust, trusting yourself, helps with any endeavours to communicate with the more-than-human.

Agreements with the more-than-human are just as important as those within yourself and with human peers. If you make a promise to Pine that you will return and sit with it again soon, if you make a promise to Pansy that you will plant its seed, if you make a promise to Badger that you will dance naked at dawn, then you must keep that promise. Failing to keep a promise to the more-than-human will only break trust down further between species and, to be honest, humankind do not have a great track record here. The more you can show up as a person of integrity, the more other species will respond and the deeper your communications will go.

Clarity Of Your Question & Knowledge Of Self

You may be approaching a being to express your gratitude for its presence in the world and all that it does by being here. You may be expressing your joy at seeing it. You may be expressing your great love for it. You may have gone to that being with a question. Communication is an exercise in reciprocity. Once you have expressed your piece, to honour the exchange, you must listen for a response.

Other species work with feeling. Where do your strongest feelings lead? That is the question you must keep asking yourself, as no matter what words come out of your mouth, it will be your strongest feelings that the more-than-human is responding to. So, even when you don't intend to ask a question the response you receive will be addressing that which you feel most strongly in your heart. This has lead me to understand that when opening to and developing relationships with other species, one of the most important things is clarity. You must know what it is that is in your heart, to understand the response.

There is inevitably an element of self healing involved as you communicate with the more-than-human. Gaia wants you to be well, as in your wellness comes greater wellness to the whole. With each piece of Gaia that is functioning efficiently, it clearly follows that the whole functions more efficiently. And so, through healing your sweet piece of it, healing takes place on a deeper Gaian level.

I have discovered, from personal experience, that you can spend years going around asking a hundred different plants (or other species) a hundred different questions and they will all be offering their medicine for what your soul most needs. You may think you are asking a different question and the medicine offered will differ from plant to plant, species to species, but once you really break it down they are all offering a different aspect, a different angle, from which you can work with your primary issue. Each will offer the unique element it has to contribute to the healing of the greatest wound that you are holding.

You will learn much about yourself in your pursuit of clarity. The communications you have may well uncover your sacred wound, the pain you hid so well from yourself that you had forgotten that it was there, underlying everything else. You will get medicine for that same thing again and again and again. Until eventually deeper understanding kicks in and you take the medicine, see to that wound, face the shadow. It is not until that point, where that personal awakening and healing has taken place, that you can move on to the next level. The next wound.

Your primary wound, when you do uncover it, may not appear that grandiose, it could be that you were called ugly at school. But if that is something that cut deep at the time and in response you buried the pain away, it may still be informing so much of your experience of life. That wound may be contributing to behaviour patterns that although intended to protect you, may be causing greater harm, may be keeping you remote and separate, afraid of meeting your potential.

Wounds and what we present to the more-than-human as such can change as our focus changes. In one moment your deepest pain and wounding may seem to be coming from the divorce you are currently going through, or the loss of a loved one. But underneath that current pain your deepest, untended wounding will be informing how you deal with that pain in the moment. *And for most of us, somewhere underlying and informing it all, is the pain of our dissociation from wider nature, from all our relations.*

You may go to the more-than-human with a very specific question or intention, so to be sure that your primary wound is not what yet again is addressed you must be very clear. Perhaps try smudging or meditating before you approach, so that you are truly focussed on that one thing alone. Intention will guide what you see and where the other being takes you. When setting an intention don't forget to remain open, alert and to listen for the response. From experience I know that it may even be instant.

You may worry that the messages coming to you are a projection but think about it, even if it is projection, that is still a message to you from the universe about yourself. You may also wonder whether it is the single Elm or the Elm archetype with which you are communicating. To be true, it is a bit of both.

As you perhaps enquire as to a plants medicine you will tap into the archetype – the medicine of Rosemary will (in part) be revealed. But, the "part" that is revealed is the part that is most relevant to you on your personal healing quest (even if you didn't know you were on one). So again and again and again you will discover that personal clarity is essential. By now you may be beginning to understand the reason for the emphasis on self-examination and shadow work in the Personal Rewilding Chapter. If you know what is going on inside you, you will understand what is coming back at you. It will be easier to understand and interpret.

Truly loving and knowing yourself, healing your relationship with yourself, and having clear communication with yourself, is essential. Especially so if you do any healing or land-based restoration work, as otherwise, despite good intentions, a subconscious intent to heal one's own wound will *always* get in the way.

The Body & Its Wisdom

Your physical body is a piece of Earth. Your physical body is a highly tuned instrument, even if you are not listening. In fact, your physical body is an organ of perception. Never overlook the physical body's role, either the other beings, or your own, for giving or receiving information.

We all know how to use the body for a kinaesthetic response, a physical sensation. You touch a plate, it feels hots, your fingers retreat rapidly. You touch the fur of an animal, it feels soft and warm, your fingers linger luxuriating in the pleasure of the moment. But there is something more. Your body also perceives a deeper feeling. Your fingers would not linger amongst the fur if the animal turned and hissed at you, no matter how soft it felt. In fact something would have probably stopped you from touching the fur if you sensed danger or felt uncertainty in the first place. This is blending physical, felt sensation and the feeling sense where we pick up on deeper, more environmental perception, the feeling of the thing. It is actually pretty impossible to separate out the different levels that we have for perceiving, just as it is almost impossible to focus on one sense alone, everything is a blending, a synaesthesia. We are so much more complex than we give ourselves credit for.

We are very used to using physical sensation, we rely on it a lot, to keep us safe, keep our fingers intact. The human body, though, has a much greater level of intelligence, wisdom and awareness than physical sensation alone.

We get into habits with our bodies. Holding ourselves in a certain way, moving in a certain way. Sometimes the way we use and work with our body is not the most efficient and can even be damaging. The most obvious that comes to mind for me personally is slouching. Having a posture where the top of my back is rolled forward. This is one of my long held body habits. If I am not being conscious of how I move, I find my shoulders rolled forward and upper body in a state of semi-collapse. When I draw my attention to it and roll my shoulders back, straighten my spine, I immediately feel better. I feel more open and stand taller. My organs have the space that was originally intended for them so that they can work efficiently, not constricted by bad posture. But the most interesting thing of all is that I *feel* different in myself. Not just physically, but I am suddenly presenting a different person to the world. One with more confidence, one who is brighter. This is the power of our body and how we use it.

You tell a story about yourself in the way that you move and the way that you stand. Just by walking across the treatment room of an expert bodywork practitioner they will be half way through their diagnosis of your psychological trauma and symptoms before you even make it to the chair to sit down and begin to speak. Such is the connection between the physical body and the other layers of our personality. We protect old wounds, physical and emotional, in the way that we hold ourselves. And sometimes those wounds, and that level of protection, no longer serves us; on both the physical and emotional level. Suddenly we find ourselves dealing with shadows all over again, as it seems they can also hide themselves in the way we stand and move. I find it fascinating.

If you notice quirks that you have physically, play around a little bit, taking care not to strain or hurt yourself of course. But try standing, moving or walking differently and note any differences you feel in how you are experiencing yourself. Just as with your inner self, it pays to understand where and how you are holding trauma or other emotions in your physical body. It pays to know yourself well. The whole body has memory, awareness, intelligence. If you ever think to stop and ask, it can tell you what it needs. Reclamation of your own body is a way into yourself. Drop into your body and use it as a connection to the outside world. Reclamation of your body, in the end, is the reclamation of the planet.

Although physical sensation is generally never in question, body wisdom is regularly sidelined. Certainly listening to the physical body and what it is telling you. And yet the body is a great barometer of the world and our surroundings. The body holds and generates great wisdom and insight.

The chronic traumatic stress which we are all party to, has dissociation as one of its symptoms – the spirit popping up and out, working in spite of, as opposed to along with, the body. Notice if you are most attracted to the practices in later chapters that are working outside of the body in the visionary realms; shamanic journey work and dream work. This is not wrong, but see it as an indicator that your dissociation is strong and your symptoms of chronic traumatic stress are present and real. Be sure to balance dream and visionary enquiries with physical and sensory ones. Directly communicating with other species, face to face, helps us to ground a bit more inside our own bodies. This is especially so when communicating with plants, as their roots reach deeply into the ground and as we learn from them, we learn to be a little bit more like them.

The more you come to know your body, the more you will realise when there is a perturbation – when something, even very subtle, changes. This is greatly beneficial when communicating with the more-than-human as communications may come in any form, not necessarily in language you understand. It may instead be transferred as a sensation, a tingle, an ache, a pain, a deep sigh, a cough or just acute awareness of a certain part or function of your body. Any of this can be an incoming communication from the one you are communicating with, so be vigilant. Know your body well and you will begin to understand when something is triggered within your body from outside of yourself.

I have had many experiences where my physical body gave me very strong messages about plants I was communicating with. One time I was walking, enjoying the gentle warmth of the autumn sun on a mountain trail. I was called in very strongly by a plant high up, growing from the branches of a tree, it wouldn't let me pass. So, I sat for a few moments responding to its call. Introducing myself, noticing, admiring, asking of its medicine. Almost instantaneously, after asking of its medicine, I had to run for the nearest bush where I had an extreme diarrhoea event. My whole body emptied in that moment. It came from absolutely nowhere, it did not persist, it was just a single extreme event in that moment, the rest of the day my bowels were totally back to normal. Later I discovered that the plant I had been working with was known as a diarrhoea remedy, but also that it was used for cleansing, as a purgative. The plant had very graphically communicated this to my body.

Another example was when I fell in love with an unassuming little plant populating the banks of a dry river bed. I was there for quite a while absolutely falling into the pure and beautiful dream of this plant. I surrendered to it entirely. But then, after some time, I began to be crippled with a sharp pain in my abdomen. Pain so severe that I had to close down the exchange and drag myself home where I lay on the sofa for two and a half hours before the pain subsided. Again this had come from "nowhere" and after it had left my body I was back to feeling absolutely normal, no residual pain, or recurrence, whatsoever. I listened, knowing that this had arrived in my body in response to the communication with the plant. It took me a lot of searching before I found just one single research paper about this plant and how its properties and actions had been shown to work well on colon cancer, research was ongoing as to whether it could be perhaps developed into a cancer medication. There was no other known or recorded medicinal uses for this plant, but it told me itself exactly where and what it could help in the physical body.

A third example, occurred when I happened across a gnarled and ancient tree clinging to a steep sided valley. Almost instantly on meeting this tree I felt an intense heaviness in my left arm and shoulder, I could barely lift my arm or turn my neck, at the same time my pulse boomed urgently and loudly in my ears. The whole experience was so unpleasant that I asked it to stop. I thanked the tree and walked away in a bit of a state. Later I spoke with an herbalist friend who told me that the tree is often used as medicine for people who experience heavy limbs due to poor circulation. Well, yet again, the tree could not have made it more clear in my body exactly what it was medicine for and its intense strength.

My lesson in all of those examples was to listen, absolutely, to my body and its reaction when in communication with the more-than-human. The physical sensation I experienced in each circumstance did not come out of "nowhere", it came directly and very strongly from the plant. It came as a very clear communication about what each specific plant can be used to heal or treat as a physical medicine. If my trust in myself and the messages from the plants was not intact, or if my attention to what my physical body was clearly and acutely communicating, had been ignored, I would have missed the communication. Pay attention. Your body can be a very effective receiver of information.

Allow your body to have its say. Let your body inform you. Don't forget that the body has language too, not just your body, but the body of others. Make time to listen.

Sensory Acuity

Drop into bodyfulness. Let your senses fill you up. Open to them, rather than ignoring them. See, hear, touch, taste and smell the rich deep sights, sounds, textures, flavours and fragrances. Let them flood in and overwhelm you. How did you ever hold them back so effectively, and why? As you allow your senses freedom to explore unrestrained they will inform you of many things and you will begin to feel your body more strongly than your mind. Then, you will start paying attention to their voices and their wisdom.

The more attention you give to your senses the more sensitive you become. It is worth spending lots of time here, don't just scoot through with a brief moment dedicated to each sense. There are so many messages from the more-than-human that our senses are constantly being bombarded with, but just like the rest of our wise body and the messages it brings to us, we often overlook them. Practise using your senses, one by one. Observe, not just what is happening at the surface level, but drop deeply and for that you will need to devote real time to each one.

How often do you look at the underside of a leaf? I mean really look. Notice how the nearby leaves cast shadows upon that which you study; how the light falling on the topside ignites a rainbow of colour underneath. The detail; the veins, the cells and segments. The fine hair of spider silk, the edges, the shapes. Then widening out to see the shapes and shadows of a wider selection of leaves and the dancing interplay with direct sun and momentary shade, the breeze that ripples through. These are the kind of things that you probably won't notice on your first visit. Or maybe your second, or even your third. It really does take a long time to notice everything. To touch every millimetre of that plant with your eyes.

Don't miss out anything that you see, not just on and of the other itself, but its surrounds, its community. For example, noticing a certain plant likes to grow in damp locations will indicate something of its character. Look everywhere, then look again. From the most tiny microscopic detail to the broader, wider view. Keep looking.

If you spend, say thirty minutes, just looking at all the different species growing in a circle of grass you are sat in the middle of, you won't be so quick to call a patch of grass a green desert. So much, even species diversity, is hidden in plain sight. Don't overlook what's right under your nose.

It is the same with all of the senses. We don't have them by accident. Learn how to use them. How to use them well and with acuity. Pay attention to the sounds that surround you. Listen well. Listen at different times of day and night, different times of the year. Use your hands to form a cup around your ear so that you can hone in on a sound and work out where it is coming from, who is making it. Become familiar with the sounds all of the plants and creatures, the birds and insects in your neighbourhood make. Close your eyes and just listen.

Make physical contact with the other using all parts of your body, not just your fingers. Roll up your sleeves and use your forearm. Your bare feet and toes. Your forehead, lips and cheeks. Each part of your body is sensitive in a different way. Touching the more-than-human with more than just your fingers brings in another level of intimacy often just reserved for human lovers.

Touching is of course more intrusive than looking or listening, so keep communicating, let the other know your intentions, ask if you can touch. During the first shamanic journey I did to the lower world, I found myself at a small lake surrounded by a tropical paradise. The colours in the foreground were vivid but this scene was backed by a rich velvety blackness, which made the plants and animals surrounding the lake stand out that much more. I walked to the back of the lake and dropped my clothes to the ground, ready for a swim. I paused a moment to take a handful of leaves in my hand to touch and let them run through my fingers; I always did this in mundane reality when I saw a plant I liked. But when the leaves had passed through my hand I noticed that my palm was lacerated, my skin ripped to shreds by the leaves. The lesson I took from the spirit world was to always communicate if I wish to handle a plant, to take a piece of its body into my hand.

Tasting is even more intrusive and so communication before the act is even more essential. Once you have asked and been granted permission, take a piece and let it sit on your lips a moment first, before you take it into your mouth. And then hold it in your mouth for a moment before you start to chew and truly taste. This slows you down and gives you time to begin to absorb the energy, so that you really notice well as you crunch, grind and swallow. Of course certain things cannot be chewed or even bitten off, certain things you can simply lick or suck. Others may not want you to taste them at all. And that is fine. But when you are wishing to understand something that *can* be tasted fully, don't miss the opportunity to take it in to your mouth and notice every nuance of flavour and texture, as each piece of the whole holds part of the message.

Often when tasting is not an option, smelling is. Get in close and smell each different part. Smell the old leaf and the new, the bark and the bloom. When you become aware of a fragrance, follow it. Allow it to draw you in and reveal the source. Who is it that smells so good? Who is trying to capture your attention and unfold themselves before you? Smell and smell again. Smell at all times of the day and year. Keep smelling.

Perception, by its very nature, involves the melding of our different senses and how they inform each other. It is through this sharing of information that we find ourselves able to go deeper into, and discover more about, the meaning of the thing.

> *As I smell the tincture I am finding it hard to distinguish you and your character from the strong pervasiveness of the alcohol. So, I let one drop sit on the back of my hand for a few moments. Again the overriding sensation is a pervasive strength and heat that I am associating with the medical grade alcohol. And so I taste, that one single drop. It is not until then that I can feel you with all of my being. That one drop seems immediately inward, downward and upward. The strength of your taste almost overwhelming, so strong, warm and pervasive. It was you that I felt all along, only my head told me that I was wrong, that I was feeling the alcohol. My senses combined*

finally broke through and informed me that what I had been experiencing all along was you...

To truly know takes time. It cannot be rushed. There is always something more, something new, a change, but also that which you overlooked on your early visits. With each new noticing, each new deepening of the familiarity between you, the further you will fall under the spell of the other. The more you will understand its language, its subtle whisperings. The more you will fall in love...

The more sensitivity we cultivate to sensory flows, the more directly we perceive with our senses and the wider the door opens.

Stephen Harrod Buhner

The Brain

Body wisdom, the physical senses and the feeling sense (I will speak more of this in a moment) are the foundations of communication and the common language between species. The brain is what brings things together and extracts meaning from them.

The brain's right hemisphere sees the wholeness of things and the connections between them, whereas the left hemisphere simply sees the "things". So the right takes in new information and sends it to the left for processing or categorising. This is achieved based on prior experience, the information is then returned to the right hemisphere to perceive meaning. But, it can get stuck in the left, in processing, in automatically categorising according to past experience, rather than experiencing as new and as what it really is. To avoid this, it is essential to recognise that every moment in time presents an opportunity for new conditions.

You can work to increase the activity of the right hemisphere. This requires introducing high frequency inputs to help expand the consciousness. And, no surprises, that involves a step toward the wild side, a diet rich with natural plant foods, medicinal herbs, essential oils and flower essences as they are all high frequency. It's energetics. Plants eat light, we eat plants; we are made of light via the plants that we eat.

Habits and habitual ways of thinking are well travelled pathways in the brain, the routes that our brain finds most easy to take. Every time we think, feel, or do, something within our regular realm of experience those well travelled pathways are strengthened. New activities, thoughts and skills begin to create new pathways. With repetition and practice of the new, these new pathways are strengthened and new habits formed. As the old pathways become less travelled they weaken. With repeated and direct attention towards change, the brain rewires.

As previously discussed, some people may find interspecies communication tricky at first but as you retrain your brain, create new pathways, it becomes easier.

The Heart

> *Shut your eyes so the heart may become your eye, and with that vision look upon another world.*
>
> **Rumi**

One thing we lost when our lives became more tame and domesticated was the understanding that we are living in a world of meaning, not things. As you shift from a brain-centred approach where life is a mystery to solve, and drop into your heart, you find that life becomes a mystery to experience.

It is essential when communicating with another that you adopt a "kindergarten state of mind". That is to rid yourself of anything you *think* you know and meet it as if for the first time. Try not to learn too much about anything initially in an intellectual way. Do not read up about the medicinal qualities or value as a vibrational/emotional/spirit medicine, of another being. Do not learn from recordings what each different call of a bird means. *Feel* into it instead – let "it" tell you. This requires developing a sensitivity to the feelings that emerge when around the being you intend to communicate with. Noticing tension, joy, relaxation, fear. Again I want to point out that as we have lived domesticated lives we have been trained out of paying attention to such feelings as they arise, but that is in part what holds us separate. Tuning back in to the feelings that arise in you as you experience the world and the beings around you is absolutely key to your own personal rewilding process and essential to effective interspecies communication. The feeling sense is expanded and fine tuned through using the heart as the organ of perception, not as is our cultural norm, the brain.

The heart is surrounded by an energy field. This is comprised of electric and magnetic fields generated by the heart. The field surrounding the heart, or heart-field, communicates with all the organs of the body including the brain. The heart-field is greater in size than the field generated by the brain which is why the brain responds to signals generated by the heart. The communications emanating from the heart go beyond the brain and our other body organs into the wider world where they interact as a series of electrical and magnetic waves, or vibrations. In fact the electrical power of heart signal (EKG) is up to sixty times stronger than electrical signal of the brain (EEG). While the magnetic field of the heart is five thousand times stronger than that of brain[30].

In essence the heart is a stronger communicator than the brain. So instead of ignoring the validity of feelings, the language of the heart, and bypassing them for logic, when it comes to more-than-human communication using the heart as the sender and receiver of information will get us better and more reliable results. The heart is all about feeling. Once you have mastered dropping into your heart and *feeling* your way around the world you will begin to be able to perceive directly

My brain is not wired to effectively intellectually describe the precise science behind the intelligence of the heart. But what I can, and do, is live it and so can describe it from my felt dimension, my perspective. If you need explanations and science to make it real for you, for it to have value, then I recommend reading *The Secret Teachings Of Plants* by Stephen Harrod Buhner. In this book Stephen takes a really detailed look into the mechanics of using the heart as the primary organ of perception.

Equally I don't want to overwhelm you with too much head stuff, as it is the heart and feeling, where you need to be for this work. If you are open minded and open hearted enough to try, and willing to be persistent, then the results will speak for themselves...

Communication with the heart, despite having science behind it, does not require technical knowledge or grandiose technique. However, feeling with the heart is something we must relearn.

My approach for dropping into my heart and out of my head, is to let go of thinking and instead focus my energy on feeling. I visualise my heart-field, the energy of my heart, pulsating outwards and enveloping the subject of my attention. Pushing out the feeling, the heart-felt feeling. The love. The gratitude. And sitting in that expanded heart space and noticing what I receive in return. Anything. Anything at all.

It takes practise. Practise, practise, practise. The more you do it the better you will become at it and the more you will ground your skills into your primary way of being.

At some point I become familiar with the one I am sat with. Start to recognise them touching my heart back and in that moment I know connection has been made. I can *feel* something other than myself in my heart space. That is what this is all about. Making that connection. Waiting, being patient, being persistent, until that feeling comes in. Someone has noticed me and is responding. I am still very clumsy, no doubt, but I feel other beings constantly these days and as I acknowledge them, I almost instantaneously, notice them acknowledging me back.

This, absolutely for me, is the primary building block, the gateway to more elegant communications. Without this starting point it is almost always coming from my head.

So to access the intelligence of the wild, first I recommend connecting with your heart. This is the only way. Feelings don't lie. And the heart, stronger than the brain, can open doors to the other realms. To the secrets hidden in plain sight. To the magic and mystery of interspecies communication.

Feelings are how you touch the world and it touches you back. As you fine tune working with feeling you will learn to notice every touch upon you and how each of those things that touched you makes you feel. Taking back mastery of your body wisdom, of your senses, and ultimately of your ability to feel, is a somewhat subversive act, as suddenly we are back in play. Suddenly we begin to understand the world we are embedded within and our place there. We begin to understand the wants and needs of the other beings we share this life with and begin to respond to that. We become more wild.

Make time to notice how other beings feel and your response. You could use that five minutes barefoot practice first thing in your day. Be still, be there, breathe, relax. Go from being to being and notice how each one feels, how they make you feel. Notice the differences and distinctions between the feelings you pick up from each one. The more you practise the more you notice when a new feeling hits you. The more sophisticated you get at using your heart, the more you will know and understand where that feeling came from and eventually begin to decipher what it perhaps means.

When you approach another being with the intention of communicating, find the feeling first. Notice how they feel, how you feel sat with them. As you sink into the feeling you will begin to come into sync, the electro-magnetic field generated by your heart and the electro-magnetic field of the other will sync and in that moment a flow of information can occur. That is what you are looking for here. A direct communication of feeling.

With the heart at the helm, using your feelings as your indicator, you will learn the ways of direct perception. It stops being all about you and what you think you know. It becomes instead biognosis – knowledge direct from the wild heart of the world. Your brain at this point will be jumping up and down to get involved, to start analysing and categorising, but just keep with it. Stay with your heart and feel a little deeper. A little longer. Eventually you can train your mind to relax and trust the heart.

Trust the feelings. And by letting them wash over and through you, you begin to communicate with the more-than-human world.

These communications will embed themselves within you. Your mind memory may forget, but your heart and body memory will not. I do however recommend writing it all down, at first at least, to help trigger those memories and to sate your mind that you are doing something of value.

The heart is the primary organ of perception, the brain offers a secondary and essential supportive role. It provides the words to fit the feelings and to fill the descriptions. Remember that engaging the brain alone will not allow for the depth of communication that the heart can reach.

Knowledge is finite. Wonder is infinite.
Matt Haig

We have spent our whole lives training ourselves, our brains, to go into overdrive as soon as we have an inkling about something to fill in the gaps, so that you can say you know, or intellectually deduce something. So it is most likely that you are not very skilled at adopting the "kindergarten state of mind". But this work and personal rewilding in general demands it. Turning off that learnt intellectual reductionism and instead focussing solely (initially at least) on experience. On how it feels, how it affects your senses and your body, and what that can tell you through the analysis that naturally comes later. Above all feeling with the heart is beyond emotion. Emotion is what we attach to the underlying feeling state due to our personal unresolved stuff. At the beginning emotion will probably be hard to differentiate from the underlying feeling state, but that again is where personal shadow work will show its value.

Feeling, feeling, feeling. That, and only that, is where direct and original knowing comes from. Intellectual knowing will never even come close, even though you will be able to reduce the thing to its "constituents" and "uses" more readily. Knowing with the heart is to know the whole person as you do with your family, friends and lovers. And that is where true knowing lies, true value, because that is when you really do begin to understand that other being as a person in their own right, not just a plant with medicinal properties (be they emotional, physical and/or spiritual). Intellectual knowing is useful of course, if you graze your knee you need to know who can help you fix it. But this work is about going way way beyond that. Knowledge is of the mind; whereas wisdom is of the heart.

Direct Perception

Any perception is an interchange between the perceiver and that which is perceived – it is an exchange, a communication. To touch is to be touched remember, and so to perceive then, is also a two way street. It is not an inanimate, inert thing that you are perceiving but a sentient life-form that noticed you back. If you find yourself caught up in your head you can miss everything, which is why it is essential to use the heart as the organ of perception; to feel, not think. Once again, this is about unlearning our perceived separation and reintegrating with other life as sentient relations, rather than inanimate objects. It is necessary to learn how to see and feel what is really there before you. The less you are burdened with a mental filter, the more direct access to the other being you develop. Direct perception is that knowledge that enters you as a result of directed and uninterrupted focus with the heart, of noticing with the heart.

Being able to perceive directly does require a certain amount of effort, quite a lot of it directed at calming the mind and getting it to wait patiently for its turn. It is also essential to approach the other being directly, as discussed earlier in this chapter, without this you will not get anywhere. In addition you need to approach without any preconceptions, with an absolute willingness to be ignorant. This is a skill, and is where you will have to engage any mind calming techniques you have to hand, as already it will be enthusiastically jumping in with "facts and information" about your subject. Knowing nothing is an absolute gift in this circumstance.

When I first began using my heart to communicate, in pursuit of direct communication, I had the absolute advantage of being far, far away from home, in high altitude desert. None of the plants were familiar, I didn't know anyone, not a single plant, stone or animal. So lucky for me, my mind had no chance of getting involved. So if you can't stop yourself from thinking, your mind from popping up with what it "knows", and sabotaging your attempts at receiving, then try with a plant or animal or place you know nothing about. Do it while on holiday. Seek out the unfamiliar. Give yourself a real chance to know nothing.

Once you have engaged with the more-than-human directly, have used your physical senses and paid attention to your wise body, then comes feeling with the heart. It is well known that if you focus intensely on something then allow yourself to rest, to defocus, then repeat this process again and again, eventually, all being well, you will have that eureka moment. The moment when the meaning of the thing drops into your consciousness. That is to say that you will suddenly gain an understanding of the essential nature of the other with whom you are communicating. In this moment lies the extraction of meaning. All of the stages you have worked through coalesce in that moment and understanding drops in. Not just intellectually, but viscerally.

Your understanding suddenly goes way beyond an intellectual knowing. This is a knowing grounded in every cell of the body, the heart and beyond that, the soul. It is a soul knowing. A recognition. A remembering. A wild homecoming.

Intuition

Intuition does not come from the conscious, rational mind, it is more an instinct, an animal knowing. It is knowing without knowing how you know, and that that doesn't actually matter. Intuition becomes stronger and we notice it more once all of the other senses, heart cognition and direct perception are all being exercised and are in place.

When I am doing ongoing work with a group, such as a several days long retreat, participants often begin to pick up what the next plant will be. In some cases this can be even before I know. Sometimes the plan I have may be rejected by a plant at the last minute; another plant steps in and surprise, surprise, it is the one people had been picking up on that afternoon or on the drive over. During a retreat, perhaps on day three in the afternoon, people will begin to notice the plant that is lined up for study the following day; they will begin talking about that plant. By day four, already during the morning tea break the plant for day five has entered their consciousness and they begin cooing over it and smelling it as they pass by during their break; almost 24 hours before we begin the work with it. Sometimes I even have people display a plants medicine in their behaviour before class begins. I once had two ladies that would drive two hours together for my evening series. They would turn up complaining of tiredness, shortness of breath, fits of the giggles, prophetic dreams or any number of other properties that the plant we were about to study had in its kit bag. Sometimes these symptoms would begin to emerge a full day before and certainly for the entirety of their two hour drive. Why is this? Maybe because the plant is getting excited and has been calling to me so very loudly for a long time and they begin to hear it too, especially now that they are primed and sensitive to their sixth sense, their intuition.

As you learn to trust your intuition, those pieces of the puzzle that seem to land within you from seemingly nowhere, your communication with the wider world expands. If you can trust that it is possible to just know, without questioning why or how, your personal wildness will go up to the next level; you are returning home.

Listening & Common Blocks To Hearing

When communicating with this animate Earth and its inhabitants it is important to trust. Don't rush. Start small. Be prepared for it to be slow. Eventually you will reach the essential essence of the thing.

Working with the heart and feeling is about entering the dreaming of the other, the dreaming of Gaia, but that does not mean it's not real. Gaia has dreamed it all, everything. Working with meaning *always* involves dreaming. So allow yourself to fall in love. Fall into the dream. I don't think one comes without the other. You cannot get there cerebrally or logically *only* through the heart. The heart provides a much more direct and visceral approach. Being overly intellectual can obscure the ability to hear clearly, we already know that the brain cannot reach the depths that the heart can. If your brain is the only organ you are using you will miss and misinterpret so much, you will not get close to the whole story.

Assuming that you already know something, as I have said before, can block your perception of what is truly before you. Sometimes you receive a plain and clear response and feel replete, know that this particular interaction is complete and that now is the time to walk away. Sometimes the conversation is very simple. Don't over-seek and look incessantly for hidden mystical meanings in every exchange as when you look too hard sometimes you miss the simplicity of the message. *But* that can only happen with a very specific inquiry, with anything that is more general or broad, there will never be enough time. If your enquiry was a general one check for more layers, for something you may have missed. There is no end to the depth of any being, there is always more.

Some connections you will make with other beings may require more than one attempt. Again try not to make assumptions that you have the answer, or that there is no message for you. Only come to that conclusion when you absolutely know it. If it is just that you are not getting much, then relax, and let it go for now; returning when you are ready to try again. Thinking you know it all already will *always* block you from noticing anything new.

This is an abundant Earth, Gaia is abundant, and yet it is very common to feel lack. To feel a deficit of time or spirituality. To feel that you are not enough. Any feelings of lack will block your ability to rewild, your ability to connect with your more-than-human relations. We already know that you will be stopped by feelings that you are not good enough, that you can't do it, that a herbalist or someone who is shamanically trained will be better than you. The thing is no one else is you, your relationships with other beings are shared only between you and that other being – no one else can ever know exactly what you share, or take it away from you, neither can they tell you that you are wrong.

You have to be open otherwise you miss the communications. One of my closest friends was single throughout most of her 30's, nearly every time we went out in a group we would get home and I would say "didn't you notice that he liked you?". Each time she would respond with a "no". Something inside her had closed to those communications and so she missed everything – she had blinkers on. For most people this is how we are with the more-than-human, most of the time. This is where your work on being open and vulnerable is essential, to remove those shields, those layers of armour you have built around yourself, possibly to protect yourself from the intensity of feeling in the first place.

It can be fear underlying that personal layer of protection. If you have an inkling this could be so, then you will need another root around in your personal shadowlands, to see if you can discover what you are afraid of and whether it is justified in this circumstance. If your fear is misplaced, you can work to reassure yourself, to defuse it and thus essentially remove your fear as a block to communicating. If something inside has closed off, clear and obvious communications can be missed, but that doesn't mean it's not happening. Keep working on it.

The other strong block I have noticed is expectations. Messages from the more-than-human can come in so many forms, some of them exceptionally subtle. If you are expecting a big booming voice coming from behind the curtain, prepare to be disappointed. Communication can arrive as an explosion of feeling, but if that is not what you are "expecting" you may not realise that what you are receiving is a direct communication, and miss it entirely. It is attention to detail, to swings in your mood, to twitches in the furthest reaches of your body, to feeling hungry, bored, sleepy or frustrated. Pay attention to how you feel (on all levels physical and otherwise) before you attempt to communicate, monitor this constantly during, and then again when the communication has concluded. If there is *any* change in you at all, then at least consider that this could be the communication. Write it all down, even if it does not seem to be much, then you can return to it. If you return to the same being and you get the same or similar reactions again, then it would be safe to conclude that it is very likely coming from the one that you are communicating with.

Expectations can lead you to miss the essential gems that were meant for you in that moment, as you overlooked them or simply didn't recognise them for what they were. This is the greatest loss. Those who do not see what is there for want of something more. I have witnessed this many times, and literally argued with the person that they *did* receive a communication, that the tears rolling down their face are a testament to that, but if the person is not ready for the lesson, no matter how clearly it comes, they will not hear it. Again and again and again, part of this goes back to clarity. Because if you don't realise what you are asking, the answer will make little sense. Notice and celebrate with joy any and all communications you become aware of.

It would be so much more simple if all beings spoke in the Queen's English, but they don't. So, drop that expectation and open to the myriad ways that information may reach you. Then, suddenly, you will become aware that communications *are* flowing, without unrealistic expectations blocking them.

Changes In You

When you open up to communication from other life forms and begin to actively stalk connection, something in you begins to change. And although you are unlikely to sprout feathers or talons, or even tendrils and leaves, you certainly start to feel more at home among other life forms, more relaxed and integrated. You are becoming more wild.

In quantifiable terms there are physiological changes that can be measured. Such as a drop in cortisol levels, lowered blood pressure, a lower pulse rate, greater parasympathetic nerve activity[31], lower sympathetic nerve activity. Together these effects translate as reduced levels of stress, depression and anxiety, improved mood, lowered feelings of hostility and a feeling of belonging to something greater than oneself. Just as with Shinrin Yoku, the Japanese practice of "forest bathing", there are physical, emotional and mental benefits. They tie in with how we were built to be, getting us back to factory settings as we perhaps now would understand it, a reboot to our wild beginnings.

It is the ineffable that changes the most though, and *that* cannot be measured with instruments. You will notice it nonetheless, *if* you are paying attention. That change is the wildness creeping back into your soul, claiming you tiny bit by tiny bit as you tune back in to the wild world, the only world your ancient ancestors, who once stood in this land, knew. As wildness claims you more wholly and you realign with the rest of the natural world you will become more adept at moving back and forth between the seen and the unseen worlds, between the sensory and the non-sensory. As you release your learned and domestic beliefs one by one, your natural capacities will return.

The wild part of you, the part that is waking up inside, needs company. You will have to learn to live from this place to fully embody your wild self, otherwise the danger is that you go back to how you were, except that now the nagging feeling that there is something more will be almost unbearable. You have to find a way for this to become a way of life, so that your whole life becomes a living communication, and for that you need to do this all the time. And when you make that breakthrough you will know what each patch of soil needs no matter where you stand on this planet.

One thing I know for sure is that there is no right way or wrong way when it comes to interspecies communication. As with every art, as long as you have the necessary materials; in this case desire, passion and an open heart, then it will begin to flow through you. With practice you will develop your skill, you will become more articulate, your technique will become more uniquely your own.

Some people have a natural affinity for communication with plants, others have to work hard to quiet their nagging logic telling them they are making it all up. Others find their affinity lies not with plants but crystals or animals perhaps. The good news is that the skill set, your art, is transferable between all life forms and as you become more elegant in your style, there will be a crossover and you will begin to be able to hear the voices of all your relations. It just takes persistence, practice and time.

Personally when I find myself immersed in wild, and deep in communication with other species, I find myself falling in love over and over and over again. Even when I then find myself in an area densely populated with humans. It is not just every plant I fall in love with, although they as a collective facilitate me arriving in this state, but it is every human too. The old man on the bus, the cute kid in the park, the shy woman in the shop. I notice them and I smile, not just on my face but deep in my heart. Spreading all through my being like the tide coming in and warm tropical waters touching toe to crown. In fact, *exactly* like the first flush of a love affair – those moments that are pure – before your head gets involved with a new lover. Just that warm all encompassing feeling that puts a permasmile on your face. The only thing I can conclude is that opening to interspecies communication increases your capacity for compassion.

Actual techniques and methods are not what is important, it is the approach and attitude that underpins the whole thing, and that includes knowledge of self. So although I outline various methods and techniques in the chapters that follow, I don't go into huge detail on any one. The most important thing is for this to become a state of being, a way of life. That is where the real magic, change and communication begins.

Delving into interspecies communication, weaving it into your being, living it so that your life becomes a living dancing interweaving with all other species, is deeply healing work, it brings you back to your rightful place amongst all your relations. This way of life doesn't just allow you a glimpse of the divine, but allows you to bask in the presence of all the gods and goddesses all day every day. The process of two-way communication allows you to live in intimacy with the Earth.

Practising perpetual interspecies communication, as a way of being, is where each of us can begin to heal the state of chronic traumatic stress that our life, separate from wider nature, birthed within us as we emerged from the womb. We begin to develop our missing sense of belonging, security and trust in the world. Our individual sense of self is expanded to being felt within the context of relationship. We feel more centred, capable and whole, as we take back two hundred percent responsibility for ourselves and in that become more able to meet challenges. And then, of course, we begin to be able to draw meaning from our encounters with the more-than-human. Our sense of connectedness goes through the roof as we regain all of these facets of our personality that we were raised lacking as a product of the domestic blandscapes which we have inhabited to this point. Ultimately we gain awareness of meaning in the world and our place within that.

It is imperative that we start to experience other species as relations. As you become more aware of all your relations, as relations, everything about you and your daily habits and rituals will gradually change until you are living a life of sacred acts, a life where truly every breath is a prayer. Allow this journey, this reawakening to the ongoing conversation with all species, to become a pilgrimage. A deep journey into creating the life you want. A sacred life filled with sacred relations. An experiencing of the sacredness in all things.

The art of interspecies communication necessitates entering into the imaginal realms, those liminal spaces inhabited by images and dreams and stories. Populated by archetypes and synchronicities. And it requires that you do not judge the information that you gather in this place, as it is as real as anything you experience in both the waking realms and in the deep night time dreaming realms, in fact I think it exists somewhere between the two and is just as important as either. When you learn the language of another you fall into its dream, it does not matter how you get there, but once there you suddenly just know things, the same way you do when you dream at night. You are entering the dream of the other, it is sharing its dream with you and gifting you insights, that arise within you from simply being allowed access. This inbetween place is exactly where we can access the Gaia mind and communicate freely with all our relations.

Every tree, every river, every stone is as different as we are. Each has their own unique experiencing of the world. Who are you noticing? Who is calling to you? The ones that capture your attention are encoded with meaning, they have something to teach you. Are you attracted or repulsed? Falling in love or fearful? That in itself is the beginning of the communication and holds many truths that you can later unpick.

Meet the land; meet the plant; meet the stone. Never forget that off planet entities, the stars and comets, the other planets; are alive and possible to connect and communicate with too.

We live in a responsive world. Gaia is alive, is responsive. We can't save it; can't take control of how we think things should be. It is autonomous, we can only take control of our own direction; but never forget there is no separation. That is the Gaian paradox...

IV
Flower

The flower emerges to attract pollinators to this maturing, fertile, alluring, beauty. Successful fertilisation leads to a time of gestation, a time of creation.

5. The Art Of Plant Whispering

Plant whispering is understanding the language of plants. It is being able to discern something within you change when you see a flower, taste a herbal tea or sit under a tree. *And* to understand that the change within you is a response to the plant. This is communication. This is being able to notice the whispers that the plant is putting out into the world. To notice them, and from them be able to understand a little more about that plant itself, but also how the plant affects you. Plant whispering can also be taking that basic level of communication further. It can be asking a direct question, receiving a direct response and understanding the meaning.

My personal experiences, the interactions I have had with plants over the years, I now recognise as an apprenticeship of sorts, led by the plants themselves. At the time many of the experiences that I had, although memorable and enshrouded with a kind of luminescence, buried themselves in my being. It was not until later, with the benefit of hindsight, that I began to trace back and notice the golden thread weaving through my life. The theme of plants. Of deep connection with plants. Of communication with plants. That is my golden thread. I was not always necessarily conscious that these individual moments and incidences, were of a greater relevance at the time, but now I can see that the role of plant whisperer has always been weaving through me, drawing the fabric of my life closer into the realms of plants, weaving us tightly together until I see no end to them and the beginning of me. We are not isolated, me an outsider with interest looking in, we are fully entangled. Every thread of my life is coloured by plants.

> *It is an early February evening, 2004. I am sat as part of a small group, there are perhaps six or seven of us in the room. The air is cold, even inside, where we sit upstairs in an old stone mill at the narrow bottom of a damp, shaded Cotswold valley, England. We are attending a herb class and have just made our first herbal cream in the dank, dimly lit room. We are all fascinated and excited, making notes and feeling empowered and liberated, learning the long forgotten art of herbal medicine making. Somehow it is connecting us with our deep ancestral past, with things the establishment would rather remain forgotten. Forgotten, so that the agenda of big pharma*

can continue to be pushed while the population remain disempowered regarding their own health and health care. The increasing reliance on finite oil resources and pharmaceutical products that are made, packaged and transported by this dwindling resource, is keeping us slaves to black gold. Keeping us complicit in wars that rage across the globe for the last drops of this ancient sunlight. There is a rebellious stirring among us in the room, in rekindling the ancient knowing of our plant relations, the other lives we share this island with. It feels ultimately subversive, edgy while at the same time folksy. Most of all it feels real. It is bringing us back in touch with our roots as members of a Gaian community, not just a human one.

The excitement of our practical exercise and demonstration, our deep learning and ancient remembering, begins to ebb just a little as we settle for more left brain words and information. But, that is not what our teacher has in store for us. Close your eyes, he requests, as he leads us on a guided meditation; a meditation that will lead us to meet with a plant spirit.

My eyes softly close and I can hear my teachers voice; as clear, strong and focused as the finest quartz. I fall backwards, inwards, through darkness. When I open my eyes I am in a beautiful rich wild flower meadow, edged on all sides and at some distance by mixed deciduous woodland. In the distance I can see the flutterings of Oak and Chestnut and Beech, moving gently in the mid summer breeze. It is bright. The sun is at its zenith and the heat is warming to my core. It is then that I notice her. Moving, gliding, towards me through the dancing clouds of bees and butterflies, a beautiful maiden. She has pale skin and rosy cheeks, her golden hair falls loosely over her shoulders. Her lips are full and rose pink. She is ethereal and surrounded by a golden aura.

She extends her delicate white hand to me and in an instant we are in the deep lush cooling shade of the trees at the meadow edge. This is where she lives. she points to my feet which are surrounded by deep purple flower spikes, they are short and close to the ground but vibrant with small dark waxy leaves of emerald green. Without opening her mouth to speak I can hear her voice in my head: sing to me, she requests. There is no pause for uncertainty, for self-consciousness, for my left brain to wonder what should I sing? Because already it is issuing forth from me. No words but an unfamiliar and haunting melody. My hairs are standing on end. Something truly magical is happening. This unassuming plant is teaching me her song. She is singing through me. Time stands still as I sing forever, only me and her exist, in a bed of her physical manifestation, this beautiful purple flower.

It is then that I begin to notice a ripple breaking through the scene, like a pebble dropped into a pond, except the pond is the meadow and the first ripple is advancing on my position at it's tree-lined edge. In the very far distance I can hear a soft clear voice calling me back into a different reality; come back into the room, back into your chair, open your eyes. And as quickly as that I am back in the deep winter of the Cotswolds, contained within old stone walls, sat on a plastic chair, with others, perhaps six or seven in the room.

Until this experience, I had never realised how thin the veil was, how access could be so simple and so easy. From this point on, it became an even more prominent part of my life path to see beyond the veil. To know what lies beyond and freely interact with that which exists there, beyond the usual frame of reference. To draw it into my day to day existence freely exchanging and communicating, existing between realms, one foot in each.

The art of plant whispering is one specialised strand of interspecies communication. It is something we all once did, one way or another. If you have been hearing the call of the plants, if they have been there for you again and again in any number of ways, then this is your invitation to whisper back to them. To remember the skills you were born with, unlearn your cultural conditioning and let your wild Gaian soul breathe and flow in the life stream with all beings once more. Remember yourself not just as Gaia but as wild plant whisperer.

Once you begin to remember yourself as plant whisperer you may just be able to look back and see the green thread weaving through *you* all along, since your earliest wild rememberings...

Our rooted relations experience things that we do not. Stood so apparently still for such a long, long time. Only they can teach us those things. And the wisdom in their knowing? You will not know until you ask.

Plant whispering is an art because it is a skill, a skill that you will fine tune with practice. The more time you dedicate, the more elegant and more uniquely your own the art becomes. Your relationships become the masterpieces. The plants, naturally, the muse.

Why Plants?

Plants, because without them there is no life for humankind; it is really that simple. From our very first breath to our very last we rely on them for life itself. Without plants there would be no oxygen which anchors us to life with breath. Every oxygen laden in-breath allows our body to function and is followed by a carbon dioxide rich out-breath, used and needed for the functioning of plants. At the very base of human life itself then, is our relationship with plants. We don't just take oxygen, we give back carbon dioxide. It's a symbiotic relationship. We need each other.

Equally without plants there would be no food. As even if we only eat animal flesh, and that animal only eats animal, at some point in the food chain there is plants. As we eat plants and use them as medicines, we take them inside our body. And so our connection is not just from the outside but also from the inside as the plant body feeds, builds and helps repair, our body. They are our body. So, also, our relationship to our body. If your relationship with plants becomes sacred then, your relationship with your physical body also becomes sacred, as does every other relationship in your life.

Plants truly are our relations, not just what feeds us oxygen and converts into our cells and blood as we eat them, but more than that they are like us. We are mainly plant after all.

Without plants we are nothing. We would cease to exist and for that we owe them everything. Plants are our ancestors, they were on Earth way before humankind. Thus the relationship between humanity and plants is a long, and constantly evolving one. Working with plants is both our heritage and our future.

Some plants have been favoured more than others, these have been nurtured and given special attention for the gifts they give in return.

The plants we love to eat the most, those we use for medicines, those with eye-catching blooms or incredible fragrance. Plants we build with, make shelter from, use their fibres to make clothing with. Once you look around in your living space, in your fridge, in your garden, in your kitchen apothecary, the presence of plants is overwhelming, we really do absolutely rely upon them for almost everything.

As humankind spread out from the African rift valley, across every continent, we took their seed with us. Sometimes we intentionally collected their seed, so that we could have our favourite foods in our new habitats. But we also transported the seed in our hair, on our clothes, amongst our belongings and in our body waste. Plants migrated around the world piggybacking a ride with the humans. It's not just us using them, again we find mutually beneficial relationships. Plants are more participatory and clever than we tend to give them credit for.

As you know by now my mind was blown by Yuval Noah Harari's discussion that wheat played a role in domesticating us. So think perhaps also of our love for roses, for all plants that we cultivate. Just like in each human relationship you enjoy, you both play a role in cementing that relationship, you both participate. The plants role in the relationships that we share with them begin as they capture our attention; as they draw us in and encourage us to fall in love.

> *Each spring you pass a Lilac bush in bloom and stop to deeply drink in the fragrance with all of your being, until you fall so deeply in love that one day you buy a Lilac bush for your own garden.* Nothing happens by chance.

Bacteria secrete acids which break down rocks, which then become available to the plants with the help of mycelium networks. And so Plants take the broken down rocks, the minerals of the Earth, into their bodies. These minerals then help build the animals (such as humans) that eat them. We eat silica in plants and express it in our hair and nails, those plants become us but as they do so, so do the rocks that became the plants. There is infinity in you, it is what we are all made of, available to us through eating plants that eat sunlight and rocks.

Another reason for "why plants?" is because they are reaching out to humans. In recent years Ayahuasca has emerged from the Amazon to present herself to the spiritually bereft of Europe, North America and Australasia. Although the first botanical samples of *Banisteriopsis caapi* (the Ayahuasca vine) were collected in the 1850's, this potent brew only came to the wider attention of industrialised nations during the 1960s and 70s*. She is not the only one that has stepped forward, but I would say she has become the most widely imbibed and well known, of the entheogenic plant teachers migrating from their tribal lands to remind Younger Brother** of a better, more real, life.

Ayahuasca, and others like her, speak to those that can feel themselves dying for lack of meaning in their lives. Living spiritually isolated lives, as we tend to in current consensus reality, eventually we weaken, wither and die (in spirit). Ayahuasca may just have come to save us from ourselves, and save the rest of Gaia from our unconscious and destructive behaviour.

This medicine has come forth and activated people: opening and waking them. Reminding them of rich, rich, lives filled with endless possibilities. In that moment, when we are open and clear, we begin to recognise ourselves once more as an integral part of the tapestry of life, intricately interwoven and inter-dependent on all others.

Interestingly Cacao also travelled the world intoxicating us with her pleasures but had a different approach to Ayahuasca, allowing her beauty and mystery to initially be cloaked in the mix with sugar, milk and all sorts of other ingredients. She then waited, literally hundreds of years, before she began to reveal herself to those outside of her natural habitat with her voluptuous depth.

Raw Cacao didn't really hit the shelves here in Europe until the early noughties. Cacao ceremonies, that is drinking Cacao in a form similar to that which was historically enjoyed by the Mayans and Aztecs of Central America for over 5000 years, not arriving in any significant way until around 2012 or thereafter. Interestingly the date that Cacao chose to reveal her true self to the rest of the world coincided with the Mayan end of time. The end of one cycle, of course, always preceding the beginning of a new one, a new time here on Earth. We were already intoxicated by her, and now in her glorious naked form we find ourselves falling ever more deeply in love with this wise elder from the plant realms.

Closer to home, has been the powerful emergence of Mugwort (*Artemesia vulgaris*). Mugwort has the magical capacity to remain invisible despite being in full sight *until* you have met for the first time. After that

---

* *Banisteriopsis caapi had been known and used alongside various other medicinal plants by native Amazonians for many many generations before this "discovery".*

** *Younger Brother is a term used by the Kogi peoples of the Sierra Nevada de Santa Marta in Colombia. The Kogi people care for the heart of the world. They name the inhabitants of outside civilisations as Younger Brother. They believe that the lifestyle and behaviours of Younger Brother are destroying the integrity and health of the world. We are Younger Brother.*

you will see Mugwort inhabiting waysides all over the place leading the way, directing and illuminating the path. Once you have met you will find each other everywhere.

Chinese Mugwort (*Artemesia argyi*) stepped forward to work with humans at least 3000 years ago. There is evidence of Chinese Mugwort's presence alongside acupuncture as moxa, since the conception of acupuncture in ancient China. It has been in the background of human culture, working with and alongside us (almost invisibly) all that time.

More recently, as our departure from our wild beginnings has become wider and the consequences more extreme, Mugwort has become increasingly visible. In the UK this has happened in the last 15 years primarily, I believe, through the Plant Spirit Medicine work of Eliot Cowan. Eliot had trained in five element acupuncture before the plant spirits began sharing their medicine through him. Mugwort, initially through the Chinese Mugwort used in moxa, invisibly and stealthily entered Eliot and to this day plays an essential role in his medicine form. Mugwort is strong and direct, and is very keen to get out there and spread its medicine among us. Guiding us toward a more animistic, sustainable, plant appreciating and balanced direction. Mugwort, through this exposure, most certainly has spoken strongly and directly to me.

My final point on the "why plants?" theme is because they remain more or less in the same spot for long enough to strike up a conversation (unlike animals, insects and birds), and most often will still be there if we choose to revisit them.

I have not yet mentioned fungi. They are distinct from plants but also great communicators and easy to build relationships with. I in no way mean to sideline them, I have mushroom allies of the highest order and I would never disrespect them. However to talk of the art of plant and fungi whispering is a little clumsy. And so know that when I speak of plants, I also speak of fungi. Absolutely all of the suggestions I raise for working with plants can also be used in work with fungi, without exception.

So What Is Plant Whispering?

Fundamentally the art of plant whispering, as with all communications with the more-than-human, is about states of mind, states of being, not information. It is not specific techniques and methods to get all caught up in your head about, more a quiet awareness where you simply let go of all the "shoulds" going on in your mind and just take time to feel with all parts of your being, time to notice and to listen.

It is opening up to the dreaming of the world. We have spent our domestic lives thus far in a dulled and sleep walking state, but even breaking a fresh lettuce leaf from the plant and taking in the smell of the white sappy residue that rises to fill and heal the lettuce scar will lift you. Carry you, even for just one moment, out and up, into the dream. This is why I know all plants are messengers, are psychedelic[32], and can lead us (if we let them) into the dreaming of the Earth.

Each plant has its own voice. Its own growing location, preferred growing partners, chemical make up, smell, look, shape, texture, response to perturbation within its environs. Plants speak through their biology and chemical messaging systems, their taste and their character. They *also* speak through feeling and dreaming.

Look at a Californian Poppy. For me I feel joy, instantly, just looking at the bright and simple but beautiful flower and silvery foliage. From observation logic tells me that it is delicate and yet resilient. That is all communication. However plant whispering can take you deeper. Give you access to what is beyond the obvious. This requires dedicated time, trust, and clear questioning; all of the things I wrote of in the previous chapter. The immediately apparent communications are exactly that – you just have to be interested enough to notice. But, if you want to know more about a plant, or yourself (as fundamentally there is no separation), that's where the art of plant whispering comes in.

I will give you a variety of suggestions that can help you take your communications deeper. You don't have to use them all for each plant you work with, not at all. Some of my suggestions may not work for you; but that is why I have listed all the different methods that I have personally found useful, so that you get an idea of the great variety of different ways "in". Often I use multiple techniques with a single plant, so that I can take my communications deeper and deeper. Sometimes it all pops in very swiftly; as much as I want, or need, to work with in that moment at least. Other times it can be more difficult. Just the same as with people. Some people you will have an instant connection with, and within a single evening together feel you have always known them. Others years later you are still finding your way in. It doesn't mean you give up on the more difficult ones, unless you get the message to go away. It just means that the treasures inside take more effort to reach...

Real relationship, as we all know, takes time, but more than that, and what I have not yet mentioned, essential chemistry. As no matter how much time you give it, if you just don't like each other your relationship will never get off the starting blocks... You carry the relationships inside of you even before you meet, you simply unlock them when you begin to share with each other.

Our vegetal relations do not behave, or think, or feel, like humankind (thank goodness). As you spend time striving to communicate, you will soon discover that there is something there beyond the physical, the material, that is real, that you can feel, and that can feel you. Our very anthropocentric and limited vocabulary does not quite have the words to explore or describe it, as since we collectively cut ourselves off from wild we lost the need for such language. We don't understand it fully so how can we accurately describe it in a language that doesn't believe in it? It is like trying to describe your first LSD trip to all your friends who are sat drinking cider. It is a different level that exists but until you peel back the layers of reality to find it you won't know, and even when you do, you can't describe succinctly in human language. The good news is that the more confidence you gain in your ability to whisper with the plants the less you will have a need to describe your experiences and relationships in human words.

If you are called by the wild whisperings of the plants and listen hard enough, you will find not only that plants can care about you (yes you!), but also that they may have something to tell you, to teach you about you, your soul and your soul's journey. Plants are the best kind of teachers, as they don't teach you directly, instead they guide and inspire you to discover what you already know. For that reason never allow anyone to stand in between you and the plants, to tell you how a certain plant is. It is a sacred relationship between yourself and the plant. When it becomes so, you will find that you are not so much *learning* about or even from the plants, but *remembering*. Eventually, once clear communications are flowing, it will become your undertaking to learn how to honour the teachings, healing and insights you have been gifted.

Throughout my life I have personally felt a distinct deficit of raw wilderness, I am imagining it is similar for you. Even attempts to rewild our land and redress this, occur mainly in parks and protected areas. And so I cannot find the wilderness I seek. It is all contained, all directed with limits to its extent. That is what I feel is happening to me. The more I notice and connect, the more I feel this from everything I communicate with. Great to be alive, but with the underlying feeling of limitations and constraint, of less than optimal health and performance. Like a slow suffocation. And as we splutter our last few laboured breaths I am aware of more and more fellow humans around me opening their eyes in dismay and powerlessness; some choosing to close them right back up. Others fighting to stand and turn things around. Like a beached pod of whales there appears to be an inevitability about our fate. Yet there can be hope. The angels from other realms (plant spirits) that stay by our sides bathing us in water until the tide turns and they can help ease us back into the sea. What is my role? What can I learn? What can I do? If you have questions like these, the plants, if you ask them, can help you remember the answers. Can guide you, help your unlearn your social conditioning, peel back the layers of it until what you find underneath is the truth, the essence of you and a clear vision of what you came here to do. They can help ease us back to the sea.

Plants As Medicines

You will find that the path of plant whisperer is a medicine path. Because of this I will talk about the medicine of the plants a lot. It is an important facet to explore.

Medicine can mean so many things on so many levels. Medicine, in the context that I use it, goes way beyond the physical. It can be *anything* that will positively benefit your life; an insight that helps you forgive, for example.

Every plant contains medicine. Really? I can hear you thinking. Every human, every storm, every insect and yes, every plant, contains medicine. All communications with plants are medicine; soul medicine. Medicine for your wild Gaian soul. They will teach you about yourself, about community and belonging; where and how you fit in. They will gift you insights that will help you understand actions that you need to take. All of this is healing; where healing is the process of making or becoming sound or healthy again. Healing is not necessarily curing, but it *is* medicine.

Plants themselves don't actually even heal us, they help awaken us, both physically and spiritually, so that we can heal ourselves. Plants inspire and guide us on our healing journey when we ask for their help. The simple action of eating a fresh raw leaf straight from a plant will cause chemical reactions and a physical response within the human body. If you brew a cup of herbal tea and take the time to smell it, even before you think to drink it, the body of the plant will inform your body of the action it will have once imbibed. If I smell a plant tea and within one or two big whiffs my mouth starts watering, I know that it will have an astringent action on my body – this is a communication, it is also medicine.

Plant medicines, certainly in the form of herbal remedies, are experiencing somewhat of a renaissance as people are losing trust and hope in allopathic medicine, in big pharma. This resurgence in the use of natural medicine is to be applauded and encouraged, as although the large scale production, processing and disposal of plant medicines does have an environmental impact, on the whole it is much more benign than the chemical-based counterparts. The danger is that with a more widespread use plant medicines become misinterpreted, and instead of being respected as living beings that can be called on to help guide the individual through their healing, are being pulled off the shelf and used for symptomatic treatment in much the same way as allopathic medicines are. It has become so that we present a symptom and want an instant and dramatic fix without taking a deeper look at the cause.

Symptomatic treatment is a kind of one size fits all approach. This way dictates that if you have ailment A then using either drug B or plant C at the correct dose, for long enough, will make it go away. This approach though is faulty. We all know that drugs may well suppress or remove the symptoms but may also leave the cause untreated, especially on any level other than the physical. Plants act more intelligently if you choose to work with them in an intelligent way. They can help you take it to a much deeper level. A level that still works on the physical but also picks away at what lies beneath.

At this point I briefly want to mention herbalists, as of course from time to time we all need help with a diagnosis and advice on what we can do to help ourselves. Beware any herbalist, or plant medicine practitioner, who has no contact with the actual living plants, instead just dusty bottles on shelves. How can you even be an herbalist if you don't have a relationship with the living plant? Ask questions so that you can discern whether your herbalist is simply using plants to follow an allopathic-style symptomatic approach. Ask what their relationship to the living plants is, before you trust what they prescribe. There are many herbalists who work in a deeply intuitive way with plants and not symptomatically; when looking for a herbalist ask the right questions and you will find one of these.

Use your wisdom and plant connections to dig deeper. To help you move it beyond medicine for physical symptoms alone, to the imbalances and scars and hurts at the very core of your being. Use the plant medicine you've been prescribed by your trusted herbalist, or gifted by the plant itself; but talk to the medicine, to the plant, pray to it as you take it. And more than that, go outside and invite a plant to step forward to help you heal the other (non-physical) layers of what ails you.

Even the global surge in Ayahuasca use is partly because people think they are getting a quick and dramatic fix. The truth is that although

Ayahuasca may help create new brain pathways, Ayahuasca or any other plant, can't and won't fix you, only you can do that. We are so busy looking outside of ourselves for that cure for our broken and injured souls and yet it is *we* that have the answer, the cure. All the plants can do is show us what we need to address, only we can address it.

Foraging & Nurturing

One danger, as we work hard to avoid prescribed allopathic medication, is that we find ourselves obsessing and gorging on imported exotics, from entheogens and so-called superfoods to the more well known herbal remedies. This goes beyond Ayahuasca, to other plants such as Echinacea and Cordyceps (so mushrooms too). Some of these plants have gained the reputation as wonder cures. And all the while, as we look to plants that are flown in from across the planet and fixate on them, we miss locally available plants that have equally impressive medicine. Observe what grows wildly in your locale. Learning about plants and their medicine is power. It allows us freedom to make decisions for ourselves based on who is growing nearby. This in itself helps build our broken relationship with wild and feeds our own wild core.

Wild, locally foraged plants can gift you with sustenance on both a physical and spiritual level. They contain wild nutrients that are impossible to find on supermarket shelves and in foraging for them you gain the deep connections that come from observing and noticing where and when a plant thrives. Finding and gathering plants helps you connect with ancestral ways, with the local landscape and the therapeutic benefits thereof. Each one of us has to fall in love with the medicine of our own land. It is a wild beauty, and a privilege, to experience.

Foraging in the wild lands of my home country (UK) and in fact increasingly wherever you are, has the potential to become detrimental as more and more people turn to the wild for medicines and nutrition. I have been witness to over-harvesting in my local woods. A place where once Ransoms were so abundant they existed in vast swathes as far as the eye could see, with leaves as large as oval dinner plates. Bare patches of soil between the remaining islands of baby-sized leaves are now a common sight in those once abundant woodlands. This change is testament to the quantity of leaf now being harvested.

We know wild spaces are pressured and limited. So when it comes to wild harvesting or foraging, caution is recommended. The reason being that there are so many people, and often inexperienced foragers take much more than they personally need or can use. In addition, if everyone went and foraged they would mostly forage in the same areas, those with a proximity to residential areas.

One incident that informed me to advise caution when foraging occurred a couple of years ago. There was a gorgeous little patch of Mugwort that had popped up near my house, I had noticed, admired and been in communication with this patch for the whole growing season. One day I was called really strongly to go and harvest some. As I approached I noticed two ladies approaching with intent from the opposite direction, so I held back and sat on a bench within full view of Mugwort to observe. They took their time gathering stems here and there, standing back and pausing before returning for more. In the end they took all but two stems from the entire patch. Mugwort wanted me to be witness to this. Why? Perhaps so that I would share it some years later with you, here, in this book. Perhaps as a cautionary tale for myself and how I personally gather. Perhaps as a prompt to get me to plant my own patch, as that is what I then went on to do. Perhaps all or none of the above, but it does demonstrate perfectly why, if we are to forage, we should do so with consciousness and attention to the local abundance or scarceness of the plant in question.

In some instances, especially with highly prized imported exotics, wild populations have become endangered due to over harvesting for commercial gain; plants such as Asian Ginseng, Hawaiian Sandalwood, alongside many Ayurvedic herbs are perfect examples. Even locally, thinking back to the wild garlic I was just speaking of, I recently visited a friends restaurant where three carrier bags stuffed full of fresh wild garlic leaves sat at the entrance to his kitchen, while the woodland floor was lacking. For these reasons, it is important to avoid any commercially foraged or wild crafted products (even local ones) so that you are not party to large scale over harvesting of wild plants.

When gathering for yourself think about quantity, how rare or bountiful is this plant? Gain permission from the plant itself before gathering. Make the whole process conscious. When you forage from the wild, do it with awareness.

> *Wild food is not about seeking out the rare but connecting with the hyperabundance that surrounds us all the time, and allowing it to nourish us mentally and physically.*
> **Mark Williams**

Personally when I find there is a plant I really love and connect with, whose medicine I use as a physical remedy or as food, year in year out, I encourage it to grow in my garden or allotment. I allow the grass to grow long and wild, the edges unkempt. I may create a space by removing a plant that is already growing in that location. Cleared soil never lasts long in the wild, a volunteer plant will always find the space and fill it at the earliest opportunity. Wild plants grow where they want. I pay attention to who arrives and what messages they may have for me.

If there is a specific plant I wish to have close by I will ask it to come, I will gather seed or maybe take a cutting and I will plant it. If it doesn't want to stay it will go. However if it is happy to stay and be medicine, it will grow and it will spread. So look to local plants for medicine; plants that you could cultivate or encourage, whose seed you could collect and scatter, whom you could purchase as plug plants and introduce to your garden or to pots on your balcony.

Cultivating the plants you love to consume, safeguards the wild ones and will also serve to cultivate your personal and direct relations. You can, after all, ask a plant where it would like to be sited, whom it wishes to grow alongside, the communication can be ongoing throughout the process. Despite having been located by you the plants still have personality, spirit, will. They still have lessons to teach and respond to communication. And just perhaps, when you have the thought to cultivate a patch of a certain plant, it is the plant itself directing you to do so.

When you nurture a plant from seed, you can hold that seed in your mouth and think about the potential, of all that plant can be, infuse it with yourself; all your hopes, wishes and dreams for that plant. Your gratitude. At the same time it is infusing you with its raw, wild potential. If you sow a large number of plants, it will not be possible to do this with every seed. However, you can still be talking to and thanking while sowing the seeds and passing them through your hands. This level of communication during the sowing process turns your relationship with that which you nurture into a respectful one, into a living communication. A living relationship, which is quite opposed to the conventional cultivation of plants where we are simply factory farmers, pillagers and the grim reaper.

House plants are yet another matter and a further level of domestication. But for some plants with which you wish to cultivate a relationship, plants that are not natives, it is the only way. If you do this and are adept at the art of plant whispering your house plants soon become fully integrated family members, with as much presence and contribution as household animal companions.

Any plant that you encourage to grow is an opportunity for communication. An opportunity to deepen your relationship. As you witness the plant and nurture it through its annual cycle, through its life cycle, something special blossoms within you. You come to know that plant as a true friend and companion, one that you return to again and again and again. Your relationship is reciprocal as you give it a space in which to grow, and nurture it; in return you receive the fruits and leaves, the medicine and the wisdom. For me cultivating plants has infinitely deepened my love and respect for them. Has allowed me to come to know certain plants more wholly than I ever would have, had I just visited each autumn to gather the ripe berries. It has added depth and richness to my relationships with them beyond measure and has increased my capacity for plant whispering.

Cultivating plants for food and medicine may not sound that wild on the surface. It may sound irrelevant to the path of the plant whisperer. But when you really work on a conscious and personal level with every plant it can elevate your relationships further. Then it is not just local low footprint organic food, but it is already something of you before you ever take it into you body. And you are already something of it before it has the chance to merge with your body fluids.

As I write of nurturing plants in this book about rewilding I am fully aware of the conflict. The wild not wild aspect. The fact that the dawn of agriculture also spawned our separation from wider nature. So it may seem a contradiction, but perhaps it is about resetting that relationship where it first fell apart. In any case it is the wild plants themselves whom have guided me in this, in locating and nurturing them. Within me there is no conflict as I do so, as I trust the plants. I don't question. I trust that they are guiding me to do the right thing.

Motivation

On some level we are all looking for a quick fix to our brokenness. But the break goes back generations and deep into our relationship with the Earth, it cannot be fixed with a magic wand. We need to isolate what is broken before we begin and then work out what is necessary to fix it. That is where the inner keystone species comes in, our inner wolf. The one thing that will change everything.

To become a master in this art, a true plant whisperer, as I have already mentioned many times, requires rigorous self-examination. If shadows are lurking unexplored and unacknowledged they will hold you back from full connection, from your full, wild ability to read the text of the world, to know what things mean and to feel them wholly. The clearer you are with knowing yourself, your strengths, your weaknesses, your wounds; the clearer your transactions with other species can and will be.

Anyone can replicate a series of techniques, but to go really deep, to change things from "what can I get from this plant" to "how can I serve this plant/Gaia" you need to know yourself, check your motivations, again explore those shadows. Because otherwise there is always going to be an unconscious part of you, the part that wants to be healed, running the show. Until you take a hard look at yourself and begin to recognise that part, this will always be the case, without exception. Once you have started to recognise your patterns, your behaviours, your triggers, the things about your personality that no longer serve you; *then* you can begin the process of self healing.

When you are ready to begin this deeply healing work the plants will assist you. Call out for a plant ally to step forward and help you with your primary issue. The more conscious you are of your issue the more you will understand the medicine being offered, be able to utilise it, and at some point heal or change that and move on. The reason plants will help us in this is because they want to help us see in the dark, understand our own grisly underbelly. Because to be truly wild you have to be able to see and feel in all directions, the full 360°. Plants want us to be whole, want us to be well. Because then we will once again treat them with respect, as sacred relations. If you can do that work on yourself, your interactions with plants will always be cleaner. When your interactions are clean you will see a truer reflection of who the plant before you is, rather than simply what it can offer you in your bid to become whole.

> *To love a single flower, you must love the whole plant: not only its stem, its leaves, its roots, but also its environment, its history, and its distant origin.*
>
> **George Ohsawa**

How far you really want to go depends on what brought you here and what you intend to do with this work. Just be aware that in the background all of this stuff is going on, and that you can use it to generate a deeply healing personal evolution.

Medicine For Others

Very occasionally, it has been the case that on asking a plant for medicine (for myself) I have received very detailed instructions and protocols relating to another human who is in need. I have literally been asked to step away from the plant and lie on the Earth. As I lay there I have received huge downloads. The plants know when someone close to you has a greater need than yourself. They help you get out of the way so that the medicine can come through for that third person. This has only happened to me when I am already working closely with that third person and already have a deep relationship with the plant, although that doesn't necessarily mean it will be that way for you.

Generally, if you are wanting to work with plants as medicines for other humans, you must initially make your question very clear, that you wish to learn of medicine for treating *other* people, *not* medicine for yourself. If you have received medicine for yourself, be wary of jumping to conclusions that the medicine offered to you will work in the same way for someone else. The only way to be sure is to ask the plant a clear and direct question about that other person, or persons.

To provide a template for your clients you must be clear, and know your wounded parts, so that you can recognise when they turn up. That way you can give those parts of yourself the love they need, so that they can stand back without wanting the healing for themselves, allowing you to get on with the job of sharing this work cleanly. Otherwise your reaction to the people and their interactions with the plants is going to be coloured by your unattended wound *always*.

When asking the plants for medicine for other people you will be offered appropriate medicine for them, *but* the clients you attract will all be presenting different aspects of what ails you. They are attracted to you rather than the plethora of other healers because they recognise something of themselves in you. And as a healer you can only take them as far as you yourself have managed to go. They too may have been called by the plants to assist *your* healing and as you help them, if you are clear, open and aware, it may just be that they also help you.

Your Sacred Contract

When you receive medicine from plants your give away in return for receiving this information is that you will use it. That you will bring it into your life and use it to make yourself more whole. And in so doing repair a part of Gaia, your own sweet piece of it. This is your sacred contract. So, never feel that to ask of a plant's medicine is a situation where you are simply taking, simply receiving. You are gifted that medicine and your side of the contract is that you use it, making the Earth more whole again. Making Earth a place where that plant can thrive and be loved and appreciated; rather than it being disrespected or ignored, being ripped up, or sprayed, or its habitat destroyed. Never slip in to the arrogance of thinking that you are simply taking, that it is one way; it never is.

Why I Don't Tell You Which Plant Is For What

The reason why I don't tell you which plant for what, in one simple sentence, is because it removes you from having your own independent direct experience. My human mentors taught me ways to honour the plants. Told me how they connect. But none of them taught me which plant was for what. As I have matured in my own practice and teachings, I have understood more and more so, why. It would have robbed me of my direct experience, and thus, I do not tell you.

If you read about the properties of this plant or that plant, then you will look for them. It will not be your direct communication because it will be choreographed by what someone else, somewhere else, experienced and recorded. And yes no doubt those properties are there to be felt, to be witnessed, by you; but in seeking reconfirmation that they indeed are the properties, you may well miss all the other messages embedded in the communication, perhaps ones that have more meaning and relevance for you.

It has to be your journey and the truth you find will differ from mine. This is not a text book telling you what's what, but a guide as to how to find for yourself what's what. What's true for you.

In addition, as we have already partially explored, language is complex. How I describe something will be different from how you would. This leads to different interpretations, and therefore meanings and so misinterpretations. If you rely on what a book or another human has told you, your interpretation may lead you far from the plants original message. Whenever possible, always seek a direct personal experience with the plant.

The only way to *really* know a plant is through direct experience. You will never be imbued with the wisdom of a plant without that. In the same way you can not *know* a person by reading their CV or biography. Always take time to ask "what am I actually experiencing, what am I *feeling*?". In the end that is all there is, all that is true. If you find the answer to be "nothing", then it is most likely that you simply have not looked hard enough or that you haven't found it yet.

Developing your communication skills opens up a world that is so rich, it is always changing and evolving with you. Through the simple act of asking a question you influence the response (basic quantum physics[33]). Trusting the interpretation of another human about what a plant (or any other being) can do for you spiritually will always leave you short changed, as that was merely their interpretation, their truth. Nothing is set in stone and unchanging – not even the stone. There are no short cuts in this work, in developing your art, there is you and only you.

There are thousands of books out there that can tell you which plant to use for which ailment. I know, as do many, that gargling with Sage will ease your sore throat. In times of acute and specific illness, plants are more than willing to help us. So, yes a cough, a cold, a grazed knee can be looked up in a herb book and relief be found.

Taking it beyond minor injuries and ailments, the symptomatic approach, as I have just mentioned, does not work. Everything is interwoven with different layers of reality and function. Cells (in the body) act and respond to chemicals (from the plants) on every level of the system, not just the physical. This is where the layers of complexity come in.

Thus when we look deeper, we find that there is no such thing as plant A for ailment B, nice perhaps as it might sound, that simply cannot exist. In part because ailment B is never the same in two individuals, it never came from the same point or incident with the same background story or physical circumstances. You may have eczema, or a backache, or a headache for a very different reason than your neighbour who is displaying the same symptoms, so the plant that can help each of you will be different.

The human body, with all its different levels of existence and consciousness, cannot just be treated as a standard physical body with a standard case of B. An outbreak of eczema, for example, may come from a change in washing powder, diet, lifestyle, but also a physical manifestation of some deep dis-ease. Something perhaps on a spirit or soul level. A reaction caused by an unresolved emotional trauma perhaps. And this is where we begin to enter the realms of plant spirit or sacred plant medicine, call it what you will.

The simplicity of plant A for ailment B is also a fallacy, because plant A is never the same. For a start, as we know, it too is a living being with different levels of existence. A plant and the conditions within which it grows are never static. Even on a strictly physical level, an individual plants physical properties will alter slightly year on year. The chemical proportions will change in response to the amount of rain and sunshine, shade and wind, insect infestations and humus the plant receives in said year. Plants, and the herbal remedies created from them, cannot always be assumed to have the same quantity of active ingredient C. This is the reason why people have tried to standardise herbs, to make it more predictable. The problem is that living beings don't respond well to factory farming, to being treated as things.

When I was about to graduate from my Plant Spirit Medicine training I had to present a client in class and give the relevant treatment. We were using the Chinese 5 elements as a diagnostic framework. In effect I needed a minimum of one plant per element. I kept finding medicine for all the elements bar water. In the hour before my exam I went to a most wonderful tree that was over 350 years old. This tree was strong, proud and true. I knew that if I presented my problem there would be some kind of solution forthcoming. I asked somewhat desperately whether the tree could be medicine for the water element. "Do not worry" was the response, "we are all medicine for all of the elements". Immediately I relaxed. Just as any illness can *come* from any cause, it can be *treated* with any plant! Of course certain plants will be better than others at certain things, most certainly physical conditions, however, we all hold the universe within us and thus any point can be touched.

Plants are so much more than a set of specific remedies for specific ailments. Each plant is distinct and unique. You are distinct and unique. So there will be a distinct and unique relationship that can be fostered between you and the plant. A medicine for your unique place and needs. If there is something in your constitution, in your make up, or even in your mental and emotional well-being, or your lifestyle, that is causing repetitive weakness, an underlying condition or an ongoing complaint; then you must go to the meadows and the woods *yourself* to find the ones that can help you.

When you enter into a relationship with a plant it becomes a living relationship that has the capacity to grow, evolve, deepen, change; *if you let it*. Just like your human relationships. And as such, the medicine offered to you will change as you change.

In the end, speaking of what plants are "for" holds us within the great illusion, as separate from other life, where we merely consider plants as "things" with beneficial properties. The paradigm shift will come when people talking of plants speak of *who* they are, as opposed to what they are good for. So this is yet another reason why I don't talk about who (which plant) said what, offered my spirit this or that, promised to soothe my emotions and ease my pain in this way or that way. You may talk of people in this way – oh yes Katie, she's a master herbalist, you must see her. Oh, Tim, yes a fantastic acupuncturist, he can surely help you. David the grief councillor is fab. Jackie will take you out for a good night, always gets me laughing. If you are great at something you will get a reputation for that thing; become known, loved and respected for it. That is in essence what has happened to the plants. But that is never the whole picture, it is just one facet of who you are. Don't forget the personality in there, the need to build relationship. Otherwise you become in danger of using the plants as resources, as things, with a specific function, a very allopathic approach. Sarah might get the knots out of my shoulders every time but you may meet her and instantly get the creeps. One size does not fit all, never did. So even when you have heard that Turmeric is great for inflammation, before you blindly start drinking golden milk every morning, ask. Ask the Turmeric whether it is the right medicine for you and listen for the response.

Spirit medicine is even less quantifiable than physical medicine. I feel it is essential not to state that plant X can help with confidence even if it offered that medicine to me; because my lack of confidence may be in a very different place to yours. In addition, reading of plants that are exotic to your region that can help with emotional trauma Y or mental affliction

Z, will lead you to overlook the plethora of appropriate assistance you are living amongst, and could be in direct relations with, that live right on your doorstep. For all of these reasons, I generally don't and won't write publicly about my personal interactions with specific plants. Even writing of the physical medicinal properties is becoming more difficult for me.

As more people delve into sacred plant medicine and plant essences, be on your guard for spiritual herbals; there are already plenty out there. Go instead to the source and learn for yourself. I can not stress this enough. There is nothing as real and as valuable as first hand knowledge, as a living relationship. And in addition, through making your own relations a deeper healing has the chance to manifest; that of becoming infused with wild native wisdom, rewilding.

Buying a book on what a plant does is a snapshot in time of the author's relationship with that plant, rather than a true reflection of all the layers of that plant. Layers that author may have missed or that have evolved and changed within that plant since. I get it for medicinal uses but even then it strictly limits the way we look at plants and understand their gifts, giveaways and potential. Limiting them to what that herbalist in the 1600's said, or what science can prove. There will always be more, especially if you make your own personal relationship with that plant. So, if you have heard something about the spiritual aspects of a plants medicine, put it out of your mind. It is the same with physical medicine, unless you intend to become a medical herbalist.

It is so exciting that people are getting involved with plants and setting up workshops and ceremonies to share the medicine and magic. But all too often they tell you what the medicine will be in advance. This is helpful if you are looking for that specific healing as it will help you choose the most beneficial workshop to attend. If however you are going along because you wish to learn about that plant, to build a personal relationship with it and to develop your plant whispering skills, this fore knowledge can hold you back as it is brain stuff, not heart stuff, just the same as reading a book.

To truly know a plant you have to let all of the fore knowledge, all of the "brain stuff" go, and ask the plant yourself; with your heart. If a plant at a workshop has been recommended for clearing ancestral blockages ask the facilitator how that has manifested in their life. Then you will understand how authentic their relationship with the plant is. It is all too easy to reel off what a plant is "good for", what it does, because we heard it, read it or were told it by another human. Become an expert at ignoring such "information" and experience the plant for yourself. Ask from your heart, as that is where the true medicine lies. No doubt the offering direct from the plant will somehow fit the description, but perhaps not in the way you interpreted the description. I don't even tell my students which plant they are working with on a particular day, because then there is no opportunity for the brain to sit at the front, it becomes all about the heart.

By advising you to avoid reading up about the spiritual medicine of a plant, I don't mean to infer that the information is wrong. I am sure we have all enjoyed and been helped by various plant essences that are prescribed for certain conditions of body and spirit, I certainly have. However, interpretation is entirely subjective, no matter how hard anyone tries to be objective, subjectivity is an intrinsic part of the human condition. We cannot separate ourselves from ourselves and our entirely unique individual perspective and life experience, with which we use to decode and interpret any and all incoming communications. So by accepting someone else's interpretation of a plant's medicine (especially spiritual), what you will gain may just be surface level, a proving of what someone else already told you. What's more it may divert you from your own direct relationship and from gaining you own sweet soul medicine. And so although the physical remedy, essence and plant spirit books do have value, don't start there; and most certainly don't stop there. If you seek to have a direct personal relationship with a plant put the books down and go to the source, to the plants themselves.

Once something is written and recorded it stops evolving. It becomes static. Even, if you are going to harvest a plant to make a remedy, you should always take time to check in with what's new, to communicate your needs, so that the plant has the opportunity to respond.

There is and can be no substitute for your direct plant relationships. Think of it like this; would you go to the forest to learn the poetry of the desert? Probably not. Take "fox walking" as an example. Many outdoor groups will adopt this quiet way of walking and stalking. It is no doubt a good thing to try and experiment with; but don't learn it from a human. Let the Fox show you. You can watch film clips if you have no friendly local Fox to observe up close and personal. Practise, wait, witness, observe, *become* Fox. Not a person doing Fox, learned from another person doing Fox, that is simply copying form. It just won't work that way, you will miss the point. Learning directly from Fox will take much longer, it will become a labour of love as you learn so many layers of Fox. As you observe and mimic, your body learns something of the Fox itself, something deep and wild. If you learn directly from Fox, *eventually* you will know what it is to be Fox. Learning the intricacies of fox movement from a human is ultimately misguided. Learning a plants properties from a book is equally so.

In the following chapter I often mention taking notes. There is absolute value in having plant journals and taking notes, notes that you can update when you have further developments and evolution of your relationships. It is important to be able to update your notes, so that rather than being static and in danger of becoming nothing more than an historic document, the meaning can flow and evolve along with your understanding and relationships.

If you give up your preconceptions and realise that you know *nothing*, release all of your abstract learning, then you create the space in which you can begin to actually *know*. And when you can approach a plant in that way, without any preconceptions, you can find medicines that no one else is using.

All of this, approaching the personalities for first hand information rather than the preconceived notion of the plants properties, is what moves you into being a master plant whisperer. Never stop asking, enquiring, giving back. Keep moving, growing, breathing, believing, and you will find yourself becoming part of the living Earth once more; not just living on it, using herbs and walking barefoot. But sinking into an evolving movement and relationship with all life. And that, my friend, is true rewilding.

6. Practical Ways Of Opening Up To The Wisdom Of Plants

The most simple and basic communication with a plant goes something like this; you meet a plant, perhaps just noticing it in passing, and it stops you, possibly just for a fraction of a second. In that fragment of time it offers you something, its beauty perhaps. You, on noticing the plant and pausing for that nanosecond, receive that gift, the beauty. And, in exchange, give something back. A brief second of attention, and possibly more than that, a spark of appreciation, of love even. This is an exchange and any exchange is a communication. This first moment is a moment of sacred connection, sacred exchange. This is the basis of *all* communications with other species. Everything discussed in the previous chapters will help you be more clear in this moment, so that you can take it further and with direction, *but* that is an extra. The sacred exchange itself is what matters most.

You are already participating in such sacred exchanges multiple times every day. Awareness of them is what makes the difference, as then you can consider your response and be conscious of where the communication takes you.

My intention is to begin with the most simple things because in my experience they are the most profound. I do not know every plant whispering method or technique, I have not participated in every ceremony. But, what I do know is that if something can be broken down to the degree that it can be used in a fraction of a second with no particular preparation then it is much more likely to be used multiple times in a day, or even in an hour, than a very grandiose form, that although utterly marvellous and thrilling, only gets worked with a few times a month, or even a year. That is why, for me, simple is best. Because then it becomes not just second nature, but our very way of being. It becomes who we are and what we do without any extra effort or thought. Just as I imagine it would have been for our ancestors living close to the land in constant deep communication with all our relations. Of course there is a time and a place for ceremony and I will discuss that later, but to be a true plant whisperer this art form needs to be lived by you all day, every day.

In the case of the most simple, sacred exchange described above the plant "chose you". By that I mean that it captured your attention. You could continue on your way after such an exchange without a second thought, but this is where paying attention to detail and developing your ability to notice become key.

We are so used to instant gratification and scanning for content, we rarely take note of the minutiae, the subtle. This is an invitation to do just that. Without it your art will have limitations as you will miss the finer hues and textures and the messages they contain. You may miss the fact that a plant called you over in the first place. Remember this is learning a whole new language and way of communicating, to become elegant in the art you must pay attention and notice at all times.

Remain vigilant for anyone who calls your attention. If a plant is calling to you, drawing your attention, that is because it has something for you, a lesson, a message, a meaning. It doesn't necessarily have to be an attraction; your attention can also be drawn by disgust, fear, revulsion. There is always a message woven into everything you feel. If I find myself feeling fear when I am called by a plant, my natural instinct is to look at my fear and ask why? Mainly because I am yet to be chased and killed by a scary plant – although there is always the chance you could get bitten by one (spines/poison) or an animal/insect that resides amongst its foliage. It is more likely that the fear is a response to something else, something that the plant has touched within me, something that the plant is perhaps indicating that it could help with. It is the same when I am called by a somewhat unattractive plant, a plant I don't like to look at or feel uncomfortable around. I am responding to something, maybe I recognise something of myself in that plant, by recognising my response it is an opportunity to dig a little deeper to discover what is really going on, why that particular plant is making me feel that way.

Initiating Contact

If *you* wish to initiate contact, to call out to a plant yourself, then first set your intention. At this point keep your intention simple, something like "I wish to meet a plant" and then take a walk. Remain alert, who is it that you notice? If you find yourself getting all caught up in your head then close your eyes and spin around slowly until you feel a presence or a pull in one direction more than any other. Then open your eyes and find the plant within your field of vision that you notice the most. Then offer something to the plant, perhaps start with gratitude. Thank the plant for being there.

Whatever it is that you choose to offer the plant in that first moment of exchange, you must feel it wholeheartedly, for it is the *feeling* that is communicated. If words, spoken aloud, or silently within yourself, are not wholeheartedly felt they have no real energy behind them and your communication will be empty. But extending gratitude, gratitude that a single flower exists, that the tree is feeding you with oxygen, when deeply felt, is a communication and can be your way of reaching out and initiating communication directly with the plant.

Next it is prudent to consider *"how does this feel?"*. In the first moments of meeting, really search into that because it holds the key to everything that follows for you two, for your relationship.

At this early stage it is necessary to overcome any self-consciousness you may find yourself feeling. You may feel uncomfortable initially because by allowing plants sentience, the ability to answer back, you are going against everything your domesticated life thus far has taught you. This is part of the stripping back process of rewilding, shedding the layers that have insulated us from wild. In unlearning what you think you know, letting it go, you are letting go of the social conditioning that has allowed the modern world to reach its current condition. What you are doing by forging ahead and seeking connection with our more-than-human relations is not only questioning consensus reality, but blowing a hole right through it and thus allowing the opportunity for change in the way humanity thinks, feels and behaves. The more self-conscious you feel, the more you will hold yourself back by keeping yourself in tame human mode, firmly rooted in your culturally informed limits of what is acceptable behaviour and what is not.

With the conversation initiated and any self-consciousness fully overcome, what next? You could sit within that state of gratitude and take time to breathe. The same as the five minute morning practice I recommended earlier. Just bring your awareness to your breath and consciously share breath with the plant. Visualise the exchange of gases, of life itself, that is happening between you. This practice will help you slow down and arrive in a shared space, a reciprocal space with the plant. If you are paying full attention you will also notice that you are beginning to feel a little different. That in taking time to notice a plant, to reach out to it and to share breath with it, you are beginning to pick up the unique signature of that plant, experience a little of what it is to be that plant, its characteristics.

Sound & Movement

You may find yourself moved to respond to the plant, to the subtle shifts you have noticed that are beginning to occur in yourself as you receive from the plant. Everything in the universe of course is a vibration, and what is a vibration anyway? Well in one part of the spectrum (20Hz - 20kHz) it manifests as audible sound. Plants, like humans, respond to sound[34].

Some people find themselves drawn to sing, to hum, to tone, to play a musical instrument even. If this is you, be exceptionally vigilant that involving sound does not become a distraction. You can use it as an offering, as a communication. As an expression perhaps of how the plant is making you feel in that moment, gifting the rapture of that feeling back to the plant. Be careful not to just blast the plant, remember to listen.

If you are drawn to hum or tone discern whether it is coming from the plant or you? Is it the plants offering or yours? It is important to know the difference.

My medium for communication is rarely sound but sometimes it comes through strong and clear directly from the plant. I interpret this as the plant's song. Essentially this is the plant's unique vibration, which of course is an expression of energy. So the plant song is the signature, the pure energetic vibration of that plant, its essence. On the occasions I have received such a gift from a vegetal cousin it feels pretty immense, as if the most private parts of that plant have been shared with me, the whole of it. It really is a gifting of the plant's soul essence, deeply sacred and wonderfully treasured.

There is much to unfold within a sound giveaway. Everything there is to know about a plant, or any being for that matter, is encoded within its unique vibration, everything. My relationship with a plant generally has to be really special before I am ever gifted the song, but we all work differently, that's why there are no rules in all of this. It may end up being how *you* receive information from the plants and how you exchange with them. But never force it. You can ask for it, invite the plant to share it with you, but in sharing this vibration the plant is sharing everything about itself, maybe you or the plant are not yet ready. If the time is right, if the plant wishes to, it can teach you its song and thereby divulge everything about itself.

Just as with all giveaways from the plants, the difficult bit then really is translating that into what you wish to know. Perhaps the song itself, in vibrating within you, is teaching you something your intellect will not grasp, or need to unfold, as your body and being has taken on what the plant had to share without needing to catalogue what it all means.

When you are gifted the pure vibration of a plant, its song, you can discover its true name. Then you can call on that plant by repeating its name over and over and over in the same rhythm and tempo that it taught you. This again is something that has happened for me only with a handful of plants, but as soon as I say that plants true name out loud, as I was taught by the plant, I can feel my consciousness altering and myself falling into the dream of that specific plant.

You may never hear the song of a plant, or be moved to gift your voice or your music in an exchange, that is the joy in all of this, the fact that every person who seeks a relationship with a certain plant will have a different relationship with it. It could be that you find yourself wanting to stretch and move, to dance, again inspired by the changes the plant is initiating within you. If you dance for a plant, as with music, make sure you don't just get carried away doing your thing. Take time to notice the plant's response. Take time to notice whether the movement is coming from you as a gift to the plant, or from the plant as a gift to you.

You may feel yourself moving *with* the plant, imitating its movements, this then becomes a little like fox walking. As you mimic you will notice the plant respond, eventually you will find that you are no longer mimicking, the plant is moving you. It requires great patience and observation. You cannot learn this from a person, the plant is the only one who can teach you how it moves. Once you can imitate the form with accuracy and find that the plant is actually moving you, you have a visceral entry point into the body of the other, you may be gifted the knowledge of how it feels to be that plant, how it thinks even. This is shape shifting.

This shape shifting generates a knowing with the body. As you know, changing posture for example rolling your shoulders back instead of allowing them to rest rounded forward (protecting your heart), will push your heart out into the world and change your experience of the world. As you mimic the plant, notice which parts of you are withdrawn and which parts exposed, how that stance makes you feel.

The movement and posture of your body unpicks secrets, allows you some access into what it feels like to be the other. As you mimic how the plant moves, how it sways in the breeze. The way the branches shuffle, arching and flexing with wind ruffled leaves, you will learn something. It may be a direct knowing, body to body; it may be a feeling; an emotion; a quality. Direct learning through movement can allow another layer, another thin veil, to rend and drop to the ground as you understand a few more communications that were always hidden in plain sight.

Trust is imperative, let yourself go, believe. If you feel self conscious you will be clumsy, you will not perfect it and you will not gain accuracy in your mimicry. Without accuracy you will never gain access to the wisdom and story enveloped within that form and its typical range of movements.

Movement is a language. Movement of the human body; movement of a plant body. It's a language and can be a doorway in. The way a human walks, how they hold themselves, can say so much about their interior landscape to one who understands this language; it's not called body language without reason. Move like a Bamboo, mimic. Persevere. Eventually you will know a little of what it is to be Bamboo.

The Value Of Comparison

I speak a lot of paying attention to how something feels. Noticing how the other being makes *you* feel. This may need a little work if you are not habituated in paying attention to your feelings. It may be that at the beginning of this journey you cannot discern how a certain tree feels. This is about practise and confidence, as you do actually know, deep inside, how different things and situations make you feel. How walking along a certain street makes you feel nervous, how on entering a certain restaurant you get a bad feeling, how some people give you the creeps while others make you feel relaxed. So within our human world we have feelings all the time, even if we then override what we feel because logic tells us to.

To develop a strong sense of how different members of the more-than-human world make you feel I recommend the following exercise:

- Clear yourself, empty your mind, do whatever you need to do to reach this state. Then go and visit a tree. This exercise can be done with any life form, but I recommend trees as they are often much stronger in presence than a smaller plant.
- Stand by or under the canopy of that tree and notice how the tree *feels* to you, how it makes you feel. Go right in, maybe touch the trunk, then work back until you are no longer under the canopy.
- How long you stay is up to you. It may be literally a matter of moments, as you want to avoid thinking. You are just looking for a first feeling impression. Just feel, nothing else. Note down the feeling. You may prefer to stay a bit longer perhaps sitting under the tree for 15 or 20 minutes. The most important point is to feel. Don't think.
- You may barely have noticed anything, but this is where the value of comparison comes in. Go to a second tree, preferably one of a different species. Do this straight away, not another day or after a cup of tea, immediately after visiting the initial tree. Again notice how you feel. The first feeling that you get. Feel it. Note it.
- And again, go straight to a third tree, preferably a third species. Notice how you feel now.

Each tree will feel different, of that I am certain. By visiting three types of tree in short succession you will have experienced three different feelings. The first, especially, you may have talked yourself out of. But as you proceeded to two further trees the fact that they all felt different is undeniable. Defining what those feelings are will become easier with practice, at the beginning just feel into it and notice the difference.

When I apprenticed with Stephen Buhner he suggested concentrating on four primary feelings and categorising the feeling you get into one of them, a bit like a multiple choice exam. The categories Stephen suggested to us were mad/sad/glad/scared. These we then worked with as the primary feeling states. Any more elaborate descriptions of the feeling, are where those feeling states combine to generate something more complex. This may help, although for some people I know it causes confusion as they suddenly fall out of feeling and into thinking in an attempt to define the feeling, but give it a go, see if it works for you.

As soon as you begin to recognise that you do indeed get a different feeling from each being you sit with, your ability to notice subtle differences between the feelings you are receiving opens up. Eventually, or maybe straight away, you will notice that the strength of feeling will be different close to the trunk, than a few steps further out, and how it begins to fade much more sharply as you step out from under the canopy of the tree. Exactly the same as with people, the closer in you are the more intensely you notice the feeling you are receiving. Play with it, with your ability to notice and differentiate between different feelings. With practise and attention you will find yourself being able to more and more acutely notice and elaborate on any slight differences in feeling that you are perceiving.

Dedicated Plant Study

If you have a more specific intention, a question for that plant, if you wish for help, medicine for yourself or others in whatever form, or simply wish to take your relationship deeper; then I recommend following a basic structure for a dedicated plant study.

As a prerequisite, make sure you feel relaxed, unhurried by other commitments and are free from distractions, including other humans. This will allow you to achieve the right state of mind for communication to flow. In short, dedicate time to be alone with the plants.

Begin by setting your intention. Be very clear about this. You may find it useful to smudge yourself or cleanse your energy with a rattle or chimes. This is to clear everything else away so that you focus entirely on the intention you have set (you may wish to revisit Chapter 4 at this point where I discussed "clarity of your question and knowledge of self").

By having a clear intention or question in advance you will have put that energy out into the energetic grid, the field. This allows the plant that can help the most, or wishes to help the most, to make itself known to you, and to start to generate a response. This is especially pertinent if you wish to gather physical medicine.

> *For it has been said among the Winnebago that when gathering plants as medicine, if you tell them what you need them to do and ask them to put forth their strength on your behalf they will do so. And among the Iroquois, it is said that when you find the plant you are looking for you should pray to it for help. It will tell the other plants what you need and when you pick them their medicine will be strong and powerful.*
> **Stephen Harrod Buhner**

Once your intention is set, go and search for the plant that calls to you, the luminous one. You will be good at discerning which plant this is by now. It is really important that you don't over think things at this stage, just take a walk and wait until you notice one plant more than any of the others, even if it is not the plant you were hoping for, or thought it would be. Try not to have any expectations and be accepting of any plant who turns up for you. In your imaginings you may have hoped an ancient Oak or a graceful Willow would respond but instead the one who does is a battered and sickly looking ragged little thing that you have never noticed before. Never let yourself be disappointed by who responds, they didn't respond by accident. Be open, be grateful and you may well learn an awful lot.

Once a plant has stepped forward to work with you identify yourself, say your name out loud. Sometimes it may be that you wish to elaborate, "daughter of ...", "son of ...", acknowledge your ancestors; your lineage to the plants. If you experiment with this more detailed identification of yourself, take time to really feel the ancestors in your body. However, don't allow this to become a distraction. I have even been stopped by a plant mid-sentence when attempting to introduce myself in this way, "I know who you are" said the plant! In general, I tend to simply introduce myself with my given name, saving this more formal introduction for occasions where it feels appropriate.

Thank the plant for inviting you, for calling you. Then, voice your intention, your question, and invite a response, do not demand. So for example you could ask "do you have any medicine to share with me?" which is much better than either "what is your medicine?" or "what medicine do you have for me?". Essentially by asking the question you are keeping yourself focussed, the plant doesn't speak in human language anyway and will already know why you are there, because of the feeling it is receiving from you.

When approaching with a specific question or intention you must give an offering in return, so that it becomes an exchange. You could ask the plant if there is something it would like from you, although I caution you to remember agreements at this point. Making a promise to a plant and then breaking it will only undermine your relations with plants further. If you cannot fulfil your promises you must always renegotiate at your earliest opportunity.

There are many offerings you can make. Your love, respect and gratitude. Your undivided attention, your time; so valuable to us modern humans. Music or dance. Something of your body, such as a hair from your head. A splash of water. Traditions from around the world offer items such as tobacco or cornmeal. Whatever it is that you offer it has to be something of value to you, to have a meaning. Following an empty ritual, gifting an item that has no resonance to you personally, has no meaning and therefore does not constitute a true exchange.

Once your offering has been made, spend some quality time with the plant. Let the energy of the plant touch you, let your electromagnetic fields combine. Listen wholeheartedly, pay attention to *everything*. Use direct perception and your heart as your primary organ of perception (as discussed in Chapter 4). Be vigilant for tiny responses throughout your body and perturbations across all of your senses, including the *feeling* sense. Note down everything.

You may find it useful to take some colouring pencils and draw what you see. This does not need to be a perfect botanical diagram of the plant and don't allow yourself to be distracted by creating a pretty picture. Drawing as a process can help you slip into the more creative mind, the more accepting and poetic, the less analytical and questioning. In addition it can help you notice the minutiae, the physical details of your new plant companion. And as you notice the tiny and the miniscule, that you would otherwise perhaps have overlooked, you may just fall deeper in love.

Notice everything. The community the plant is part of, where it is growing, the conditions in which it grows. Interact physically with the plant. Touch, smell and taste*, always gaining permission first. Note it all, every texture and note of fragrance, hint of flavour. How the plant touches you back and what that feels like both in your body and in your spirit; physically and emotionally. Also listen. Listen to the plant in the breeze, if it is a larger plant, a tree maybe, put your ear to its trunk, you may be surprised at what you can hear.

You can try imagining hands coming out of your heart and touching all parts of the plant. This way you can go further and beyond what your eyes can see; to the crown of the highest tree, below the deepest tap root, you can enclose it all within the touch of your heart. Ask the plant to enter you, ask it to tell you, notice what you feel in your body. Allow yourself to become so absorbed by the plant that you merge with it. While you are in this state you are in the dream of the plant, it has brought you into its dream. It is here that your answer, or any medicine gifted to you by the plant, will be revealed.

Notice, notice and notice some more. Take your time.

Eventually you will return to your normal sense of self. You will either feel replete or find yourself drifting, day dreaming about what you need to do when you get home or what you are going to cook for dinner. If you cannot refocus, it is time to stop. At this point write everything about

---

* *If you are going to taste a plant you must identify it first to ensure that it is not poisonous.*

your experience down, you will soon forget otherwise. You can use this information later to go back in and discover the meaning.

Even if you do not begin your exchange with an expression of gratitude, you must always close it with one, even if you didn't like what you learned.

If you asked a question and didn't feel that you received a response, it could be that you are not ready for that answer, or that you missed it. That is why taking notes is useful, because you can review your notes and in so doing something may become clear. Perhaps the necessary response was silence, quiet or stillness? Sit with that for a moment.

The essentials for this kind of study are being totally present and undistracted, whole heartedness, gratitude (this has a physiological response in the body in that it engages the magnetic field of the heart), humility, respect, exchange. Forget to be an adult; look through the eyes of a child. The more emotionally naïve you allow yourself to be, the more successful in this process you will become. Most important of all is to engage your feeling sense. Keep asking over and over "how does this feel?". With all of this in place you enter into sacred exchange and physiologically your body will go into parasympathetic mode, a non-adrenal state. In this state peripheral vision opens up, auditory acuity is amplified, your capacity for feeling increases as does fine motor control. Your eyes will soft focus, your breathing will slow, you will feel good. In essence you become more wild and in your wildness you become more open to what is coming to you from the plant and are more able to respond.

When you engage with a plant, whether asking for help, or a question about the plant itself, what comes next is all about experiencing, about entering the dream of the plant, not about information. Plants *know*. When you approach a plant and ask a question they are feeling into your heart, they know your intent. You cannot hide your heart from a plant. Feel, don't think. If you ask and open yourself wholeheartedly you will receive a wholehearted response. If you hold back, the response will also be held back. So be full power, put everything in, don't allow your mind to sidetrack you. Come from a place of heart, follow your heart, not your mind. Pay attention to the most prominent feeling. Censor nothing. Honour your perceptions.

How long should you take for a basic plant study? An absolute minimum of twenty or thirty minutes, in which time you will get something. An hour perhaps? Much more? But to return two, three, four, twelve times over the course of a year then, only then, will you really begin to know the absolute subtleties. The high notes and accents that a brief encounter will never unveil. So take your time. What is the best quantity of time to spend? How long have you got?

A plant study can help you direct the exchange and allow you to focus on the plant. It will also give you clear time in which to focus on any shifts in your feeling state and consciousness. That to me is the exchange, the communication, the give away from the plant. Soul medicine.

Over the years I have found that when I am working with a client remotely either mentoring them or as part of an e-course (now perhaps through this book) some people have found it very difficult, or had resistance to, concentrating solely on one plant. To take an hour out of their day to sit with a plant and communicate directly; introduce themselves, ask a question or set their intention, and then spend time paying attention (learning how to listen). Of course there is no rule book that says you have to do it this way. Perhaps it comes back again to the need for instant gratification. Why spend an hour to just feel slightly more relaxed and get a gurgling tummy? However, to make deep and profound inroads you have to start somewhere.

By the age of seven most people have closed down their intuition and wild connections. So for most of us, from age seven until we consciously open back up to the more-than-human realms, we have generally been ignoring their communications. Unless you are exceptional, an incredible empath or clairsentient, you will need to work at it. Even if it is building your confidence in accepting that what you are receiving really is coming from the other and that you are not making it up. Just the same as if you had not driven a car for 30 years, it would take you a bit of concerted effort at the beginning to remember how and gain confidence, before you zoomed off on a treacherous single track mountain road full of hairpins and oncoming traffic. So I do recommend trying this basic structure, it certainly works for me.

There is a temptation for some people to run from plant to plant doing several studies a week or even in a single day. Please resist! This is not a cocktail party! Plants work on a different plane to us and as we open to their wisdom it may still be infusing into us over the course of several days. By opening up to another plant during this process you will cut the flow from the first plant off, or the two will both be working in you simultaneously, which makes it more difficult to recognise the unique signature of each.

Many times I have undertaken a dedicated plant study with a desire to get to know that plant as my intention. I have sat with the plant, admired, loved and noticed. Even in these circumstances I have had incredible break through moments of insight. I have had truths revealed to me, truths about the plant, Gaia as a whole and/or myself, often there is no divide or distinction. This is how I unequivocally know that it is what you hold closest to your heart (even if you have effectively hidden it from yourself) that is addressed when you commune directly with a plant.

Dropping Deeper – Sensory Noticing

I spoke of sensory acuity and its importance in the Interspecies Communication Chapter, it is time, if you have not already begun, to start really working with and paying attention to your senses.

I occasionally run a workshop where each physical sense is tuned into, one at a time in a woodland. By the end of a single hour I have had people moved to tears (in a good way!). Some attendees have written long letters and emails of gratitude after such workshops, exposing parts of themselves that were activated by the session. Parts usually held close and secret. And, more wonderful than that, is that almost everyone makes a pledge to repeat the experience again and again. To introduce it to husband, wife, friends or kids. What is it that is so powerful? Slowing down. Physically noticing. Becoming a part of, no longer apart from. All this instead of swiftly blundering past in a blur of busyness. As I said, simplicity can be profound. So that is how I approach plant whispering, with simplicity and humility as key.

So, for a moment, let's concentrate on the physical senses. Don't fall into the trap of thinking that using your senses is not going to take you far enough, quickly enough, that there are bigger and better things to dive into. *Slow down!* Intricacies, minutiae are hugely important and hold the coding for everything else within them. Don't overlook the small and the subtle in your rush for an otherworldly shamanic experience. When engaged with sensory noticing your mind will naturally quieten as you are occupied. This allows your senses to work as the gateway to your body and to accessing its incredible wisdom.

When we tune in to our bodies and the messages they are sending us, a huge wealth of wisdom is revealed. We are as natural and as wild as the wise and beautiful plants we seek to know of. We too are Gaia. We too are medicine for the world. Imagine that? So with that in mind it is time to invite your body to assist. It is time to start noticing what your body is telling you about what you put inside it. A very simple way to begin listening to your own body wisdom is to focus in on the changes that occur when one new thing is presented to it in a relatively controlled environment. That way, when we are out and about in the world and something tweaks one of our senses, we will be more alert to it and more able to interpret what it was that drew our attention and the nature of the incoming message.

Blind tea ceremonies are absolutely perfect for this training; for tuning in to the body and what it can tell us and also for tuning in to the subtle communications of the plant that has been presented. It is called a "blind tea" because preferably it will be a plant tea that someone else has made for you, so that you are unaware of which plant you are drinking. Of course, ensure that your friend, who is making the tea, has checked that the plant is not poisonous, before they make you tea with it! If you have no one that can make a mystery pot of tea for you, don't worry, you will just have to practice setting aside all of the things you *think* you know about the plant in the teapot. Knowledge itself is a absolute barrier to direct perception, to biognosis, as we already know.

The ceremony itself is relatively simple. Pour a cup of mystery tea and simply smell it. You may find some smells very difficult to pick up - our sense of smell has hugely atrophied in the face of all the strong artificial and chemical smells, all the unpleasant whiffs we encounter daily. But you can still smell. The more you practice the better you will become at noticing even the most tiny and subtle fragrances.

Smell and smell again. And smell again. Keep at it for twenty minutes or so. And notice. Notice everything. This is best done with eyes closed so that you can really focus in on your sense of smell and any reactions in your body. Feel for any changes, any tension, any pain. Notice where it goes in your body - up? Maybe down? Throat, temples, belly, toes? How do you feel on an emotional and energetic level? Any changes? Excitable, relaxed, happy, sad, energised? Any strange thoughts or memories? Any colours or images? Any words or physical sensations? Did you let out a deep sigh or a cough? Did you sneeze or get an itch? Anything and everything that is coming to you is a communication between the plant and your body.

How often do you notice a smell and yet do not pause, instead continue on and think nothing of it? Your sense of smell and what happens as a reaction to that in your body can tell you many, many things.

Once you have really got to the end of smell, it will be time to taste. Sip it. Swirl it in your mouth. Keep your eyes closed. Gently, slowly. Let the plant infuse into you. Cell by cell. Pay attention with your senses to what it is telling you. Don't rush or overlook this process, it is ultimately valuable. Again notice *everything*. Every thought, sensation, feeling. Its direction, its strength. Where is it in your body? What are the differences between how you feel now to how you felt when you simply smelled it?

Take your time. Take your time.

There is so much information embedded in the exchange. In a simple herbal infusion rising to meet the olfactory bulbs and again as it meets your body in your mouth and down into your gastrointestinal tract.

Acknowledge the plant and invite it to become a part of you, to teach you about itself. Acknowledge your body, its great wisdom, and ask it to help translate the message from the plant.

When you are done, if your mystery plant is a known plant for teas and herbalism you can look up its properties and check against what you experienced. This is when and where the value of books regarding the physical remedies of plants comes in, *after* your meeting. This will help you build trust in your incredible body and its wisdom.

You can try this with any tea that you drink, in fact with any plant food that you eat. It will make you more conscious of what you are putting inside your body. What you are both fuelling and medicating it with.

How often are you unconscious when you drink a herb tea, even your favourite Mint or Rosehip? How often have you drunk that cup and never noticed how far and deep it goes; what it has been saying to you; what it has been gifting your body; and what your body has been saying to you in response?

This is a sacred ceremony, but one that can be repeated daily, even multiple times daily. Whenever you *really* want to feel the medicine of a plant tea, even a plant that you drink all the time, acknowledge, invite and notice. When you want to learn about a new plant this is a fabulous way of meeting, of getting to know its character, its medicine and what it does to you.

Time and again I observe my students falling under the spell of a plant from just a few sniffs and sips. I see changes in people every time they pause and pay attention, alongside inviting the plant in. Posture, skin, eyes, words they use, all gently, subtly changing. Be vigilant for subtle responses, they can communicate many things.

> *For four days she had remained cool, in control. Her boundaries were strong, too strong. Her deep fears kept her isolated from the humans in the group. She protected herself, and kept a distance, in all that she did. But invisibly each day a different plant had been working away, eroding her defences. On the fifth day, the final morning, one plant stepped forward to push through. On inhaling the mystery plant tea she visibly began to crumble. On the first sip, the first taste of this beautiful plant's flesh, it broke through and the tears started falling.*

Falling and falling, as if with no end. The barricade around her heart had been breached. The healing could begin...

As your body opens to a plant and it infuses into you, there is an information exchange, a magical transformation, an ancient remembering. Not only of a plant your body may have encountered before or something that is a far part of yourself; but also a remembering of how to really engage with and use your body.

Pace yourself and use the wonderful tool that your physical body is. Your stomach, your lungs, your liver, your fingers and toes, your circulation, or any other part of you, may be activated by the imbibing of this plant flesh. And as it settles, as it becomes you, you become more plant. If you take time to do this you will notice the plant talking to you from the inside. That plant resides now within you. In your cells, in the intercellular spaces, in your bones. Your body has changed in response to this influx of chemicals, of sustenance, of nutrition, of medicine. Pay attention. Listen. Learn. Learn who that plant is and how to be more that plant yourself. When a new lover enters your body you learn something about them. No matter what happens after, that interaction cannot "unhappen" ~ they become part of you.

Using your senses to enquire about a plant through the inhalation and ingestion of a plant based tea, although a very simple approach, demonstrates how connected you are, how much you know, and fundamentally how much is being communicated to you in any moment, if you just pay attention

When you become elegant at using your senses and your body to pick up communications from plants, they become invaluable during your dedicated plant study. But more than that, you will find yourself to be more tuned in at all times, more aware. You are rewilding and your wildness is gaining momentum.

Plant Allies

You won't feel inclined to return to all plants that you are initially called to. Some plants will have a very succinct message for you. Some will be just short term in their lessons, their medicine, although of course once you have initiated contact they will reside within you for all time and your connection will remain.

A plant ally on the other hand, is a plant that you find yourself working with over a period of time, perhaps a year, or even a lifetime. It may be that one day you had a pertinent question, a question about some deep soul healing for yourself, possibly a persistent medical or emotional issue.

This plant called you and the lessons were such that a dedicated plant study alone was too brief, and you knew it. It will be a plant that you just cannot stop thinking about, or that has offered you something that is taking a while to unpick. A plant that returns again and again to your consciousness. A plant that keeps offering itself for many different things. Eventually you cannot ignore this plant, your relationship is destined to be something special.

When I spoke about returning again and again and again over the seasons to a plant, "two, three, four, twelve times over the course of a year", this is this one that I was speaking of. You may find it useful to keep a diary and return to your ally in the field once a month over the course of a year. It really depends on your relationship and where it is taking you, how you were drawn together in the first place. But returning each month, through the seasons to sit again and observe, learn from and offer your love, can only deepen your appreciation and understanding of the plant before you. It will give you the opportunity to notice the subtle aspects that combine to create that plants individual and unique character.

There will no doubt be properties that you admire in your ally, maybe it is strong or nurturing. If so ask the plant to guide you, to show you how you too can develop those properties within your own personality. This is alchemy, you transform, you shape shift, with your ally as your guide.

You don't really get to choose who your ally will be. You cannot pull a name out of a hat. You will find each other.

To keep your ally physically close you may wish to keep a piece of its flesh in a medicine pouch around your neck. You will first need permission from the plant to harvest a piece, be sure to let the plant know what you intend to do with it. It may not be that you have to ask at all, it may offer a piece of itself to you.

If you carry a piece of your ally in a medicine pouch the plant will be close to your heart at all times. You will be reminded of your ally as you bend forward and it slips out of your shirt. And each time you remove the pouch to take a shower or to sleep. Each time you hug your beloved and it is pressed into your chest. It helps keep the conversation flowing between the two of you and helps you feel the plants presence around you at all times.

I have a couple of different medicine pouches. One of which will only ever have one plant in at a time, this is for when I am doing specific work. When I have called in a new ally for help or guidance on something.

I wear it every day while I am working on that one thing. While I am carrying out the work suggested by the ally and receiving its medicine.

In the second pouch I keep a tiny piece of each of my plant allies. It is for use during special occasions. I wear it whenever I wish to call my allies in, for example if I am to lead a workshop or undertake a ceremony. Even just putting the pouch around my neck gives me a certain feeling and helps me focus on setting and holding sacred space. I feel and know that my allies are close at all times, but especially when I am wearing the pouch. As I place it around my neck I consciously call in my allies and I kiss the pouch to honour my beloved allies who are represented by their pieces of flesh inside. As I remove the pouch I again kiss it and thank all within for their help.

Alternatively you may have an altar that you clean and honour often as you set your intention and say your prayers for the day. Keeping a piece of your ally on an altar also reminds you of the plant and the work you are doing together.

Some people have a medicine bundle, a place where they keep pieces of all the plants they are working with, all their medicine plants. It is totally appropriate to keep your ally here if you have this practice.

If you wish to begin a medicine bundle or make a medicine pouch, if at all possible use natural materials. You can weave it. You can dye it with bark or roots or leaves. You can make your own cordage to tie it. Just remember at every stage to keep it sacred, to ask for permission and guidance.

Any plant that you have ongoing work with becomes an ally. An ally becomes part of who you are. An ally becomes deeply embedded within your personality. An ally is your companion, your medicine, your muse. An ally can become loved as deeply as a human lover. An ally can reflect the deepest aspects of your soul to you. That's why it takes time, time for you to learn to trust, to drop your defences and to learn the intricacies of that plant's language. To fall deeply in love and to accept and understand that plant's love for you.

Dream Work

I often dream of plants that have been in my heart, plants with which the lines of communication are open. Pay attention to your dreams. Note who visits you in them and what they show or tell you in those dreams. Dreams can be an incredible resource and an opportunity for the plant to teach and show us while our thinking minds are asleep and thus disengaged.

It is not just plants that I have been working with that inhabit my dreams though, sometimes an entirely unknown or unexpected visitor appears.

> *I awoke that morning repeating a strange name over and over again. As my dream memory began to fade I clung to the image of the bronzed leaves and bright berries of this squat shrub. I ran straight up to my office to my huge herb encyclopaedia to search for this mystery plant, to make sure it existed in this plane, it did; I was delighted. Shortly afterwards, as I was still reeling from the clarity of my dream, my husband awoke; he felt unwell. He had become ill in the night, the symptoms arriving suddenly and with some force. My personal kitchen apothecary was lacking and so I took a trip to my local health store to gather some supplies. As I entered the shop there was a display right by the door and at eye level on this display was a syrup made from the plant I had dreamed of. The plant I had never previously heard of. It was, it turns out, exactly the remedy he needed.*

Don't ignore your dreams. If at all possible keep a notepad and pencil at the side of the bed so any that come to you can be noted down before they are forgotten. They can be very clear communications.

You can undertake intentional dream work with plants. Within dreams the imagination is free to teach us things that the waking mind would either not accept or would try to rationalise.

Begin by communicating your intentions to the plant you wish to dream with. Ask permission and if granted gather a sprig. Take the sprig to bed, place beside or beneath your pillow. As you begin to fall asleep invite the plant to visit you in dreams. If you intend to ask a specific question of the plant, now is the time to do so. Record any dreams on waking. These days I actually just record my voice, recounting the dream onto my phone, as I can do this before I can write and so the memory is fresher. Whatever works for you.

You may get a result on the first night. You may wish to repeat each night for a week. You may not remember whether the plant appeared or not, but record your dreams anyway.

An alternative method that a student once presented, was to set an alarm a little before sunrise and drink a preparation made from the plant.

Then hold an image of the plant in your minds eye as you go back to sleep. Invite the plant to appear and ask your question as you enter conscious dream space with it. This is the most active time of the night for dreams and so may prove to be more effective than a sprig by the pillow. It will only work if, after the disturbance, you can get back to sleep.

Sacred Elixirs

Before I proceed and discuss using plants internally it is important to consider that not every plant is suitable for internal work. Even a tiny taste of something unsuitable can cause discomfort or worse.

> *The early morning sun was gently warming, taking away the stiffness of the nights camping. You called me over and I asked if you would share your medicine with me. You stood exotic and beautiful in this strange land, I could not help myself but fall for you, deeply and wildly. The longer I was with you the more you whispered to me. And then it happened. You invited me to taste a tiny red flower bud. I enthusiastically took you to my lips. Almost immediately on taking you into my mouth something felt wrong. As I swallowed, the burning sensation followed your flesh like fire into my throat. As I took my leave and hurriedly sought a human to help me, I am sure I heard you chuckle.*

The incident above happened in the Mukogodo Sacred Forest in Kenya, far from home. The plant, Popongi as it is locally known, is not for ingestion as I discovered. Luckily the Samburu medicine man that had taken me to that place was not far away. On showing him the picture I had drawn of Popongi he chuckled, just like the plant itself had done. Shortly after he found me a remedy for the discomfort. This is probably the closest I have come to a plant biting me, and it was not a plant I was in the least bit scared of! The point I am really trying to make is to not simply assume that a plant is safe to eat just because it invites you to do so.

So please, before working internally with any plant, make sure you are one hundred per cent sure of its identification and suitability for internal use. Don't let fear get in the way, but if you are to taste a plant it would be well to know of any poisonous ones in the area first – not to avoid them outright as their medicine may be strong and true in other ways, but to avoid tasting one that could cause poisoning or worse.

Once you know a plant is fine to taste, before making a remedy with it, check for any cautions or contraindications pertaining to its use and always stick to any recommended dosages. As you should realise by now plants can be incredibly potent, so don't disregard advice on dosage unless you are looking for trouble.

You may have already been making plant remedies for many years and as we all know, a simple remedy can be made with book knowledge. Remedies made with plants have great value and can be very effective. Gathering plants to make remedies certainly slips comfortably into the personal rewilding sphere. By foraging for those plants you become familiar with their territory, with their cycles of life, with their physical characteristics, with their medicinal qualities. You get outside, you use your hands, you learn and make a connection with not just plants but with the landscape and all that contains, from weather systems and fauna, to the soil itself. I love making and using remedies and through their use I most certainly feel myself becoming more connected to the plants, the place in which I live and also to my own body and what it is telling me it needs.

Ideally your kitchen apothecary cupboards and shelves are almost bare, inhabited solely by a small handful of preparations, made to preserve seasonal plants for use when they are in a different phase. Certainly not full of endless rows of jars filled with dusty dried herbs, picked and grown by someone else, somewhere else. Real food, real medicine comes straight from the ground. You, asking and thanking, as you gather. This is the rewilders kitchen and apothecary. And this will make you well and keep you in a living relationship with the plants outside your door; your true neighbours, the rooted ones.

Making remedies with plants that are in your neighbourhood, plants that you have a relationship with; that you can ask and that you can gift in return; that you can nurture, gather, love; will result in much more potent remedies. It will also mean that you are only using local medicines in your kitchen apothecary, and Gaia is not wrong; your local area will provide the medicines you need. It will mean that you are not using the last drops of ancient sunlight to transport exotic plant medicines that you have no direct relationship with to your door. It means you have an absolute handle on the plant body's provenance and whether it was grown and harvested in a sustainable way and with respect.

Once you have begun treading the plant whispering path your remedies will enliven. You will find yourself acknowledging the plant when you find the one you seek. You will be communicating; asking whether you can gather, which leaves or buds or roots you may take. You will be expressing your love and gratitude. Your remedy, because of this basic level of interaction, will become something more. It was gathered with permission.

The plant gifted you parts of its body and you were grateful. The plant is a little more alive inside the remedy and for that reason the remedy will feel more precious to you, more personal. It may be that you just need a sprig for a physical remedy, a cough for example, but when worked with as a living medicine gifted by a sentient plant, your basic cough remedy will be somewhat elevated, because the plant was acknowledged and asked.

Once you take your communications with that plant further, then you enter the realms of sacred elixir making. Your simple remedy is elevated to the sacrosanct, the holy. It is elevated from being a medicinal remedy to something magical that can touch you on many levels.

The full sacred elixir comes when you ask a plant if it has any medicine to share with you and it tells you something. Making a remedy afterwards, for the purpose indicated by the plant, will give you a scared elixir.

If you you wish to work with plants in this way, to make sacred elixirs with their flesh, then once you have already made a deep connection with the plant and been gifted medicine, ask permission to gather. If the answer is yes take only what you need, never all. Ask the plant to direct you to which parts you may gather, and when to stop. Sit quietly once harvested and thank, thank wholeheartedly for all that you have gathered, all that the plant has gifted you.

Throughout the whole process I encourage you to keep the communication flowing. Express *all* of the reasons you wish to make an elixir, any layers to your motivation beyond the medicine you were offered. It could be that the plant is asking to be made into a medicine by you, or that you wish to get to know the plant better. Perhaps it is that you wish to make money from selling tinctures, or that you feel you *should* make something with this plant, or that you want to generate a new and interesting post for your social media account. Be honest and the plant will guide you. If, for example, you are wishing to make something for commercial gain, the plant may well guide you to a different patch where it is growing more abundantly and thus has more to share. It is important to be conscious of *all* layers of your motivation and acknowledge them. Being unconscious during this process can lead to unintended consequences. Never, ever, forget that the plant is a living being and making a remedy with the living plant means taking some of the living flesh. Always honour that.

Communicate at all times. When processing into the remedy ask if the plant wants to be chopped or not. Quite often it does not. The plant may wish to remain whole. Ask the question *each* time you make a preparation. If you are communicating directly with the plant you will need to be fluid as it may change with what you are feeling from the plant in that moment. Don't do what you have always done, or have heard is the best way. Always communicate, always ask. That is what makes your handmade medicine a living medicine – you listened to what the plant wanted and acted according to the plants guidance.

As the remedy is brewing - maybe you are infusing the plant body in alcohol or oil, vinegar or honey - keep the conversation going. As you shake it each day, whisper or sing to the plant, enter the dream. Extend gratitude, feel it in your heart. Drop back into the feeling that you had when you sat in person with the plant. Repeat this every day until the remedy is ready to use. It is during this extended communication process that the medicine you were offered will be transferred into the remedy for you by the plant, not just physical medicine but medicine for your spirit, your soul, too. Your remedy becomes an elixir. So if you were gifted medicine for a broken heart, that is what your elixir will contain, even if no herbal has ever mentioned such a thing about this plant medicine, because it is personal medicine for you directly from the plant.

Treat the elixir as a living being, communicating with it to wake it up before use. When it is time for you to take the elixir; hold the remedy bottle in your hand, hold it to your heart, and speak to the spirit of the plant(s) inside. Thank them and ask them to help you. When you honour the medicine in this way and it will come alive for you. Invite the plant to infuse into you. Invite the properties the plant offered you; the plants wisdom, medicine, food. Invite the plant to become you. Be conscious. Like saying grace before meals, take a pause to connect and slip back into the dream of the plant, take time to ask and to thank. The response can be overwhelming, it certainly is a magical doorway which when opened changes everything.

Take time to notice what happens. It may not be instant, you may have forgotten your invitation when say twenty minutes later something rather profound begins to happen and all across your body you feel different sensations. When this happens sit with it, give time to it rather than just carrying on with what you were doing. Notice how that plant changes things for you and thank it for them, for the insights. Drinking a tea, eating a leaf, becomes a sacred act infused with meaning and learning.

The Seminole people wake the plant in their remedies with their breath, by gently blowing into the remedy before using. The ancient Greek word for breath, pneuma, shares its origins with psyche; both are considered words for soul. So, if you choose to breathe into a remedy, as per the Seminole tradition, to wake it up before use, you are breathing a bit of your soul in there. You and the plant once again joined, forming the unique combination that only the two of you together can make.

A sacred elixir probably sounds a lot more grandiose than it actually is. As soon as you have worked on a personal level with a plant, studied it, felt into it, observed it, acknowledged it, your relationship has begun. Any subsequent medicine you make from that plant, as long as you keep the communication open; asking, and then thanking, will become sacred medicine. The medicine has been willingly given by the plant, not simply taken. A plant communicated with in this way, treated as the intelligent, sentient being that it is, will put forward it's best efforts for you.

Because a sacred elixir comes with the promise of what that plant offered you in your exchange, it can be used differently than you would if you were to use it as a physical remedy. Feel into it and notice what you are guided to do. Perhaps you will be guided to apply the elixir to your wrists and temples, to your palms and third eye, to your chakras, to your heart, to the soles of your feet. This is sacred medicine, working on your spirit and soul; and so the way you use it may well differ from its use as a physical remedy.

I have led workshops where, after dedicated study and deeper communications with a plant, the body is then harvested and juiced before mixing 1:1 with brandy. This is a liquid extraction but also, because of the personal direct communication, a sacred elixir. The rule of thumb with dosage for a liquid extraction is 1ml three times daily, and yet, furnishing my students tongues with a single drop of sacred elixir I have witnessed each one of them fall into the dream like dominoes. Their faces may flush, or eyes become more sparkly, perhaps they fill their space by physically standing taller, straighter; potentially all of these visible physical changes after a single drop! It may be that you need very little of a sacred elixir, much, much less than you would of a traditional remedy. One time I took a single drop of an elixir that I had just made, the strength and presence of the plant spirit moving through me was such that my knees crumpled and I had to grab a nearby tabletop to steady myself! So, start small if taking internally, just one or two drops, and build up to the level that feels right.

This, again, is a form of shape shifting. You are putting energy in and a transformation is taking place. You put in energy by forming a relationship with the plant, harvesting with permission, making a remedy and asking the plant to infuse into you. The plant responded, the plant offered you something. The plant spirit is present throughout the medicine making process, as it has been approached with respect, gratitude and love; and so gifts its medicine on all the levels initially offered. You are now more that plant, a living embodiment in part of that plant. It lives not just in your cells and your bones as it becomes you, but also in your heart and mind.

I have been asked whether it is possible to make a sacred elixir for someone else, the short answer is no. You can approach the plant with a request for medicine for a third party, you can undertake a dedicated study and journey work on behalf of this other person. If you do so the remedy you create for them will certainly be greatly elevated, it will be much more than a simple physical remedy that they could buy off the shelf. It will be infused with what that plant has put forth specifically on that third persons behalf. However a remedy only truly becomes a sacred elixir through personal relationship with that plant. Only a one on one relationship can reach those sacred depths.

Using a medicine pouch or bundle, incorporating dreamwork, and making remedies and elixirs are not exclusively for use with an ally plant. You may be drawn to undertake those activities with any plant you make contact with. However, they certainly help you cement your relationship and deepen your knowledge of the plant and its medicine. And so often form an illuminating element of work with those somewhat special relationships, with your allies. The more practices you undertake with a single plant, the further your relationship, your knowing of that plant, will go.

Preparing The Soil
The art of plant whispering is an everyday pursuit. A life way. To encourage and allow for this there are certain behaviours you may wish to adopt, or to deepen, to make the conditions within yourself more favourable for this life way to establish.

Humankind on the whole has moved away from a natural, local, seasonal diet; from surviving on what we can hunt and forage in our immediate locale. But imagine a time when everything we ate, grew or roamed within miles of where we stood. Imagine how deeply in tune with the landscape, with the seasons, with the rain and sun, with day and night, with the rocks, the soil and the insects we once were. As we eat a more and more exotic or processed diet, we move further and further away from our natural way of being and our connection with the more-than-human becomes more and more tenuous. The more local, organic, wild and unprocessed we eat, the more our wild connections have a chance to re-establish and the plants have a greater chance to live in and through us.

> *The Wheat becomes human because humans eat it. The Blackberry becomes human because humans eat it. The Sorrel becomes human because humans eat it, and on and on. They all become human.*

Local food holds, encoded within it, the message of the land upon which you stand. It holds the character of your locale; the rain, the microclimate, the soil minerals and bacteria, the ground water. When you eat locally grown foods it ties you in, the land reclaims you. Certainly on a personal level by eating local plants I feel myself more a part of the local landscape. Just as through eating wild plants I feel myself becoming that little bit wilder.

> *As I eat the local landscape, the soil and climate, through the wild leaves; ancient whisperings settle in my bones and I know I belong here.*

As I meditate upon what I can do for our planet in this time of ecocide, of destruction and chaos, one simple phrase keeps returning to me ~ *become more plant*. And so that is what I strive to do. On gathering my green relations, placing the leaves on my lips as I quietly acknowledge everything I feel, know and imagine it is to be that plant, then eat with gratitude, I can feel my wild connection growing. As I eat my raw plant supper I do indeed feel myself becoming more plant.

The Alkaline State

To receive a good and clear message from any communication with the more-than-human you will need to be clear and clean yourself. We have talked about internal work to reach that place spiritually and emotionally. But to maximise your potential for interspecies communication there is another level that you absolutely need to consider and that is your body. If your body is clean and clear you will also find your mind naturally falls in and becomes less cluttered. The cleaner you eat, the less your body will be working to digest and cope with toxins, the more clearly it will be able to work for you in picking up and interpreting incoming communications.

It is not just a clean body, but a body in its natural alkaline state that potentiates clear communication. As you have worked with and begun to understand the great wisdom of your body, there comes a time when you understand that it deserves the best fuel possible to function at its optimum. With your body operating in that condition everything becomes clear and communication is free flowing. More than that you begin to *just know* on a much higher level. Understanding does not take energy and processing, it simply clicks in because there is nothing in the way, nothing slowing it down or stalling its assimilation.

To achieve an alkaline state you will need to eat a high proportion of alkaline-forming foods and reduce your intake of acid-forming foods. A diet composed mainly of fresh and raw fruits and vegetables will be alkaline-forming. Lightly steamed vegetables, sprouted seeds and legumes, cooked quinoa and millet (both are seeds, not grains) and herbal teas are all also alkaline-forming. Dark green leaves are especially alkaline-forming. Foods that are acid-forming include all animal flesh, including river and marine life. All dairy and egg products. Alcohol. Fried and roasted foods. Refined sugar and anything containing it. Processed foods. Grains and anything made from them (for example bread and pasta). Coffee and black tea.

It is still possible to eat acid-forming foods (in moderation) and achieve an overall alkaline balance. To do this you will need to eat raw dark greens alongside pretty much everything that is acid-forming. But simply put, the more acid-forming foods you eat the less chance you have of maintaining an overall alkaline balance.

As with everything it is of course up to you. You can eat, drink, smoke (which is also acid-forming whether Tobacco or Marijuana), whatever you like and still communicate, of course you can; the plants can shout rather loudly and cut through your body and mind fog if they feel to. That is why this section did not appear at the beginning of this chapter, because plant whispering is possible without taking it this far. But, it is all about how far you are personally willing to go. As with everything, the more you put in, the more you get out. With regards to having a clean and alkaline system, if you have not ventured into these realms before and are willing to start experimenting, you will discover an entirely new level to your abilities, and become party to so much more of the ongoing Gaian dialogue.

Chlorophyll is essential. Not just for keeping our bodies in their natural alkaline state and for the cell building that it affords, but also because the more chlorophyll we consume the more plant we become and the greater access to the wisdom of the plants we gain. An alkaline and high chlorophyll diet both help push it to the next level.

Very early on my path as plant whisperer I was directed by the plants that to take my relationships with them to the next level I needed to eat plants in their natural form.

> *Eat raw plants, they will root you directly to the divine within.*

I was told.

> *Become a clean, crystal clear, vessel for messages from the divine. Be raw, be pure, keep your mind clear.*

The plants directed.

These messages have not just come once, but repeatedly to me over the years, from different plants in different circumstances and at different stages in my life. Most recently after a difficult time of great personal loss, where I found myself eating less well and reaching for the wine glass a little too often. An ally I have been working with for over 15 years, stepped in to remind me. All it said to me, over and over, was:

chlorophyll, chlorophyll, chlorophyll.

Another time I was several days into a wilderness immersion. I was absolutely tuned in to all the beings around me. Time and space was twinkling as I lived from moment to moment within the dream of Gaia. I *felt* everything around me. The livingness of everything was rushing through me as a life force. I had been hiking and fasting all morning but had become hungry, so I paused to eat. I had some cheese in my bag, almost instantaneously the moment this passed my lips it was as if someone turned the switch off. The immense feeling of connectivity dropped out and I became "human", a lonely human again. All on my own on that mountain path. The only thing that had changed was that I had eaten a few bites of an acid-forming animal product, a piece of cheese. That alone was enough to close everything down, immediately. An alkaline body and following a mainly raw, plant based diet, turns up the volume immeasurably, no question.

> *The cleaner the body, the purer the instinct; instinct is infinite intelligence working through the living being.*
> **David Wolfe**

Cleansing & Fasting

To reset your current habits in the pursuit of a clear and clean body and mind, you may find it useful to undertake a cleanse or an occasional fast. This doesn't have to be a one off. I find that regular cycles of cleansing and fasting, at least annually, help remind my body and mind of exactly how clearly and efficiently they can function when working at their optimum.

> *One of the primary things that happens during a fast is the re-establishment of a sophisticated relationship with your body.*
> **Stephen Harrod Buhner**

Fasting and cleansing is an in depth subject which I will just touch on here. I have found it has tremendous value when seeking clear two-way communications with the more-than-human.

If your diet is currently rather toxic, approach it very gently. Start by cutting caffeine, alcohol, animal products, fried food, salt, sugar one by one. If you cut everything at the same time you may feel horribly ill as your body goes through the detoxification process and you may not be able to stick with it. So cut down and gradually cut out the previously mentioned offenders over the course of two or three weeks. Don't cheat as you will only be cheating yourself.

If you have a serious medical condition or are on long term medication it is advisable to discuss this process with a natural health care practitioner before you begin, and follow their advice. Otherwise just take it gently, cutting down toxins gradually until by the end of the third week you are eating only plant based foods, either raw or gently steamed. This may be as far as you wish to go.

If you wish to take it further, cut out all solid food and spend the next seven days drinking green juices made from fresh vegetables and fruits. At some point you may even consider spending 24 hours drinking only water.

When you have settled in at the furthest level you are willing or able to go, you will notice exactly how much clearer you are. How your intuition is much stronger. How much more rapid your interpretation of everything that touches you is. You will gain clarity in everything, all your behaviours, all your relationships, all your communications.

Ideally when you return to eating, incorporate wild dark greens whenever you can, drink wild plant teas and juice chlorophyll every day. By following this as a general template you will ensure that you are receiving enough chlorophyll and not slipping away from your plant relations.

When you undertake deeply cleansing work with your body, be it by changing your diet, a juice fast or a water fast, you will find that deep shadow work becomes inevitable, unavoidable. As your body lets go of long stored toxins, long held emotions are also released. It can be quite a roller coaster, but because you are cleansing and immersed within the process of letting go, those old feelings just pass on through and are released. It is a genuinely incredible experience that I wholeheartedly recommend. And through it all, your connections and communications with plants and others go yet one step further.

However far you choose to go in cleaning up your diet, every now and then take the time with each mouthful to conjure up an image of the plant you are eating in your minds eye. It helps if you have met this plant in the flesh, if this is not possible make yourself aware of how the growing plant looks with online photos. Think about the plant this food came from and thank it. Really go in to detail, the flowers, the fruit, the leaves, the plant through the seasons. If the plant is an annual, go through the life cycle. Consider what it took to create this piece of plant flesh that you are about to eat, then once you have offered your gratitude, consciously invite the plant to become you as you take a bite. Stay in the zone, go with it, how deep will it take you? How far can you go? Quite far actually from my experience, but always further with a plant that you know just a little bit, even if it is a banana that you have only ever seen growing once while on holiday, that familiarity, no matter how passing, does help.

All life should be considered sacred, and thanked as it gives its life so that we may live. Just as one day we will give our life and if not then stuffed full of embalming fluids and other chemicals in a hard-to-breakdown wooden box, we will go back to feed Gaia. Whatever you choose to eat becomes you, so choose well. If you feed yourself with chemicals, industry and fear, then that will affect you on many levels. Live with grace. Eat less. Eat local. Eat organic. Eat alkaline-forming foods. Treat every meal as a sacred offering, every life that contributed to that meal to be offered your wholehearted gratitude in return. That is how we need to live if we wish to live in a better world.

The clearer you become, the more able you are to notice when you are being called or instructed by the plants to do certain things. There may come a time when, for a specific reason, you may need to go deeper or further and wish to involve ceremony or ritual. The springboard to change generated by this can be immense.

Shamanic Journey

Throughout history, hypnotic, repetitive beats have been recognised and employed to induce trance-like states. Even in popular youth culture, people making and listening to electronic music are aware of the trance-like states that can be achieved when dancing for prolonged periods to music with a certain range of beats per minute. That was where I had my introduction. The genre I was listening and dancing to loosely referred to as trance music, which indeed makes the point in its name. Through dancing all night to this music, I regularly reached an ecstatic state where my physical form was transcended; conscious thoughts and concerns were left behind as I seemed to move and merge, as one with the crowd. This can be explained by the physiological effects that a repetitive beat of a certain tempo has on upon us, it follows that this is also what happens when a shaman bangs their drum or shakes their rattle.

Through the process of shamanic journey we gain access to the dreaming of the world, to the spirit realm. It is common practice to use a drum, but a rattle or even a didgeridoo can be used to generate a rhythm that in turn alters the way our brains function. With altered brain function, mind chatter is silenced. In the space created, the doorway to dreaming, to the spirit realm, is fully opened. This allows us to tap into Gaia mind, Earth intelligence, all that is. It allows us to dream in the sacred language of spirit.

Physiologically, a repetitive beat of around 3 to 4 beats per second will create changes in the central nervous system and facilitate the production of brain waves in the alpha and theta ranges. Simply put, brain waves are the pulsing vibrations of the brain. Different rates of vibration or pulse rates within the brain have their own characteristics. Alpha and theta are just two of the five types of brain wave that we experience. The production of alpha and theta brainwaves, although distinct, both relate to creativity and vivid imagery.

Alpha waves are naturally higher during wakeful relaxation with closed eyes. Your brain will generate alpha waves when meditating, sunbathing, daydreaming and during deep relaxation. The theta frequency wave is deeper than alpha.

> *The theta state…the twilight phase when linear thought succumbs to free-form images, and awareness of the narrowly defined self is supplanted by identification with the shifting fields of an organic whole.*
> **Jesse Wolfe Hardin**

Theta brain waves are associated with early stages of sleep and the process of dreaming. They are experienced during REM sleep (whilst we dream), lucid dreaming, hypnosis, and the barely conscious state between sleep and waking. The theta state is also entered when having a spiritual experience, when experiencing powerful surges of emotion and when in a highly creative state. Interestingly it is also the state where your extra sensory perception operates. They allow a direct connection to the subconscious mind and subconscious processing. It is the liminal edge between the conscious and subconscious mind.

How To Journey
If you have never undertaken a shamanic journey it is best to experience one initially with a guide, perhaps in a group, just to get a feel for how it

works. The method is safe, so embarking upon a shamanic journey alone will be fine once you have a handle on the method; all that will happen if you fail to maintain focus is that you will simply return to your normal sense of self.

To journey to the spirit of a plant, first you will need to have a clear intention. Say it out loud or in your mind before you begin. It will most likely be something along the lines of "I wish to meet with the spirit of this plant"; you may also have a question for the plant, the same as when you undertake a dedicated plant study. "Do you have any medicine to share with me?" for example.

The next step, is to imagine yourself in a place that can act as an entry point into the Earth. So a cave, a rabbit hole or a tree root, for example. Once the drum starts beating, imagine entering into the Earth and descending to the lower world, the place where the spirits of plants reside. On arrival in the lower world you must ask to meet the spirit of the plant and ask your question again. The drum is typically played at a steady rate for ten to fifteen minutes or so, it is during this time that your interaction with the plants spirit will occur. As the drum signals you to return to mundane reality, it is essential that you express your gratitude before you leave, even if you felt that nothing happened. Turn and retrace your steps, all the way back to your entrance point and back out of the Earth.

On return to your ordinary state of consciousness write everything down. Do so *before* you speak or share the experience. If you fail to do this some of the details may be lost, details that could have great meaning and significance once interpreted. Many times I have returned to plant journey notes years later and discovered a whole new layer to the communication, a layer that I didn't recognise at the time of the journey.

If you are banging the drum for yourself it takes a bit more practice to let go and enter the dream, as part of you will be concentrating on keeping the beat going. If you do choose to drum for yourself you don't have to be too precise regarding maintaining the correct number of beats per second, I have found that each plant has me drumming a slightly different rhythm and tempo. If I just relax, the spirit of the drum and the spirit of the plant take over.

Whilst within the journey it is important that if you make any promises to the plant spirits that when you return to this reality, you keep your promises, *remember agreements*. It is also important that you don't in effect "hassle" the plant; don't return and ask for more before you have acted upon what you have already been told.

When I do this deep work with a plant spirit, I can feel the spirit of the plant and the dream space lingering for much of the day. I actually enjoy this as it holds me in there with the plant spirit for longer; giving the messages a chance to work through me kinaesthetically, giving further insight to the plants character and response. If you dislike this feeling, or feel you have brought something back that you didn't want, smudge yourself to clear away any residual feelings and close the door to the dream state.

A shamanic journey can be undertaken whenever you wish to learn more about one of your plant relations, or have a specific question for a plant. I find that a journey is most effective directly after conducting a dedicated plant study: when you are still feeling the interaction you have just had in person with the plant, while its taste is still infusing into you, its flavour on your tongue and perfume in your nose, its touch on your skin.

The Journey Experience

Everyone experiences meeting with a plant spirit, during shamanic journey, differently. A journey is commonly experienced visually; but it may be auditory, physical, visceral, emotional, or any combination of these. It may be experienced by the body in a very physical way, perhaps with a shimmy and shake, minor convulsions even. Others experience it in a more oral way, expressing moans and groans, snorts and giggles. Others have a more aural experience as they hear rips and scrunching, whistling and angelic song. There are so many ways to experience, feel and express a journey. None are more right or more useful.

If you feel that you are getting nothing, finding yourself stuck in the darkness behind your closed eyes, explore that nothingness. Can you distinguish anything at all? Any variation in the darkness, such as edges, shapes or patterns? Don't be hard on yourself, you may have been relying on logic and your left brain for a long time so it may take a while, like any new skill, to even realise that something is actually happening and certainly to develop acuity.

If you don't experience images perhaps you will have a more sensory experience, feeling or hearing something. It may come to you as a wave of emotion or as a bodily sensation. Don't work too hard at it, it is the work of spirit and it will come the way it needs to for you. Have no expectations.

The first shamanic journey I was ever guided on was to a plant spirit, in a group setting. There were almost 80 people in the room. After the drumming had ceased we were invited to share our experience. I felt that I had got nothing at all and became increasingly disheartened as people shared incredibly vibrant descriptions of otherworldly scenes, of holding hands and dancing with the plant spirit, of vast colourful landscapes imbued with deep meaning. And so I raised my hand to share. I explained how I had sat in the dark and nothing happened, that I just felt increasingly sleepy as the drumming went on and on and I just sat there. It was then that the group facilitator revealed that the plant we had visited was known, amongst many other things, as being a remedy for insomnia; it was a sleep inducing plant. So, be careful to look in all corners of your experience for any slight change in how you feel, any tiny sound or sensation; despite the lack of fanfare, it could be the answer to the question that you asked.

It is quite common to disregard what occurs because you think you are making it all up. However, if you think you are just imagining it and that thought is holding you back from believing the message, consider the word imagine. It comes from "I Magus". The Latin *magus* translates as magician, learned magician. So the roots of its meaning is *I the magician*. Your imagination is very much a facet of Gaia, don't forget that. What is the world but a hologram, each piece containing the whole but from a different perspective? Our imagination contains it all; all the questions, all the answers and everything in between. As you begin your descent to the lower world when the drumming commences, you imagine it. In that moment as you are making it up, you visualise it. Imagine an opening, another world; as you start drawing the outline with your mind, spirit will come and fill the rest in.

What you seed in deep plant meditations and journeying is a product of your imagination. Everything you see in the inner realms is coming through your cultural filter, visions come in a way that you can relate to. For me that is most often meadows, clouds, fairy castles and crystals. Whereas for my Brazilian friend, who currently resides in Africa, the context is often thick jungle with a very tribal theme. Yet after the journeys that we have undertaken together, when we share our experience, the actual messages we extract from our otherworldly adventures are always remarkably similar. The truth behind them comes from the plant spirit and the collective unconscious, from the dreaming of the world.

Sometimes I have had people reject how a plant spirit appears to them and as quickly as they think "you can't be it" the being shape shifts into a different form, one they find for some reason more agreeable. This hasn't just happened once but many times. I am a great believer that you get what you need in the moment. The message comes across in the way that means most to you individually at that point in time.

The more you visit, the more you understand the language of that realm, of spirit. Eventually with experience you can become fluent. Your experiences whilst journeying become like lucid dreams, ones that feel real and within which you can control your actions and direct your adventures with the plant spirits; allowing for deeper and further questioning and knowing.

The respite from mind chatter and rational thoughts, bestowed by the drumming, is brief. As soon as the drumming ceases our little minds go into overdrive (unless we are careful), trying to interpret the messages, rather than taking time to sit with them and allow the meaning to gradually infuse into our being. Don't be in a hurry to interpret the message, it may take months or years to fully understand.

Maybe your body convulses but you get no vision or clear picture, just a few movements or shakes as you lie there. If you have asked the plant whether it has medicine to share with you, it could be that the shivers and shakes are your body's reaction to the plant spirit entering you and doing its work. Work that you have no need to really know any more about lest your brain rationalises it. It may be that through its spirit the plant has delivered its medicine directly to your physical body. Wasting time trying to work it out, or feeling that you are less than as your journey was not visual, that you "can't do it" would be a shame and a waste of energy. It is about being open and gratefully accepting whatever comes to you even if it is in a form that you cannot currently unfold with logic, or that you cannot catalogue as that plant's power or medicine.

Shamanic journey is a great tool for accessing other realms and I love it. But don't get carried away with it. After living such spiritually bereft lives and suddenly finding access to the realms of spirit, approach with respect; it is not a sideshow. Never reduce a shamanic journey to entertainment, despite the great pleasure it may bring. Remember this is sacred work. Use it when you have a genuine line of enquiry and with full acknowledgement and respect for the plant; never just for fun. Equally I would like to caution you not to become dependent on a drum. There are so many ways to enter the plant realms, a drum is not necessary to get you there.

Plant Diets

When placing a piece of a plant in your mouth and beginning to chew, you produce saliva and the plant begins to assimilate. It takes its first salivary steps to becoming you, and you take the first steps in becoming more that plant. So imagine when the relationship is already strong and this assimilation, this becoming, is conscious.

When you have consciously communicated with the plant, subsequently inviting the plant to then live in and through you becomes immense. If your plant relationships are strong and run deep, this can happen every meal time when one of your plant companions becomes your dinner. Plant diets are yet another notch up.

Plant diets can be many things. Intention is key. Being clear about what you are asking of your plant relation, or what they are asking of you, is essential if you are to learn anything of value from the practice.

I need to make the point here that plant diets as I describe them here, are significantly different from "dietas", South American jungle diets which are curated by a local medicine (wo)man or "curandera/o". Here, I discuss paths that you can follow safely by yourself and use as a portal to the plants of your land. A way to get to know and meet your local plants and their spirits. And an opportunity for those plants to work with you on the issues you have presented to them and that they have offered you medicine for.

During a plant diet you will need to consciously consume the plant you are working with every day over a period of time. To learn from your plant diet, any other foods you are consuming alongside the plant in question will typically need to be somewhat bland. No salt, sugars or fats. No animal flesh (including fish or seafood), no dairy. Very similar at this stage to the cleansing diet I recommended a few pages ago. If you are really serious you will want to add in an element of remoteness by removing yourself from distractions, electronic and human. In essence combining both a cleansing diet with a solo wilderness immersion.

I find this approach somewhat challenging unless I simply fast with a single plant; that is consuming the plant in question alone, with no other remedies, teas, drinks other than water, or food at all. This is an extreme form of plant diet and one that cannot be maintained for very long, although the length of time you can maintain will depend on the plant you are working with and your personal constitution.

You can take the plant body in the form of its fresh body (eating a leaf for example), a juice, a tea, an elixir, whatever you feel directed to do, or most comfortable with. You may choose to consume the plant in several different ways alongside each other. If you wish to explore a plant in this way it advisable to undertake a thorough cleanse first.

Even water and fresh mountain air are carriers of messages and communications, so make sure you really get a feel for the plant, for its unique signature, so that you are not getting confused. This is facilitated by being in the presence of the living plant. In fact this is preferable, as it becomes a full immersion.

Such extreme plant diets will allow you great insights into the plant you are dieting. Your relationship will expand and grow in many directions. It is however a big commitment and not something you will necessarily be called to do that often, or by that many plants, unless of course it becomes *your* way; your primary way of working deeply with a plant. Mostly it will happen with a plant that has already had a great impact on you, that has directed you to undertake this approach or that you have a deep calling to work with in a more intense and immersive manner.

Much, much, more regularly I find myself imbibing a plant for several weeks alongside my usual life. It may be that the plant has just come in to season and each time I leave my door to gather a plant to drink as tea, or eat for my supper, it calls me over and gifts itself. I am used to the usual background noise of the place that I live and the foods that I eat and so if I focus I will feel the plant I am dieting and the subtle effects it is having, the subtle communications it is gifting. I welcome the plant each time I introduce it to my system. I pay attention and notice any feelings, any changes that are occurring. As the days pass I become increasingly aware of the plants signature and movements within me. Some plants I repeat this process with for a few weeks every year as they arrive back after the winter. With those ones it has become a tradition, something we do, kind of catching up after time apart if you like. It may also be the only time we work together all year.

The results gained from working in this way are much more subtle than an extreme plant diet, but are there if you are open and paying attention. It is a much more sustainable way to work with a plant for me as I can diet in this manner without stepping outside of my daily life and routine and thus it can happen many times in a year with many different plants. It can become a way of being.

Microdosing

Essentially, much of the time when I diet a plant consciously it is in the form of what is now known as microdosing*. Microdosing is something I have employed for years without realising that was what I was doing. I was doing it before it was a "thing". Microdosing is simply taking a very small amount of the plant, by small amount I mean much, much less than would be considered an active or medicinal dose. If you have been elevating your remedies into sacred elixirs then, as I suggested, taking just a few drops each day can be enough to remind your body and drop you into the dream and the medicine of that plant.

I have worked with many different plants over the years in this way.

---

* *Microdosing is a term and practice usually used in reference to psychoactive plant medicines, and drugs such as LSD. However, by this point on your plant whispering journey I am sure you now appreciate that all plants can be psychoactive and can work to change you deeply if you are in direct relationship with them.*

One of the great benefits of microdosing is that you are taking such a small quantity of the plant you can continue working with it over long periods of time. If you are not feeling much at your starting point of one or two drops then simply ask the plant. Clear your mind, drop into the dream of the plant in question and ask how many drops you need. The length of time you work together in this way will be personal to you and the plant in question. After working together for some weeks or months, one day you may feel that the work is complete, if so simply thank the plant for its lessons and stop taking it. You may find that after several months of religiously microdosing each day you have suddenly forgotten and a whole week has passed since you took any; this I take as a sign that the job is done, for now at least. Always remember to communicate, to say that you are stopping and to offer your gratitude for all that has passed between you.

It is essential to invite the plant to become you each time you take it and give undivided attention as you assimilate the drops, the way you would with a blind tea tasting. This takes time each day, not just a drop and go, but as with everything the more you put in the more you get out. So, the more you consciously invite and take time to notice, the greater you will understand the medicine and its effect upon you and the less likely it is to get lost in the daily maelstrom of events that is this life.

Working with a plant in this way can be subtle and can take time, although not necessarily. One time I had dramatic effects by day three. The plant I was microdosing had offered help with clear communication. On that third day, I found myself clearly debating with two highly articulate academics. I did not stumble over my words and was able to back up every argument I made with clear facts; something my lack of self-confidence would never previously have allowed me to do. It really was something quite special, it changed me deeply. The one I was working with however was an ally which had been in my life for thirty years! We had worked closely together on many things and so our connection was already strong.

Other times it has taken longer and been less dramatic. It varies immensely from plant to plant. I would say that in general, the plants that you know more fully before embarking on a microdosing adventure with, will have a much more noticeable effect within a much shorter time frame. I am pretty convinced that this is because the relationship is strong and by already knowing their character, their unique signature, you recognise them and their work within you very quickly.

The most important thing is to work consciously and even then, at the beginning, it may be hard to distinguish anything distinct. It could take time to realise the changes that manifest within you in response to the plant, sometimes it will only be on reflection after the microdosing journey has ended. Do not be disappointed. With the benefit of hindsight it becomes possible to look back and notice the subtle directing of the plant upon you. For this reason I recommend keeping a diary whilst the process is ongoing, take notes of anything you notice each day. So that after the month or six weeks or three months that you work with the plant, you can look back and extract where and what the changes within you were.

Microdosing is a very interesting way to work. This process becomes hugely magnified if you know the plant, even just a little, in advance. That is, if you have sat with the plant, communicated with it, been offered its medicine and then harvested the plant and produced a sacred elixir. Because then, as you take the drops and invite the spirit into you, to become you, to show you, to teach you; you can't help but drop back into that moment of presence with the plant and all that it told you and showed you. But, you can try this method without that. If you have no direct access to the plant but feel it calling to you anyway, feel this method is the correct one for the start of your relationship, then follow your intuition and give it a go. Get hold of a bottle of remedy such as a tincture or an essence made from the plant. Sit with the bottle as you would the living plant. Honour it. Communicate with it. Thank it. Ask it. Taste it. When you have thoroughly introduced yourself and enlivened the remedy bottle, feel that the plant has been awoken and is responding to you, then you may begin.

This method is perfect for long-term fine tuning of your relationship with a plant. For understanding who the plant is and how it works, for receiving the personal medicine that it has offered you. If you are looking for a dramatic fast track into the wisdom of this plant you are unlikely to find it in this method, although that can happen. What it does give is a deep organic knowing, something that will help you make permanent changes in your life and that you will carry within you for all time.

General wisdom is that it takes somewhere between 21-90 days to break a habit and integrate new behaviour. Personally, if an old habit is deeply instilled it takes even longer. Maybe it is just that I am a little slow on the uptake, on letting go of the old and inviting the new in. But either way, I recommend that when you are working with a plant that you wish to go a little deeper with, working initially for a minimum of 3 weeks and onwards to a year or beyond is a good start. There really is no limit, only that which you choose; or when the plant itself chooses to retreat, decides that for now this is all it wants to give, to share.

Single Plant Immersion

Following on from plant diets is single plant immersion, I touched upon it when I spoke of extreme plant diets. A single plant immersion can be in the form of a diet then, but is not restricted to that.

A dedicated plant study can be regarded as a single plant immersion, even if in a city park for a single hour, as long as you are focussed. A single plant immersion is actually a form of wilderness immersion, again even if it is just in a city park, as long as you are focussed.

Spending a full day with a single plant allows for deeper immersion. Drinking tea and taking other remedies made from the plant whilst focussing with the blind tea method, then undertaking a dedicated plant study, a shamanic journey, followed by harvesting the plant and making an elixir with it, will really immerse you. As you can imagine, as the hours peel away you fall deeper and deeper into the dream of the plant. By the end of the day you have a deep feeling for, and understanding of, that plant.

One time some friends and I rented a field in a place called Coot-la, a few hours walk almost vertically upwards from the small village of Tosh, on a side branch off the Parvati Valley, in the Indian Himalayas. We rented the field (and its contents) for a full month. We were living in a tiny wood and stone built cabin. There was no electricity or running water, just our hammocks strung up to provide us with beds, a fire both to warm us and over which we cooked our simple diet of dal and chapattis. A fresh mountain stream gurgled past the cabin door. We were surrounded with snow capped peaks which towered above us every which way. The air was fresh and clean, the skies bright blue. The nearest road ended a full days walk away. During the whole month not one other human walked by our happy enclave. It was just us, the mountains and the plants. Each morning we would rise and freshen up in the ice cool mountain stream, we would imbibe some plant medicine and once nourished we would head to the field. Day after day after day, without variation, for a whole month we maintained exactly the same routine. Each day we stayed harvesting in the field until early afternoon when the sun dipped below the mountains in the west and left our valley to rapidly cool during the remaining hours of daylight.

This time became a single plant immersion. We each fell deeply into the dream and the medicine of this one plant that filled our days. Hands and fingers clothed and sticky with resin which was being absorbed through skin. We received the medicine with our lungs all day long as the sickly sweet smell of sun warmed buds pervaded the air. My eyes seeing rainbows sparkling through giant crystal adorned buds all day, they also populated my night time dreams. I fell into deep appreciation of the minutiae, intense noticing. It was full immersion.

With no electricity we had no music or other "modern" entertainment, we could not even read books at night as the room was dimly lit with only a candle or two. So, with no distractions we simply lived the rhythm of the mountain and drifted deeply within the dream of this plant for weeks. Falling in love in that thin mountain air, over and over again, day after day after day.

It is difficult to find, or make, opportunities such as this as we enter deeply into adulthood with all of the responsibilities financial and otherwise that often saddle this section of our lives. But deep single plant immersion like this is great medicine for the soul. And as with all my other steps along the road less travelled, the wild path, entwined my life ever more deeply with my green cousins.

It was moments in time such as that which I have just shared, that formed some of my formative training as a plant whisperer. The initial attentive noticing, heart opening, falling deeply in love. I have come to understand that without care and attentiveness, how can you listen? How can you whisper with meaning if you are not motivated by love? If it is not love that drives you then why would you devote yourself, why would you give full attention?

Nathaniel Hughes, in his book *Weeds In The Heart,* suggests wild camping in a Wild Garlic wood to learn of Wild Garlic. This practice can form a beautiful single plant immersion and is within a time frame that we can all manage. You could do this with any plant that grows prolifically in one area, a huge great patch that you can swing above in a hammock or bed down amongst. You will learn aspects about the plant that you would not know through daytime observation alone. You will know that plants territory and you will become infused with its presence.

Sleeping under the canopy of a tree is another wonderful form of immersion and can lead to a full initiation with that being; even if the sleep is a nap of a couple of hours during the daytime. I have had incredible results every time I have slept under a tree. In essence it is another way to do dreamwork with plants and download vast amounts of medicine and information whilst forming a deep and lasting connection.

Immersion, then, can come in many forms. One that I have yet to describe is when you are undertaking a single plant diet in the extreme form and then take a medicinal dose of plant elixir within a ceremonial setting. This is often the way entheogens are consumed (I will discuss entheogens in depth later). It can be undertaken though with any plant, by combining dedicated plant study and plant journey with the single plant fast. Even just one day of this with a ceremony in the evening is incredibly powerful and will take you and your relationship with the plant infinitely further than just undertaking one of the practices with that plant as a one off. To undertake this kind of ceremonial work for an extended length of time; a few days, a fortnight or a month has the potential to radically change your life.

Involving a ceremony during, or at the end of, an immersion helps you focus and gain more clarity. By ceremony, what I really mean is that alongside your clear and focussed intention, you create a sacred space and then consume the plant in elixir or other medicine form. How you create a sacred space will absolutely depend on any tradition you may already have. You may clear the energy of yourself and the space with smudge. You may invite the spirits of place, plant, ancestors, other living beings, Gaia, to join you and guide you. You may open the directions. You may say prayers. You may have something present to honour the elements; fire, water, earth, air. You may have built an altar specifically for the occasion. I won't tell you how or what to do, just be sure that everything you bring in to create your sacred space has meaning for you. Many people follow traditions from indigenous people of distant lands, calling in the spirits of animals perhaps that are unknown to you. This is OK if it feels right to you, maybe it is how you have always done it. If you are new to creating sacred space and ceremony why not ask Gaia to guide you? Ask the land you are standing on, ask the plant spirit.

Many contemporary cultures including my own, have lost the rituals practised by our ancestors, the traditions that were followed and passed down between generations for hundreds and thousands of years. This is tragic, but also in some senses a liberation, as we are not tied to long known wisdom and practices that have become static. Gaia will always be evolving, always, as the land changes, as the challenges facing the plants change and as the challenges facing humankind change. We have been challenged by the loss of ritual and tradition because we need to be during this dreadful time for the planet. We need to be strong, powerful, resourceful, with the ability to dig deeper, not just follow prescribed practices and traditions. Nothing has happened by accident.

Create your ceremony, take the plant medicine. Listen to everything it tells you and honour that by making the necessary changes in your life. The deeper your immersion, the stronger the relationship with that plant you will develop and the more clearly you will hear its voice and receive its medicine. You cannot go back to being who you were before, the plant lives within you so strongly now, your souls have become entwined.

Oscillation

I have not yet mentioned what to do with the whispers you have shared with a plant; how you interpret the feelings you receive and turn them into useable information. Of course in some instances the communications may be very clear, with no real interpretation necessary. The clearer you are, the better you know yourself, and the clearer your question, the more likely this is. However there will be times when either it is not so clear or that you want to search deeper, to see if there was anything more under your initial surface level understanding.

When in the field, working in person with a plant, if you find yourself a bit stuck, as if you are not getting anywhere, one technique I recommend for breaking through is to get up and have a stretch, walk away from the plant for a moment, and then return and focus once again. You may need to repeat this focus and relax cycle a few times but eventually you will have a breakthrough moment and be able to discern something coming to you from the plant. This in essence is the oscillation technique. A controlled movement in and out of focussed attention, with the intention of achieving a deeper understanding.

When working with meaning it is no different. You no longer need to be in the presence of a plant, but what you do need is a clear memory of the feeling that you received from the plant. How you felt when you were enveloped within its dream. Use that initial feeling and concentrate upon it. Feel it in your heart, this is not yet an exercise about thinking. Grow the feeling to the strongest you can muster then back off. Then repeat. And again. Repeat this cycle of feeling deeply and then letting it go, ten or twenty times and then totally let it go. Each cycle of feeling and backing off does not need to take ages, just as long as it takes to really feel it and release. This way a sequence of ten or twenty oscillations may only take as many minutes. You can do this as you are lying in bed before sleep, as you are jogging or walking in the park, as you wash your car even. You will need persistence to break through. That means repeating your sequence of ten or twenty oscillations, twice or three times each day for several days or weeks.

You will only be inspired to undertake this practice with something that is niggling. Something that is on the tip of your tongue and yet you can't quite grasp it. The meaning is there, it is close, and yet for the moment it eludes you. This is exactly what happens when you are speaking with a friend about an actor or a film, you both know the one but neither of you can remember the name, no matter how hard you try. It is not until later that evening, when you have forgotten all about it, maybe while you are driving home, that the name suddenly floods in.

What happens during the oscillation technique is that during the moments of focussing intensely on the feeling, your heart blasts your brain. As you blast again and again and again, maybe over the course of days or weeks or months, eventually you will get a burst of knowledge. The burst of feeling blasting the brain gets turned into useful information.

You can envision it as an ember that you carry in your heart. That ember is what the plant gave you of itself when you fell in love with it. An ember that is glowing away in the background. By focussing in on your encounter with the plant, by focussing on how it made you feel, it is as if you are blowing on that ember. Each time you focus it is as if you blow and the ember glows a little stronger, until eventually it bursts back into life taking the kindling with it. It is at that moment you suddenly flood with feeling; more intense, stronger and clearer, than when you were originally making the sacred connection with the plant. And it is from here, this point of intense feeling, that your brain is flooded and you can extract meaning. That you can find intricacies that you did not notice during the time you spent in person with the plant.

You can use this technique with anything that you wish to know more deeply. But it requires commitment and that is why you will find yourself reserving it only for those most special of plant relations, or for where you know there is a wisp of something on the outer edges of your grasp and you can't let it go, you need to unfold it.

Entheogens

A hallucinogen is something that takes you out of reality, even TV can be considered an hallucinogen. Entheogens, however, take you deeper in to reality.

John Perkins

Entheogens are known by some as the "master plants" or the "teacher plants". They are a group of plants that are profoundly psychoactive. Plants who on ingestion act on the central nervous system, where they alter brain function, resulting in temporary changes in mood, behaviour, perception and consciousness. Of course, as plant whisperer, it becomes clear that any plant can have such effects, however with entheogens, the effects are more marked and more intense. In addition I would argue that although the intensity is temporary, some of the effects experienced with entheogens, such as the changes in perception and consciousness, can be permanent.

Imbibing entheogenic plants can make you feel like you are spending the whole night (or many life times) making love to the universe over and over and over again. It can however also feel like you are being called into the headmasters office for a dressing down. It can even be a bit of both.

Entheogens enhance your ability to work with your heart. They help us remove our assumptions about the nature of reality and see what is really there, clearly for what it truly is. They help us recognise the livingness of the world. They help us see the true nature of our individual realities and so can help people to face and tackle their addictions. For many seeing their reality more clearly will generate a lifestyle change, making a move from living in the city to the countryside, for example. For some it manifests as an even more radical lifestyle change such as becoming an advocate for plants and the more-than-human. The plants have a conscious part in all of this. It is not really so much you using the plant for self-healing, as the plant using you for the wider aspects of self-healing. Healing our relationship with the more-than-human and thus making Gaia more whole and more well.

Entheogens can be a doorway to plant whispering, to the magical plant realms, to Gaian consciousness. In this polluted, disconnected, confused world they can form a fast track to Earth wisdom. Without them, for many people, it would take much longer and be much more challenging to reconnect. They provide a big boom, a full shake up, something that we desensitised modern humans can relate and respond to.

Entheogens can be the way back in to the remembering of other realms parallel to and as real as, consensus reality. Realms that in our mundane reality we stopped dreaming of when we stopped believing in fairy stories. In meeting with an entheogen, access is gained and once more we stroll shoulder to shoulder with fey and giants, with magical serpents, with rainbows and unicorns. Perhaps also we join with darkness, nightmares, facing difficult truths and our greatest fears. It is, it's safe to say, jumping in at the deep end. But it can be the beginning of the story. Whereupon realising, remembering, these sacred realms of kaleidoscopic patterns and felt tip colour saturation, lies the memory of connection to these realms and an existence within them at all times. And there begins the hunger to forge that perpetual access and connection.

Certain entheogens have allowed me to feel, see and experience the world from the perspective of another being; if only temporarily. This way you can go beyond considering the notion of to touch is to be touched, not just layer it in your imagination, but actually *know* it. Know that what you see is also seeing you. You can also access this perspective within a shamanic drum journey. It can also be achieved with direct perception, although this requires great patience and persistence, but eventually you can drop into the feeling of the being so deeply that you find yourself inside of it looking back out (at yourself). Work with entheogens is just another method, another access point into the plant realms; another option that you may or may not choose to take as your plant whispering matures and deepens.

> *I can hear you approaching, feel your vibration in my head. As it intensifies it becomes clear that nothing is solid and I slip into another realm. One of sensuous felt sensation, of direct perception and feeling. A place where I transcend the human condition. No longer thinking; just being and receiving.*

Research has found that with ingestion of psilocybin, found within certain mushrooms native to the UK, the way that information moves through the brain is changed. Cross brain activity is freed from its usual framework. Parts of the brain become flooded with signals that are normally filtered out. New links across previously disconnected brain regions are formed whilst previous connections become muted[35]. Thus psilocybin acts to increase connectivity in the brain. What is more interesting is that the effects are not just temporary but can cause lasting changes in perception and consequentially behaviour.

The results perhaps are that this rewiring of the brain gives us access to what is always there but we usually filter out to protect ourselves from information overload. It allows us, not to perceive what *isn't* there, but more or a different aspect of what *is*. It could be that the usual filtering process is formatted by what we as domesticated humans prioritise. So if we are prioritising self-advancement and accumulation of resources, over connection with the wider natural world, then that is what our brain becomes hard wired to do. If however, as the aforementioned research demonstrates, new brain pathways can be built which allow us to perceive other aspects of reality, could we not train our brains to stay that way and perceive the other aspects of reality more readily at all times? With repeated ingestion, entheogens can allow these pathways in the brain to become more familiar, and eventually can allow access to those realms at will. I don't have proof for this beyond my own personal experience, although perhaps research that proves as much is already out there. In essence what I am trying to say is that there are other realms existent and parallel to this one and that entheogens allow you access. And, with new brain pathways available, you can access them at will and enjoy a deeper knowledge of wider nature, energy and the universe.

Research has also found that the ingestion of Ayhuasca can stimulate the birth of new neurons (brain cells) in the hippocampus, the region of the brain associated with memory. In addition it accelerates the development of newly formed neurons into mature cells[36]. These changes in the brain can help you recover from trauma but also, with new pathways engaged, bring memories together with other parts of the brain that are concerned with insight and awareness, allowing one to feel through past experiences in a new way.

I fully believe that in our wild native state that consumption of entheogens would have been part of our natural lives. Living within deep wilderness immersion for our whole lives, eating the wild of the land, having a perpetual alkaline-state and knowing all beings as our relations: consumption of entheogens would have been part of our existence. We would have existed in an open and deeply connected state, in between realms that for us today, and the way we currently live, are distinct and separate places. Through simply consuming these plants there is the potential for lasting change within us, possibly taking us to a wilder version of ourselves, closer to our natural way of being.

Exotics

You may find yourself being called by the exotics. A particular plant keeps arriving on your path, in your dreams. Feel deeply into it, you know enough by now to call out to the plant spirit and ask, *are you calling me?* Be sure.

Exotic entheogens provide the entrance point to this world for the majority of people in Western nations. It is common to meet them within a ceremonial setting, resided over by people native to the lands of the plant. Peoples who have an unbroken lineage; generation upon generation of reciprocal relationship with the plant. This forms part of the attraction, the traditions and relationships, which provide a safe place for this work. Strict protocols and a deep respect for the plant are in place and agreements made between the humans and the plant, have been upheld for generations. There is a deep and respectful relationship. You will understand this if you have close relations with any plant. You may have had close relations with a plant for a short time, a month, a couple of years, and already there are invisible ties and promises between you. That is the way of things, the way of the plant whisperer.

Closer To Home

Exotics that are still part of an unbroken living tradition can show us how amazing things can be, that is undisputed. But then it becomes our responsibility to enliven our own land, rediscover our medicine plants, work with our own entheogenic teachers. That is the true worth of initially working with exotics; to help us fall back in love with our own land. Allowing the whole of Gaia to be sacred once more, not just one or two plants in one place that the whole planet is craving for.

Local plants will always be more appropriate and suit your constitution better, teach you the medicine of the land upon which you stand. Plants that experience the same weather and stand in the same soil as you. The same as with any other plant, relationship with an entheogen will be elevated into a much more bespoke and personal experience if you have communicated. If you have gathered. If you have prepared with intent. If you know and love that plant.

It saddens me that our local entheogenic plants, plants that people of these lands once held as sacred, plants who inspired the art and calligraphy of our ancestors are being totally overlooked; even to the extent of being looked down upon or outright dismissed. I am their cheer leader. I wish for people to know of and love the medicine of the land they stand upon, as well as the exotic cousin. But I guess we are all drawn by the rock star while that quirky band playing the local clubs gets overlooked for years. Even though in the background, it steadily and wonderfully continues on, mainly unacknowledged, doing its thing.

If you wish, or are called, to work with entheogens from lands where there is no unbroken tradition or lineage, you must initially make those relationships with the plant yourself; those agreements, imbued with respect and reciprocity. In these circumstances you must work closely with the plant allowing it to guide your ceremony. Be sure to take time to generate a clear intention. And as always when working with plant spirits you must proceed with an open heart, no expectations and an attitude of gratitude.

There are a few general safety guidelines you may wish to consider if you are called to work in this way. Create a safe and sacred space. Make sure you are warm and comfortable, fit, healthy and well. That you are aware of the recommended dose. That someone knows you are going to be undertaking the ceremony; you may wish for them to be with you in person, or just to check in on you the following day. I also recommend following a cleansing diet for a few days beforehand and fasting for at least several hours before your ceremony begins, preferably all day or longer. It is also useful to have some grounding food prepared, ready for when you need to eat after the ceremony.

Whichever kind of ceremony you find yourself involved in, once complete and you are ready, which is usually not until the following day, write down everything you can remember. Just like the notes you make from a dedicated plant study or a shamanic journey, these details can otherwise be lost. You can return to your notes again and again as you work through and unpick various layers of meaning as the memories fade.

Excepting Antarctica, there is not a land on Earth that does not have indigenous entheogens. Consider working with local plants and re-enlivening the magic and mystery of your homeland. Give yourself the opportunity to build these relationships over time where the plants grow and know that your ensuing relationships will be strong and deep and filled with meaning.

Doorways To The Inner Realms

Many of us need the initial sharp slap to the face, that entheogens provide, to awaken us. To allow us even the vaguest sense of awareness that the minutiae that we live alongside every single day can also be doorways to the inner realms of self, to the deeply psychedelic plant realms.

If entheogens have been your entry point into interspecies communication you will have had a massive download to begin with. Subsequently, tightening your art can initially be immensely challenging. However, entheogens are not the only plants that can help you find your way, secure your re-emergence as wild and connected. And, if you rely on them alone, you will potentially miss so very very much that is occurring.

Never overlook the messages in the subtle micro-perturbations, in the fragrance, in the tingle and multitudinous variety of feelings. Entheogens are not the whole picture, not by a long way. In believing that they are, you will be in danger of missing much of the art of plant whispering and the gifts that such communications can bring you. The groundedness, sense of being and place, belongingness, livingness, aliveness and wildness that a multifaceted being with a million eyeballs all looking in different directions, times and realms can impart. These are the properties a well-versed and skilled plant whisperer will eventually develop and use to direct and inform their wild life with. There is value in the subtle, the communications embedded within that can be just as powerful, self-assuring, useful and life changing as any psychedelic blast that has you on all fours vomiting and crying for 15 hours...

What is right for one is not right for another. And so whether you began this journey with entheogens or if you began it with teas, that is perfect, there is no right way or wrong way. Gaia knows best and would have found you the way you needed to be found in that moment, so that you would respond.

If your plant whispering journey began more subtly, with gently building awareness of the senses and the felt sense, entheogens can help fill in even more blanks. By introducing entheogens later on, you will most likely have an easier time assimilating the messages gifted by the entheogens. As you already know the language, the territory. You know how to communicate, how to ask, how to listen. You are not just open mouthed and astonished, you have legs and can work this new realm. You can bring back useable information much more easily than someone who is catapulted in and then has to work backwards to understand the full implications.

Entheogens can take you beyond the limits of what you thought possible, and give you the wisdom of the full Gaian hologram, sometimes in what can be more or less an instant. Working with entheogens may blow your mind and make you change the way you think, may blow open your perception. But it is you that must work out what it all means and use that information to change yourself and make those changes with compassion, with love.

From whichever angle you began this journey entheogens add another dimension just as subtle noticing does. Each has its part to play in reintegrating your wild Gaian soul and with your path as plant whisperer. Entheogens had an early and fundamental role in my path as plant whisperer, opening up my mind to another track through the woods; introducing me in a very unsubtle way to this art.

Meeting the sacred other in the form of an entheogen can really help humanity wake back up to our relations and our responsibilities. As this is happening, these plants are being banned by the powers that be, because they are too powerful. Imagine if we all woke up, we all spoke all the time with all our relations. There would be a huge revolution. We would turn our back on so many of the multinationals whose actions and chemicals wantonly destroy the Earth and they of course have a great hand in steering government policy and even what gets reported in the press and how. Plant medicines are powerful instigators of change, remember that next and every time, you hear about a plant being classified as a drug and scheduled. Conspiracy or not, it serves someone somewhere to keep the majority of humanity dulled and sleeping through life. It has to, otherwise plants and their medicine in all their great range of capacities and forms would never have been attacked and made illegal, and neither would those who work most closely with them (think witches...).

Cautions
What is unfortunately happening now, with the spread of exotics across the globe, is that these plants are often presented without the traditional ceremony and teaching. Medicine out of context leads to misuse and abuse, because we don't understand the respectful relationship and so it becomes something else. We just need to look at the history of Tobacco, one of the most sacred plants across the Americas, to know this is true. The relationship becomes unbalanced.

The Ayahuasca vine, more than any other exotic entheogen, has become somewhat of a global phenomenon. It has certainly woken many thousands of people up across the planet to the magical plant realms. However, there are other plants that can help you access those realms. In fact, those realms are here and accessible all the time and there are many plants that will step forward to assist you in accessing them; instead Ayahuasca itself has become the next big consumable thing.

There is not an endless supply of any plant. The voracious global appetite for the handful of exotic entheogens is clearly unsustainable and if it remains unchecked will eventually destroy the homelands, culture and traditions from whence they came. Maybe it is the conscious and selfless act of these few plants giving their lives, lands and culture to help wake the rest of the planet up. But it is a high price, one that I hope doesn't have to be paid. This in part returns us to personal responsibility, all two hundred percent of it. Responsibility for all that you consume and knowing when enough is enough.

Unfortunately a kind of cultishness has begun to surround some of the exotic entheogens, I believe this is a reflection of human frailty within the modern world. It's all caught up with the need to belong. There is also the sense of entitlement despite the environmental and cultural kickback. These factors indicate a soul entangled within a tame and domesticated life, isolated and dissociated from wild reality and connections. Like all plants, exotic entheogens are sentient and can show you visions, can bless you with medicine for your soul. However, people have to start waking up and looking beyond the exotic; even though those plants initially stepped forward to help us rub our sleepy eyes.

It is essential not to become single minded, to be blind to who else may be calling your soul home, to feel that there is only one medicine. To not care if it is destroying that plants homeland as long as you get your next hit. It may sound like I am describing an extreme here but I have actually come across *many* people who fit this description. People who wholeheartedly overlook and disregard that there is any other medicine in the world, and personally I find that quite frightening.

If you are busy consuming exotic food, medicines and entheogens yet feel like you don't connect with the myth, mystery and magic of the land where you live, why do you think that could be? Think about it...

Gifts & Challenges

If you respond to a genuine calling but then find yourself returning to the same entheogen again and again, week in week out, you may well be missing something. It could be that you're not listening attentively. Too much entheogen, even with intent, can become a distraction. If you find yourself in this situation undertake some rigorous self-examination, check your motivation. It could of course be that this plant has stepped up to be your ally and requires continuous ongoing work. But because the experience is so rich and strong it could also be impatience, ego, joy rider mentality or greed. If you are unsure, go back to what the medicine has been telling you, go back to the notes you made, if you did not make any it is time to start doing so. Ask yourself what is it that you are not getting from the ceremony, what feels so incomplete that you have to keep returning for the next layer? It could be that in ceremony you receive so much that you mistake that for the fix, rather than seeing so much and going home to do the fixing. It will often take you quite some time to both digest and assimilate messages from the entheogens into your life as action.

Entheogens can open a door for you. Your contract is then to enter this place in your waking realms, to go through the treasures that were revealed to you, and place them in your day to day life. This can be the greatest challenge, to bring back the ecstasy. To keep the feeling and draw it into this dimension. To achieve this you will need to traverse the initial fantasy landscape revealed by the entheogens and see what lies beyond. This may be challenging to achieve at first but eventually you will need to if you wish to take your work with entheogens to a deeper level.

It is not the vision itself that is most important but what you do with it. How you bring that into your day to day life and use it to make the changes that you need to make. Entheogens can show you unknowable realms of richness and beauty very quickly, but it will still be up to you to translate that into useable information. It will be you that must do the work when the medicine wears off. If they show you the horror of your addictions, or the challenges of your relationships; it is *you* that must go cold turkey or apologise to your mum... What they can do is show you, in no uncertain terms, the corrections you need to make; much more clearly than in the silty tides of your waking mind.

It may take a long time for you to interpret what you receive. Sometimes work with entheogens can generate confusion because they may reveal more than you are willing to see or acknowledge. There must be no expectations when embarking on such a mission in the far realms (whether it is through entheogen use or other deep plant whispering methods). But I believe the plants will show you or tell you exactly what you most need to see or know at the time. It is not all rainbows and unicorns walking hand in hand through sweeping mountain meadows rich with wild flowers; far from it. What you see is what you need to address first; the question that you have been asking all along. And, once again, if you are not clear within yourself, do not know that you are asking that question, you may not understand the significance of the response.

It is true to say, and I am not shy to say it, that this section of the journey into the realms of plant whispering is not for all. This is where the path twists and turns a bit quicker, in and out of revelation and self reflection, ecstatic joy and the terrifying dark. But it can be an incredible part of the journey and, even if ventured into but the once, can be truly life changing on a multitude of levels.

In the end, despite the cautionary notes pertaining to exotic entheogen use, they have indeed begun a movement with great effect. Turning people on to the incredible invisible realms; realms of meaning, communication, medicine, light and life. As a plant whisperer you now know how much deeper and further that can go, with every plant, every more-than-human life, in every moment.

Through developing your skills as a plant whisperer you will eventually gain the skills to access those realms at will. Those realms presented by the entheogens, even when no entheogen is present. As you develop the multitude of ways of listening and interacting using the language of plants, you will become skilled and articulate. Then, if and when, you do work with an entheogen you can connect deeply and bring back all the lessons and wisdom with clarity and in an actionable form.

Another Way Of Working With Entheogens

Never forget that you already know the way in to direct communication with any plant spirit. Entheogenic plants are no different. If you have access to the living plant you can approach communicating with an entheogen in exactly the same way that you would approach any plant. You can conduct a dedicated plant study, or dream with the plant. You can hold a piece of the plant in your medicine pouch to keep it close. You can make an elixir, perhaps a salve to spread over your temples or chakras, maybe an essence or tincture that you could microdose with. You can journey to the spirit. There are so many ways to access the wisdom and medicine of an entheogen, it does not have to be by ingesting a full ceremonial dose. I love working with entheogens using these more subtle approaches and have introduced this way of working to many of my students over the years. The medicine arrives in a much more gentle way, but that is not to say that it is not as profound. In addition working in this way in advance of a ceremony, will help you get a feeling for the unique signature and character of the plant you are working with. It will help you gain familiarity. It will help you begin the long and fruitful journey of falling in love.

Tying It Together – The Next Level

> *...mind, or intelligence, is located throughout your body.*
> **Sharon Blackie.**

I want to bring you all the way back round to the most simple kind of approach. As once you have experimented with different tools and techniques, you will find access to a very deep level with the most simple of activities. In this instance I am suggesting that when you are called to a certain plant that you take a living leaf, *one that is still attached to the living plant*, into your mouth. No crunching or chewing, just hold the leaf on your lips, your tongue, in your mouth. Close you eyes and allow yourself to drop into the dream of the plant. Trust, see how far you will be taken. Listen to what the plant has to say to you. Ask the plant to tell you about itself, how it can help you, what you need to do. This is quite advanced work despite being so simple. You do need to have developed some experience and confidence for this to flow.

> *I was invited into a dome made from the leaves of the plant. It was bright inside. The plant wrapped me from*

head to toe in its leaves. After some time, the leaves were removed. I emerged much brighter and more energetic than I had been before. Then, hand in hand with the green skinned plant spirit, we walked through flowering meadows. Ahead we saw a mountain made of crystals and rainbows. We rushed towards it and merged with them. In an instant I felt that I had direct access to all of the wisdom in the universe. The plant told me, and more than that took me on this journey to illustrate, that it could provide direct connection with source.

No ingestion, no journey, no dedicated plant study. And yet all of this gifted in an instant of connection with a living leaf attached to a living plant.

With your new sensitivity to your body and its wisdom you can ask a body part directly how it is, what it needs. Choose a part that is perhaps in trouble, a joint that aches from an old injury, your stomach that struggles with digestion; and work with it, dialogue with it. Feel into it. Communicate the same way that you would with a plant. Give time to this. Listen. You can even journey to that body part to learn more. Then ask that part, be it perhaps liver or shoulder, to lead you to a plant that can help. It is essential that your head is fully out of the way here. Let your body part guide you to a plant. Let it take you to the plant it needs. Then, sit with that plant and place a leaf *that is still attached to the plant* into your mouth.

The first time I presented this exercise to a class of my apprentices I was blown away with the results. It was their graduation week and graduate they did! Each apprentice, despite different levels of capacity, articulation and ability in the art; got it. They all got taken to a relevant plant and were gifted its medicine. This is revolutionary. As behind every ache and pain; every ignored strain and unrealised ailment is a different story unique to you and what has happened in your life. How you have lived your life. Your body has the wisdom to guide you to a plant that can help. You have the skill to understand which plant is calling and how to ask what you need to do next.

If you can develop this level of elegance in your communication, you can explore your body organ by organ, section by section, and find plants that will step forward to make you more whole. Never stop learning about yourself, you are the one you spend all day every day with, from conception to death. Don't overlook your own body in this process, your own sweet piece of Earth.

Once you have generated a deep connection with a specific plant you don't necessarily need to return in body to the plant if you wish to take your enquiry further. You can simply revisit the feeling that you had when originally dedicating time to the plant and use it to call the plant back so that you can work on further questions. This is also true when working with entheogens. Once those new brain pathways are deeply forged, once you know that plant as an ally, you just need to think of taking the medicine and the questions or intention you have, and the connection is suddenly there. Your answers arriving quickly and clearly with no need to imbibe because you have a direct line to that plant spirit, this is quantum entanglement.

It all comes down to noticing the unique presence of that plant, its signature on all levels of your being. Then it becomes that you can feel when it is close, as if you can smell it. The more elaborate and refined your art becomes the more you will notice when a plant is calling to you. They may call to you when you are sick and offer help, even though you may never have met. They may communicate that they need water, shade, food, or something else. They may lead you to the deep mysteries of the universe. Maybe all and maybe none of the above.

If you are working with one plant spirit, it may introduce you to another. This may happen if the plant has done all it can to help, but you still need more, something else. It may know another plant that is better equipped to assist; a bit like a human therapist referring you to a different specialist for another element of your healing. Be open to this happening.

Plants tell you the truth; although some are not as straightforward as others. Some, like Popongi whom I met in Kenya, could even be described as being a little bit tricksy. The better you know yourself the better able you are to navigate the less straightforward characters and the more able you are in discerning their communication. Plant spirits are shape shifters and may change form regularly and with ease. Pay attention at all times.

Make It Your Own

The quantity of time you dedicate to plant whispering, will inevitably change as *you* do, as your priorities and the way you choose to spend your time gets a shuffle towards the wild and the vegetal. The more willing you are to dedicate yourself to plant whispering the more you will get back and the deeper you will go...

When it comes to any tool you may use to facilitate plant whispering, for it to be effective in reactivating your wildness, you must *make it your own*. Following a set of preordained practices or a rigid framework will rarely gain you access to the true moment and the true feeling of the thing; as instead of sinking viscerally into the present, you will intellectually be ticking boxes and thereby remain separate as a remote observer. In effect you will be going through the motions of what worked for someone else. That is not to say that following another's suggestions is ineffectual (if I thought that I would not have written this book!), but that you need to go beyond simply learning and practising the tools as they have been recommended. To make them effective for you, you must breathe life into them, you must practise them until they become your own. Until there are so many idiosyncrasies you have either personally developed or dropped from the original form you were taught (or read about) that you end up with only vague similarities to the original, nothing more. What I mean to say is that the form must be true to you, not just blindly followed. Everything is always changing including yourself, so how you interact cannot remain a static practice prescribed by someone else from some place else. Your methods will become as unique as you are with time, as they become your own, and as you are guided further and deeper by the plants that choose to work with you.

The more you do in preparation, the less grandiose plant whispering becomes. However, despite all the self work that I have recommend in this book, don't be too serious when you approach a plant. After all, no one wants to hang out with a really heady, serious, person (including most plants). Being respectful, though, is an absolute. Gratitude is essential in any interaction with our vegetal cousins, most especially if you are asking something of them, their food, their oxygen, their wisdom, their medicine. Try expressing gratitude *every* time someone gifts you a teaching; whether it is very subtle, a difficult thing to learn, or anything in between. Thank the paper you write upon, that this book is printed on, and acknowledge the sacrifice the trees have made to get these words to you and your own words to another. With acknowledgement comes understanding of what "things" actually are and changes the way we appreciate and use them.

Essentially there are a million things you can do to facilitate your open two-way communication with plants. I haven't tried them all because very early on I discovered what worked well for me. The most important thing of all is not the *how* but the fact you *are* doing. By focussing on the plant and trying wholeheartedly you will be half way there, as it is you, your intention and perseverance, your "desire to know" that is *most* important; the rest should fall into place as a response. If you have persistence, then, no matter what your technique for approach, eventually the plant you study will initiate you. Will take you deeply into its world and you will become just a little bit more that plant.

Eventually, the moment will come when you no longer have to think about what you're doing, instead you are consciously communicating all the time. Your communications will be both spontaneous and elegant. You *are* plant whisperer. Once you reach that point the impact on all areas of your life will be incredibly profound. You find you are no longer a stranger looking in, but a full and essential part of the picture. Like Alice in Wonderland, as if you have drunk a psychoactive potion and the world around you is suddenly larger than life; thinking, speaking, breathing. Once you begin to see livingness in all things, at all times, there is no going back; a wild wonderland it is. And in wonderland, knowing comes as a gestalt, sudden and complete. This is true biognosis, true wisdom directly from Gaia, and true rewilding.

It is in the spaces in between, when your mind lets go and your spirit connects with all that is, and you feel it with all of you; that you finally know yourself as Earth, that you belong to it, and that all other lives are a further part of yourself. The same starry beginnings and the same Earth blood. That really is what this is all about. That and then bringing it back, embodying it.

You will be most unlikely to ever reach the full depth and complexity of any single plant. It is a life's work, I am sure. I hate to throw in such a cliché, but personally, the more years I am present with a plant, working with it alone and with clients and in group settings, the more I realise there is to know. The more insights open up, reflected by the different angles of approach that each of my students bring to class. The beauty and intricacy and absolute cleverness of the way in which the plant responds and evokes responses in the students, continues to astound, amaze and fill me with awe. To the extent that I fall another notch deeper in love with that particular green guide. I am not sure I ever even want to know everything there is to know, as it keeps the relationship magical and evolving. And actually, as with every day, every rotation of the Earth, I change, you change, the plant changes, Gaia changes. So the quest to know everything there is to know about a certain plant would be to start afresh again every morning, or indeed be to set oneself the most deliciously perfect impossible perpetual task. Beware of anyone who tells you they know everything there is to know about any living being, it simply cannot be so.

The best advice I have is to let your heart guide you in all communication with plant relations. Any or all of the techniques and tools I have outlined could become a distraction or a sideshow. The only thing that is real is what you feel, how you feel when you are with that plant, how it touches you and what that means to you. Anything that gets in the way of your awareness of feeling is superfluous. Many of the practices I have spoken of really help me, hence me talking of them in the first place, but don't force it, the most important thing here is you, the plant, and how it makes you feel.

The Possibility Of Overwhelm

Opening up to the consciousness of plants, to the consciousness of the more-than-human realms, is opening up to untold possibilities and a whole new landscape. It can be overwhelming, especially at first. You may encounter deep grief that you have lived life not ever knowing. Or knowing at the edges of your consciousness but not acknowledging, or not knowing how to acknowledge. This is quite normal. You may feel like you have been wasting time, wasting your precious life, up until this point. Acknowledge that grief, feel it and let it flow, but then allow it to transmute into the joy of the fact that you have finally found this new world. That you never need to walk an anthropocentric path again or waste another minute. That you now have friends and allies all around you and that you are communicating. Celebrate it. Celebrate this awakening and enlivening.

You may also feel overwhelm at the number of voices you are suddenly aware of. At exactly how alive everything truly is. It can feel like you are surrounded by a crowd, a rabble even. They may all seem to be vying for your attention, all with something to say and to share with you. The thing is if you wish to quiet those voices a little so that you can draw your attention down to a single plant, you already have the skills to do this, as you have been doing it all of your adult life thus far. When we get on a bus or a train or walk through a busy city street we all draw ourselves in, otherwise we would go crazy, we would pick up too much. We would know who is angry or sad and we would find all the different feelings and emotions being experienced by everyone around us overwhelming, so you automatically close down your sensory gating channels, even just a little bit. You can do the same with the more-than-human. You can feel them all, notice and acknowledge whomever is there, but then bring your focus on to that one you wish to dialogue with. Explain what you are doing if you wish but just draw your attention back inwards and send it solely in the focussed direction of that one being. Just as you can do at a noisy party when you wish to have a conversation with one single person, you basically shut the rest out and focus in. It is the same skills that you will need to employ when the voices of the more-than-human are too many or too loud. It is not being rude, it is just paying attention to the one who drew your attention more than any other.

Living in this animated and vocal world all of a sudden is exciting but not all the voices will be happy ones. When you can hear the screams of trees being felled, or of a hedgerow recently flailed, it is hard, it is really hard. In such circumstances I always find myself apologising, saying sorry, sending love. Much the same as if a human I know had received injuries due to the unconscious actions of another. Keep the communication open, talk to the damaged plants and yes, say that you are sorry. Again if it gets too much after you have said what you need to say and extended your love to them, you can of course close yourself back down a little, draw yourself back in as if you are walking that city street. Closing back up all the way is impossible. It is also cheating yourself out of touching the deep meanings in the world and your capacity for wildness. It takes courage to keep feeling and refuse to close the heart, but a full and wild life depends on it, depends on our capacity for feeling.

The thing is to experiment and keep yourself open as much as possible. We need to hear the other voices, both the excited and the distraught, so that we can feel it too. So that we can remain part of the animate living world, that place we have been missing from for so long, and have worked hard to return to. It is when we perpetually dwell in this place and really know what is going on around us, all of our behaviours become more considered. And that is when we begin speaking and acting for the whole, rather than just for ourselves.

Our Natural Way Of Being

You may have noticed that many of the practices I have outlined are actually our natural way of being. Living in a perpetually alkaline state, deep wilderness immersion and plant diets (including entheogens); would have formed our daily existence had our ancestors never left the forest. Our natural way of being, is a state characterised by high levels of intuition, of seeing energy and sensing, of knowing.

When immersed in the wild, even after a few hours walking the local woods and hills, you may notice yourself becoming slower, calmer, more attuned, more aware of unseen presences. This is considered an "altered" state. Such non-ordinary states are facilitated by our natural way of being. Not just spending time outdoors simply walking or undertaking wilderness immersion but by eating a more natural high chlorophyll diet, fasting and ingesting entheogens. In these extraordinary states of consciousness, communication with more-than-human relations flows unabated. You could say that the practices in this book are centred upon entering "altered" states. However, this implies that our natural way of being is considered an altered state in comparison to how we currently exist.

This begs the question, is what we consider a "normal" state of consciousness actually normal? What is normal? It may be that it is *usual* for us, but for our forest dwelling ancestors I boldly make the claim that our current *ordinary* or *normal* state of consciousness would not be considered normal at all. I believe it is sick, diseased, disconnected; we need to stop looking from this place as our start point. We have lost our baseline.

As we delve deeper and deeper into such altered states, we are simply delving deeper and deeper into our natural state. This is why I believe that personal rewilding practices, are very effective treatments for depression, for anxiety, for addictions and even for many inflammatory diseases and conditions. So often the distractions people choose to cope with their lives (anti-depressant medications, TV, drug and alcohol addictions, etc. etc.) are adopted in an attempt to escape current reality. Perhaps this is because *our current reality is the altered state!*

Through the adoption of our natural way of being, we find the most effective, cheapest, healthiest and long lasting remedy for our collective ennui, for getting out of it (which was what my peers and I used to call it!), for escaping our current reality. The symptoms of living in line with our natural way of being, in this so called non-ordinary state of consciousness, are happiness, calm, sense of belonging, sense of being part of something larger than oneself, beingness, compassion. We suddenly find ourselves living within a universe of richness and fullness. A beauty and depth beyond words. Where, in each awe and wonder filled day, more is revealed, seemingly without end...

When your existence comes closer in line with the natural way of being, it will not just facilitate plant whispering; but will awaken and feed the wild within. Plant communication, in fact all more-than-human communication, is a natural given once existing perpetually within this extraordinary state.

There are so many ways to invite the plant spirits in; it really doesn't matter how you do it, as long as you do it. And that you do it with integrity and love. Whomever it is that you communicate with will become part of your personal medicine journey. Every element of wider nature is a further part of yourself and in opening up to them you are drawing all those far and lost parts of yourself back together again. You as a consequence become more whole. Within this wholeness, you will be guided by the plants to become the best version of yourself. The wilder, wiser version. More able to be a positive force for change as you slip in to your natural way of being and knowing. This is what you gain and this is what the world gains. This *is* the wild path and is what we need collectively if we are to have any hope of rewilding our home and our lives. Any chance of continuing as a species on this dangerously damaged planet, or more accurately as part of this dangerously damaged organism.

V
Fruit

In an explosion of sweetness the fruit is ripe, ready for the world, ready to be eaten, to be shared. Within each fruit lies the next seed. And within each seed lies everything the next plant, and all it's descendants, will ever be.

7. Interpretation

It is intentional that I have barely mentioned interpretation, as yet. Trying to understand or tease a meaningful message from your communications with the more-than-human gives a green light for the brain to get involved. If you allow this too soon, the brain rushes to interpret, which can sully and distract you from, the true felt experience. The longer that you can hold on to the feeling, the more vividly it can be recalled (or perhaps more accurately re-felt) and the more deeply it will have embedded itself into your being. Sometimes there are no words, just feelings. And in attempting to interpret we can miss the message, the communication. Don't try too hard. Think back to the oscillation technique and use it. Recall the feeling and feel it deeply. That is the communication more than anything else. And it may not be something that you can later quantify or categorise, and that is OK. You will learn to be OK with that, the more you do this, and the more you allow for it to be feeling led.

Another reason that I have held back on discussing interpretation until now is that it is not always straightforward. Expectations (as I have mentioned before) can really block you from believing you are receiving any message at all. Sometimes it takes time to realise exactly what went on, before you can then be able to glean the wider meaning.

There have been multiple occasions when I have been leading a class and a participant has an extremely strong reaction. Most often it will be frustration, or even anger, as they believe that they can't do it. I have had people crying, or shaking, wild eyes rolling, as they insist that nothing happened, that nothing has changed at all. Others who are deeply saddened and disappointed because *all* that happened was that they fell asleep.

Incidences such as the above are exactly why I recommend writing everything down, even if it seems like nothing happened. When there is a huge response in a person, it can be that they are so deeply *in* the feeling that they cannot extract themselves from it and thus be able to realise the change in themselves. By writing through streams of tears, writing of anger, frustration or disappointment, you give yourself material to review, to return to later when the feelings have subsided. It is on review, that it is often more possible to realise exactly what occurred. When a reaction is really strong it may even be several years before the truth is found in the medicine. Interpretation comes at the time you are ready to digest it, to understand what it means, and be able to use it.

The main barrier to communication will *always* be yourself, pretty much without exception. This is why I recommend again and again rigorous self-examination. You, your level of confidence, your ego, your preconceptions, too much thinking, these are the blocks. So if you are sat there and "nothing" is coming through just let go of any attachment to an outcome, lay back and relax. Have a doze. But always remember to pay attention to how you feel. After a while say thanks to the plant anyway, get up and walk away. Notice any difference in how you feel now, to how you did when you first sat there. Don't let your mind write this off as "oh well I relaxed so of course I feel different". Become skilled at noticing the tiny nuances in how you feel and you *will* eventually begin to recognise when something from outside of you has touched you and, even just ever so slightly, changed the way you feel. It requires belief, as unless you are chugging back cup after cup of bitter entheogens, it may well be subtle, certainly at first. That is until you become more acute, your sensitivity becomes fine tuned, becomes elegant, and you begin to truly be able to feel throughout your body and heart the subtle smoky whispers of Pine and damp cushioned tickles of Sphagnum...

One time I was tending the garden of a wonderful woman, Mrs Clarke, she was 92 years old. As I weeded between her Wallflowers I cried out from my heart with my deepest wish, I wanted to be able to hear the plants, to have a two-way conversation. And that is when it began to happen. A plant name I had never heard of before arrived in my mind, repeating itself over and over and over. Was it the named plant calling me by repeating its name over and over? Or was it the Wallflowers telling me the name of a plant that could help? I don't know and does it matter? I got the message and then I worked with that. This is a perfect example of why it is important not to get bogged down with logic, let it flow. Let the plants tell you, let them lead you. Ask questions, but don't let intellectual reasoning hold you back.

When you pay attention you will notice things; that certain plants come and go in your locale for example. Many years ago I noticed a delicate and beautiful plant pop up and create a huge patch in my garden. Within months I was to discover that this plant was instrumental to the healing protocol I was training within. If you don't have a garden, pay attention to what comes and goes in the parks and along the footpaths near your home.

One time I was walking in North London with Stephen Buhner. On noticing a plant lining the pavement edge, growing against all adversity in the tiniest, driest and most polluted of places, he commented that through the abundant presence of this plant he knew what ailed the people of this area, what they needed. At the time I wished I had had my notebook with me to scribble down the name of the plant and the ailment he spoke of, the medicine the people needed. But the actual example itself was irrelevant. The fact that you can glean information by noticing which plants are present was the message I needed to take from that conversation, not what the specific remedy was. You can see here where my head could have got in the way with this interpretation. I could have got carried away with the detail of the specific and actually entirely missed the most pertinent message.

The plants speak loud and clear if you know how to listen. Recently I was in an area that had been beset with horrific wild fires. The scorched and blackened earth had just one plant left standing. As I moved through the land I saw that one plant again and again, not burnt up and crispy like all the others, but standing strong and true. I mentally noted it down, but in such a rush to pass through as the land was still smouldering, thought nothing more. A few days later, I found myself in an area ahead of the fires but under a shroud of the thickest smoke I have ever moved through, it was heavy on my lungs and cut visibility to a few meters at best. I walked down to the river to cool my feet and refresh my dry skin. On the grass was a twig covered with an old ally of mine, a plant well know as a lung remedy. Its presence reminded me of the other plant left standing in the fire zone, also a well known lung remedy. I did not need further nudging. When your eyes are open the messages you need, the medicine you need, will come to you in many ways.

Interpretation comes down to personal experience and just as everyone has little quirks, phrases and turns of speech that are unique to the way they converse, this form of communication is no different. And thus what you learn from your communications will be unique, in part because of the angle you are coming from, your interests and your character. If you went to a dinner party and Einstein was invited (and still alive!) it may be that you discuss the theory of relativity with him, while someone else will learn that he has a soft spot for the woman in blue, prefers beer to wine, and had a sore shoulder that evening...

One thing that it is really important to keep in mind is that we don't actually know. I constantly ask myself what do I know? I wonder, maybe it is 10% or 5% or 1% of what there is to know, if that, about that plant – or anything in fact. There are no definitives. The only way to know is to ask, to approach with love, and to be persistent. To gain acuity of perception you must sense the other, you must notice how they touch you. Your interpretation of that interaction will never be entirely clear if you do not know yourself. As you will not know why, when the other touched you, it generated that response. You cannot escape from working on yourself if you wish to develop sophisticated levels of interpretation.

In the end, no one can interpret your personal interactions with plants but you. There is no shortcut. Some messages will be clear and obvious, some will take time for their meaning to become apparent. However, the better you know yourself and the more often you communicate with the more-than-human, the easier it will become to recognise how things are presented to you and what they mean.

Benefits Of Group Work

I recommend working with plants in a group setting from time to time, especially at the beginning when you are first developing your art and finding your unique way with plants. If you have the opportunity, gather a group of friends, once a week or once a month, and work together with a single plant. I once ran a weekly group where we got together and the person called most strongly by a plant that evening would then take us to that plant. We would then each find an individual of the species and all ask the same question of that plant, each of us sitting with the plant for an hour, doing our individual work. We then came back together as a group, I would drum us on a shamanic journey to the lower world to meet with the spirit of that plant, after which we would share our learnings.

There is power in sharing your story, your interaction, your message. Your story may help unlock coded parts of someone else's. There are always threads that run through, even though the delivery will vary, sometimes greatly. When someone else clearly sees and grasps one of those threads, it may help you remember that you also glimpsed it.

Working in a group, with two or more people calling out to the archetype of a certain plant for wisdom and understanding, for knowledge of its nature; the response is somehow amplified, stronger. Certainly until you are skilled and confident, it is great to share in a group as it will help you gain confidence when you spot the similar in your stories.

Some plants literally seem to wake up or become more alive in response to the attention of a group. The plant may become more luscious before your eyes, visibly responding to the attention, to the love, to the energy give-away. Pay attention and you will notice.

Having said all this there is no great need to continually work within a group setting. It is personal practice in direct relationship with the plants themselves that will help you refine your art. The main reason to keep going back to a group is for the amplifier effect of group work and the camaraderie, excitement and community building that doing this work with others has.

Layers Of Meaning

A plant is *always* more than just a plant. There are many invisible relationships that allow that plant to be, and more than that, to thrive. Plants, the same as all living beings, have very complex relationships, not just with other plants but also with mycelium, with landscape and weather. They are not isolated units but live within a community, communicating with and supporting others within that community.

A plant can even be considered as a habitat and all the relationships that exist within that habitat. You can never know a plant if you treat it as an isolated unit as it cannot exist in isolation. Think of all of the invisible relationships happening within the dynamic living medium that we call soil. Think of the relationships with warmth and sunlight, shade and nutrients, moisture.

There are lessons in there for us. As we learn of others they teach us of ourselves; that we cannot survive as isolated units either. We could not survive in a dark room with no oxygen, food, water or warmth. We too are a habitat (just ask your resident bacteria) and we survive as a result of our habitat, locale and the relationships that exist within both. On the surface it may seem that our primary relationships are with our car and the supermarket. But they all, at some level, go back to plants and sunlight, be it the ancient ones (oil) or recently living ones (food). Never just look at the surface and think you know everything. There are layers upon layers in every area of life.

It follows that whatever is communicated by the plant will almost always be on many levels and tends not to be as straightforward as it initially seems. This is why it is essential to feel rather than think, to perceive directly rather than taking things literally, and to feel into the responses you get. A request from a plant for water could be a message about how you are and what you need, perhaps care, attention, nourishment, conditions conducive for a healthy life. And it may not be referring to your physical conditions either, this could be on any level.

For this reason, one should be careful of making any sweeping generalisations on the strength of what you learned from a plant. Once again think about language. Look into the words you write down about a plant. Tingly, fizzy, powerful, ancient, fluid, feminine. What do those words *mean*? What do they mean to you, and in this instance specifically? You can peel layer after layer from a few simple words that were written to capture observations. Different people will have different observations for many reasons. Use of language, descriptive ability, vocabulary, life experience, all lead to different scribblings. This is why it is best at all times to keep returning to *how does it feel?* What feeling were you trying to capture when you wrote that word and what does *that* mean? Because feelings don't lie and they are at the base of communications with plants (with all beings). Always, always, feel back into the being. It is not what you wrote that matters, but instead the feelings reviewing your writing evokes within you; and how that returns you to your original communication with the plant.

It is essential to keep going back to how does/did it feel, whilst attempting to interpret. It is the only true thing. Was it coming from you, a projection; or from the plant? Where does the plant end and the soil begin; where do you end and the plant begin? Does it even matter? It's a continuum and you and the plant are meeting and the exchange that is occurring is the meeting point. *The boundaries that separate us become ever more blurry.* Know yourself well and you will learn more about the essential essence of the plant, and yet you *are* a part of it, just as now it is a part of you...

Never underestimate how much you can glean, how far you can travel, with the most subtle, most miniscule, most short lived encounter; when you are open and aware. When you pay attention, and are becoming good at noticing, you can dissect that moment, that sensation, into a multitude of layers. Never rush over a single moment as you never know how much you will miss.

What each person indisputably has is their personal experience and relationships. No-one can belittle that, or take them away from you. If anyone ever tells you that what you got in your communications is wrong, rest assured that they have yet to develop their relationships to the level that they understand each persons relationship will be unique, and that there is no right and no wrong. Anyone who thinks they unequivocally know, is just showing their ignorance. Any one of us may indeed know a huge amount, you may have been married 50 years, and yet there are still more layers of your partner to know. More treasures to learn and to be uncovered.

When interpreting, bring all the aspects that you have discovered together as a whole, everything. Commit to journeying to ever deeper levels of meaning, and your understanding will continue to evolve and deepen. You will discover that you will never quite know everything and that nothing is as you have taken it to be...

Humility
Always remember to approach your art with humility. Communicating with the more-than-human world, by talking to the plants and being able

to hear their response, does not make you special. You are special if you *listen* to what they say and *act* on it. This was the norm for the ancestors and I believe there is a time coming when it will be the norm again.

I have met people within my culture who have been plant whispering all their life; who never stopped their inter-species communications as life beyond early childhood kicked in. And it is because these people exist that we are reminded both that it is nothing special but also that there is no need for grandiosity because anyone can do it, we are all born with the ability to do it. We can *all* re-inhabit our interbeing with the world.

All of this interspecies communication work must be undertaken with respect. This is not about playing games. The energy between you must flow and the wisdom will come. If you approach the art with a good heart, you will find a good heart waiting to greet you in the other dimensions.

Specialism

> *Tell me, what is it you plan to do with your one wild and precious life?*
>
> **Mary Oliver**

People will pop up with specialisms as plant whispering becomes more widespread, as once was, in our wilder, more deeply connected Earth based communities. Many years ago I met a medicine woman who, in essence, is what we would perhaps call a doula or a herbal midwife. She lives in a remote rural community and cannot read, so her access to "information" is strictly limited. She came into her specialisation during her own first pregnancy when certain plants called her in. The plants told her who to harvest and how to prepare them. She used all these plants, during her pregnancy and childbirth, at the times directed by the plants themselves. Something happened, the community saw her connection, her smooth and healthy pregnancy, and her reputation was born.

When you listen, really listen, when you are open and ready, the plants will guide you into the role you came here to fill. The question beyond all of your wounding, deep in your soul, that you first went to the plants with. Very often it won't quite fit with your plans. With your image of where your work with the plants would take you. You can of course override it, choose to ignore that inner calling and direction and stick with what you did your training in; what you had planned for yourself. But sticking will draw you away from the whispers, just a little; if you ask for wisdom then choose to ignore it what do you expect?

I have fallen to my knees in front of the smallest morsel of forest moss. I have returned in my heart over a thousand times to that initial moment where we shared a consciousness, a soul exchange. I returned to truly understand the teaching and the medicine that was offered. It was not entirely straightforward because the plant folk speak a different language at a different pace. They speak directly to the heart and as a typical human in the twenty first century there are defences around my heart. So to truly interpret the teachings from the other realms I had to first dismantle the fortress that I unwittingly erected as it obscured the innocent, honest, incoming messages from the plants and other life.

We wake each morning and protect ourselves from the devastation humankind has wrought. We do this so that we can continue to eat breakfast while images of Orangutans hitting mechanical diggers that are destroying their forest play on our screens. So that we can hear about a beautiful Whale that died because his whole digestive system was tied up in knots around the 40 plastic bags that were twisted within, and get on with our day. The pain, the hopelessness, otherwise would be so much that we would never be able to lift our heads again. But we need to *feel that pain* with every cell in our bodies to really make the change that we need in the world.

On this path you never stop learning about yourself. Sometimes you will find through your repeated rigorous self-examination, or maybe because a plant has told you, that you have barriers. They can sneak in and appear in places and in ways that you may not associate with defences, be vigilant. You *have* to let the barriers go, to continue to move, grow and evolve. To make space for the new that practising this art is bringing in to your life. Ego can make you feel self important and shy and inadequate and any number of things, but you must understand this work is bigger than that. Believe in yourself, keep at it, dance in the face of your fears. The plants can help. They can help us remove our defences. They can help us be the best versions of ourselves, living out the work we came here to do.

With each layer you peel back you uncover another wounding, another behavioural pattern that you have based on your own damaged and distorted belief systems. The more you work the deeper and darker you will go. The more you face and don't turn away from, or deny what you are feeling and seeing, the stronger you will grow. Plants will absolutely support you in this. In fact when you really start to let them in, and listen to them, they kind of insist on it.

Why do I yet again return to personal work when I am speaking of specialism? Because your personal medicine for the world, your personal specialism, can only become clear when you have dropped any and all expectations, when you have faced your shadow and removed your barriers. As you become more clear, the path before you will become more clear. That is when the work you came here to do, your specialism (whether that is working directly with plants or not), will suddenly become obvious.

You will find there is a difference between "wanting" to and being "compelled" to, in the context of acting on the wisdom of your interspecies communications. Some of the wisdom you have gained will require certain actions, maybe you have been given a task by a plant. I think that is what generates different layers of plant whispering. Once you start acting on those compulsions, once you see the responsibility that has been laid upon you and you understand that it is no longer about simply *wanting to* complete the task but actually *needing to*, to sate your plant allies and your own inner daemon. That is when the art of plant whispering truly becomes a way of being as opposed to an interesting diversion and pastime. That is when the green tendrils of your plant relations are reaching in and rewilding you from the inside out.

At one time my intention was to be a healer, I had romantic visions of myself as curandera. I saw these visions on a magical day in which I had bumped into a group of Kogi on a deserted beach within sight of the snow tipped sacred mountains, the Sierra Nevada de Santa Marta. I called the visions in that same evening while basking under the orange glow of a total lunar eclipse. I undertook many trainings in the proceeding years in pursuit of the role. Trainings and apprenticeships facilitated not just by human teachers but by various plants that had stepped forward to guide and train me, to become my wise elders and allies.

The plants, as I increasingly let them in and followed their guidance more and more, had a slightly different vision for me it seems. They nudged me, at times not very subtly, away from that romantic image I had naively called in on that wild beach in northern Colombia all those years ago. The plants directed me to understand that what people need right now is personal empowerment, reconnection with Gaia, and with our ancient ways of being. I have found the most profound, effective and from my point of view satisfying "healings" have always come about when I simply open up the tool box. When I give a brief demonstration and introduction of what each tool is and what it can be used for, then simply stand back, hold space and witness what unfolds. I give energy, time, guidance, but the best healings come when people are given the chance to find their way themselves. It is like they pop into another dimension, and then more vibrant, confident, shiny, and with direction, they head off to take their part in changing the world for the better.

On the surface what I offer to clients may be remedy and ferment making, calming walks in the woods and techniques for talking to plants. What underlies it all though is my main intention, made clear by communications with my plant allies, and that is to assist people as they realign how they see themselves and their relationship to the world, to the wild. It is not getting "out" into nature more, or "bringing" more nature "into" your life. It is about self-recognition. Realising self as nature, as wild. As part of the vast interconnected grid, absolutely inseparable from *everything* else. Not just reading about it and mentally agreeing with or acknowledging the concept; but feeling it, knowing it, living it with every cell of your body; your bones, your blood, your breath. As when you do so the realisation also dawns that not just every deed, but every word, every thought, ripples out into Gaia consciousness and embeds its impact within all of us.

My personal mission, as you can see, changed over time, clarified and moved from being a curandera to sharing this work. The role I originally dreamed up under quite magical circumstances, and that I worked to action, to bring into reality, has been constantly directed and refined by my plant allies and communications with them. I could have tried to ignore the plant wisdom, I could even have perhaps convinced myself to interpret it a different way. I could have continued to pursue what I had originally trained to do. But I know that what I do now reaches many more people and has the chance to inspire more, than simple one on one treatments would have. The work I do is deeply satisfying and I know somewhere deep in my soul that this is the work I came here to do.

Your teachers do not show up by accident. None of what you have learned or trained in is by accident either. You need it all. Weave it all in to what you do. And so, whatever it is that you feel inclined to do, or are instructed by the plants that you must do, let it emerge gently and organically. As you mature and develop, your offerings will naturally become more sophisticated and elegant. That can only come with depth of experience. You cannot become an authority on direct perception during a short course and then presume to be equipped to go ahead and teach it yourself, for example. Because to be able to effectively perceive directly you *must* know yourself; the ripples *you* create in the pond. Otherwise how do you know that what you are perceiving is accurate and not skewed by your own cherished blindnesses?

I know an incredible medicine man from Kenya, who from the age of six used to arise each morning at dawn to silently observe all the plants, before his human community arose. He didn't just want to do this, he was *compelled* by the plants to. He did this for ten years, learning their language slowly, letting it gradually and gently advise him, *before* he put his rich learned wisdom into practice and began using plants to heal within the community. He continues with this practice each morning, even though he has now entered middle age, because he is still learning, deepening and evolving with his plant allies.

Being able to look deeply at yourself, leaving no metaphorical stone unturned, not shying from the shadow but seeing it all and defusing any triggers, that's a life's work in itself. The more you know the more there is to know. Like reaching the peak of a hill, only to realise a further stretch of climb that has just been revealed on reaching this height, the false peak you had perceived to be the top. Depth perception work is just that and unless you are in process with the depths of yourself how can you access the depths of another?

For something to become your specialism you must be drawn by your gut. You will know in your blood and bones that it is your truth, the things you have been starved of, have been searching for all your life. You will be compelled to know more, to learn it, feel it, live it. Dipping fingers, toes, hands; going for a full body immersion in wild, with full acceptance of self as Gaia, your drive will surpass the surface level. It will go from perhaps "how can I make money, make my living from this?" to "how can I be of service to this?". When you are in that space the universe will conspire to provide you with a living. It may not be an extravagant one, but it will provide for what you need without further degradation of the planet. You will know it when you stop going out to chase "nature" or wild experiences, but when you live and breathe it, all day every day, no matter where you live.

As that realisation, that knowing, beds in, you will notice all the things that don't make you feel good that much more. If you are an urban dweller, don't be so quick to run for the hills and turn your back on urban life: within the city you are needed more than ever. Perhaps you will organise a community litter pick, become more conscious of what you eat, work to get green spaces, guerilla plant wild flowers, medicines and edibles in your neighbourhood. Live your wild, plant whispering truth and influence your peers invisibly yet effectively that way.

With the knowledge you have been gifted as plant whisperer, with a direct personal relationship to the more-than-human, comes a big responsibility. A responsibility to carry the medicine the plants have shared with you, and for you to share it... You have to tell your story. Hiding what you know and what you believe will not serve us, not now, not in these times when we need a full paradigm shift. Stand up and speak your truth, tell your stories of relations with other species. The human world needs to hear this so that we can change our collective story. It gives us all permission to have these relations and that is when the paradigm shift will happen; when we all tell our story. Then consensus reality changes, and the paradigm shifts.

> *Once we understand things in a new way, we have a new world.*
>
> **Alex Grey**

You will be guided and supported to find your medicine, your gifts to the world, what you came here to do; and to embody them. It is no mistake that you are here at this time. The more you tune in, the more you will understand what your unique medicine is and how you can share it.

Doing what you were born to do is a release, a freedom. It will bring you pleasure. You will not notice the passing of time – not be clock watching for your day to end – you will be totally absorbed in the magic of doing what you love. So much so that when the day ends you will emerge as if from a dream wondering where all the time went...

What you do with your plant whispering, with the wisdom entrusted to you by the plants, that is your business. I know that plants can provide access to all the information, knowledge and wisdom in the universe; and this has the power to embed you as an alert, wild and fully functioning integral part of Gaia. The more of us that are listening the more we can influence humanity's role in the wider changes Gaia is undergoing. We have the opportunity to be involved in something revolutionary; world changing.

8. Plant Whisperer

The art of plant whispering cannot fix the original trauma of being rent from our wild beginnings. It can, however, go part of the way, in concert with other rewilding practices. It can put those of us who are interested and are actively pursuing a wilder and more natural way of being into recovery, remission, the first stages of healing. What you will almost always find through your interactions with the more-than-human is that you will learn about taking more care of yourself. Which, if you think about it, is self-serving of the other being, and also in service to Gaia; as the more you take care of yourself, the more you take care of the world.

When you meet with a plant as an equal, you get out of the audience and join the show. This is rewilding. Not just observing, but interacting and responding to how your vegetal cousin makes you feel. Each plant will gift you with a different aspect of wholeness. Plants are really good at being their authentic selves, which is partly why they teach us so well to be who we truly are. Each plant will have a different message for each person because we all work in different ways, the answer is all tied up in who *you* are.

It is not my place to wonder why or question this knowledge when it comes, just humbly and gratefully accept it in the joy and delight that the plants have seemingly accepted me. Plant whispering will most certainly form part of your ecological restoration of the self. Even if you didn't know that was what you were looking for; the plants will guide you to it and aid the process.

The art of plant whispering will provide an access point to your own wild soul. Rekindling, nurturing the wild that already exists inside every one of us, inside of you. Encouraging it to come forth and expand. It provides access to the god(dess) within. To the wisdom of the world beyond yourself and yet held within every cell of yourself. There is no cultural misappropriation here, communicating with other species was in all of our cultural lineages once upon a time. And remember your lineage can never be fully broken because it is in, and of the Earth itself.

Interspecies communication can help you find your power. It can help you discover what it is that you came here to do. Help you find your place, what you are, who you are. No matter who you speak most fluently with (perhaps it is not a plant but a mountain, animal, crystal or ocean) they will show you what your power is and guide you in how to use it. They will help you discover how you can express it both creatively and practically. How you can feed that power and use it not just for yourself, for personal gain, but for the whole of the human community and wider than that, all your relations.

Life As Plant Whisperer

I cannot even begin to describe the richness that plant whispering has brought into my life. I just don't have the words to describe how many layers there are and how deeply this work can go. I have shared the tools and techniques that have brought me to this place, but the only thing that is real is you and your relationships. As soon as you begin to open the door and open it with your heart, let your feeling sense lead you, a whole new world of meaning will step up to greet you.

Just yesterday I was called by the seductive fragrance of a beautiful ally, and in just a fleeting moment I understood that I was being offered support in the help I was giving a distressed soul. I was offered flowers to make a tea for that person. The fragrance alone bestowed deeply sweetening and strengthening medicine for my own heart, in what was quite demanding work. This kind of interaction is what you are working towards, a deep knowing that arrives in response to even a momentary exchange with a plant ally.

Once more I wish to clarify that the tools and techniques are there to help you initiate communications and focus your attention, allowing those communications to drop deeper. The personal work is to help you be clear and confident that what you receive is not a projection, not coming from you, but a true communication. When all of this is in place it begins to flow. You begin to hear the more-than-human call and speak and offer assistance without setting aside dedicated time, because you are in the flow and communications are on-going. You are plant whisperer.

The plants have bestowed me with many treasures. But most often, and I find this easier to notice with the benefit of many years hindsight, the medicine I am gifted is insight into my place amongst them. Amongst the living breathing entity that is Gaia. They offer me wisdom in small pieces that I can now begin piecing together. Wisdom of how to live well, where I fit, how to be more plant, how to be more human.

As I communicate, expressing my love, my gratitude, my empathy, I feel their response. As I notice and acknowledge them more and more I feel them responding in kind. Acknowledging me, letting me know that I am loved, that I belong. Because that is what happens when you love and when you express that love. Whether it is a human, a dog, a place, or a plant, you feel the love coming back to you and it makes you feel more alive, more certain that you are on the right path, and that you are not alone.

Plants are medicine. Our living world is medicine. But they, and it, are so much more than that. We too are medicine, just as we too are more than that. We live, we breathe, we share, we damage, we destroy, we create, we love. We fit together, we belong together. When you are in right relationship with lover, parent, sibling, community, you feel more whole. The same is true when a plant, animal or river becomes any of those things to you. You grow richer and stronger, you begin to luminesce. This is not about personal gain. About gaining mastery over plants or anything else that lives. It is about living well with all your relations.

There are many ways to learn the language. As you stand wild and barefoot the communication can be felt through your feet, it is not all sitting "talking" to plants. As you kayak wild waters the swell beneath your vessel is the wild language of ocean, river, lake. As your fingers, clothed with soil, nurture seedlings, the cycle of day and night, of seasons, another wild facet of language, infuses into you. There are so many ways. But make it conscious. Take time to listen so that you can clearly hear, respond and interpret.

Everything Sacred

The insistent and eternal ebb and flow of sea on sand. The whoosh and suck as grain rides over grain. Rolling over the bodies of all the other minute grains, wearing down, wearing into smooth tiny specks. Again and again with their salty companions, riding up, gently breaking down, drawing back in. Ancient tides, rhythms of moon and sea, of land and water. Ancient as our own wild bones and the cyclical nature of day and night. The rhythm of our own sacred breath, in and out, in and out, without conscious thought, occurring in the background as our blood flows. A lullaby all day, all night. From dawn until the end of time.

Where does more-than-human end and you begin? I once sat with a plant, not for long even, I just sat there one sunny afternoon in the middle of Regents Park in the centre of London. It was in a very public place, right next to the path. Many people were wandering past, dog walkers, nannies with buggies; but this plant had a loud voice and beguiling looks. Almost prehistoric the deep purples and large leaves with a silken sheen, spiky protection around the slowly maturing seed; it drew me in very rapidly. As I introduced myself I acknowledged my ancestors, opening up my family line in my minds eye. I was suddenly catapulted on a visual journey back through my known relatives and then plunged into the unknown, the mix of cultures and ages that have come together in me. I travelled further and further back along my timeline, beyond the human. Spiralling, spiralling, further and further until I was simple bacteria in the primordial soup at the beginning of time. I was given just enough time to register this before I was thrown back in the opposite direction. Spiralling, spiralling outwards towards the present. From the same bacterial source but in a slightly different trajectory until I found myself to be that beguiling and incredible plant, looking out at human me. I realised with the plant that *I am you*; you are an unknown and forgotten part of myself. Remind me of you. Tell me. I want to know. Amazing medicine, amazing tutorial. This is what happens when you become plant whisperer.

Whenever I spend time deeply immersed with plants, each time I close my eyes my lashes leave a trail of jewels. And there are psychedelic patterns in pastel shades behind my eyes. And I can feel every breeze, every sensation heightened to an extraordinary degree. This is the world of plant whispering.

I don't talk too much of creating sacred ceremony, or grandiose ritual. There is a place for these things when you have something specific to honour. But when you are living a life of perpetual communication with the more-than-human your whole life becomes a sacred ceremony. Every waking breath becomes a ceremony and a celebration of your gratitude and relationship. Every action a sacred ritual. When you splash your face with water and in a short fraction of a moment images of everything that water is – the mountains, clouds, oceans, streams, reservoirs, even the pipework that brings it to your house; all of it flashes through your minds eye and is greeted with recognition and conscious gratitude. This is how your life becomes a sacred prayer.

Personal Rebalance

Adeptness in the art of plant whispering will not just help you be a better herbalist, gardener, forager, plants person, but also a more integrated wild Gaian soul. In addition it will benefit *all* your relationships as you become more astute, more practised in the art of noticing hidden messages (although of course *nothing* is truly hidden...). You will unfold untold layers of communication. You will be sensitive to unspoken undercurrents, psychic hints and nudges, body language. So, yes, you will understand the more-than-human more clearly and directly in all its forms; but *also* your human peers.

You will notice the games people play and be able to defuse them before your buttons are pressed. It will help you become a more understanding human, able to make choices based on what is real, not the side show, not the sleight of hand or the charade you have been believing or reacting to all this time. Most people do not consciously know they are giving so much away about their truth, their inner private feelings and confusions, especially those deep secrets they have even hidden from themselves. But you, armed with the skills of a plant whisperer, will be able to interpret the signs and through fully knowing what is going on, be able to make better choices yourself.

Your relationship with your lover, your best friend, your wider peers, your work colleagues, your boss, your parents and siblings will all be affected. You will have the capacity to nurture deep connections, and a widening of understanding for all your human relationships. This is all because you begin to become adept at translating that unspoken language that exists between all folk. You become more able to read the meaning in someone's face, moods, body language. The inflection in their voice and how it shows that what they say may not be the whole story or in fact may be a scant cover for what they would really like to, or are trying to, say. What all this means is that you can address things in your most important relationships without being confrontational. That you can make rapid and astute decisions about each new person you meet.

For many people there may be no initial intent when learning the art other than curiosity. But within the process of learning many of us will inadvertently uncover our own deep wounds. No matter how much work we have done on ourselves, how much we have explored our own shadow, each time you go back and check there is always something you missed. A little game or behaviour lurking, long buried and forgotten, but existing nonetheless to trip you up and sabotage your best efforts, when you are least expecting it. We need to be alert to this and to recognise it when it happens as we can then work with it. The plants (or other beings) as our guides and helpers. One lasting impact of the art, may be the progression each of us make in becoming more whole. We, all together, make up this broken world. Any piece that is fixed becomes a good thing for the whole.

And so, the lost treasures that plant whispering will bring into your life will help restore you, bring you to a place more closely resembling wholeness. Give you access to your wild knowings, buried for so long under your tameness, and yet now revitalised with strong intuition and feeling sense. The plants will lead you to better health; when perhaps you have chlorophyll shouted repeatedly in your ear as images of green juices fill your minds eye. The plants tell you what you need to live a better life, how to achieve and enjoy better health. As you do so the planet in turn will respond. The healthier the habits you engage with the better the footprint you leave (less waste, pollution etc.). Engaging in the art is an holistic approach to world healing.

Don't search the planet for plant medicine, for home, for belonging, you must find it where you stand. This is a manifestation of rebalance and integration. Earth, Gaia, needs you to find your own indigenous wisdom. Needs you to fall in love with yourself and the place where you live, and all the plants and animals and stones and soil that also live there. That co-habit with you. Don't overlook them in your search for something real and magical. They may not feel alluring or sexy, their legend may not currently be strong. We need to honour them. We need to give them energy by communicating directly with them, and by sharing our knowledge and love for them in story and song. The more energy we give, the more we connect directly, the stronger the presences, the plants, stones and animals of our homeland become. Don't be distracted by exotics; allow them to awaken you to the magic of Gaia by all means, but once your eyes are open use them to look around and discover who you stand amongst. You don't have to live in the wilderness to love the land that you are standing on.

Empathy For All Life

Our human family is incredibly dysfunctional. By each one of us waking up and working with plant spirits, with plant consciousness, and that of other life, we are making a positive step towards healing our broken and failing system and world order.

We now know that any relationship is reciprocal. As you feel the plant and its impression upon you, so the plant feels you. You are exchanging, sharing something between you. The more your awareness grows of this two way participation the more self-aware we become collectively. It is not just you and I waking up, becoming more sensitive, feeling it, falling in love; it is Gaia herself, as of course, there is no separation.

As we become more aware of the plants and their livingness we are becoming more aware of our own connection. That they are our relations, that they are far parts of ourselves. Taste the truth of it throughout your being. The more we wake up to the livingness of Gaia, of the universe, and reach out to connect, the more it responds and reaches out to connect back up with humanity.

Half the time we live in ignorance because we just don't think to ask the right questions. We behave in a way that damages Gaia without a second thought as we haven't realised that our unconscious actions are so damaging. I never thought to ask how much water it takes to make a simple cotton t-shirt, did you? Well, at least 2700 litres apparently, roughly the same amount that it would take the average human 900 days to drink![37]

As soon as you are in possession of such a fact then you have to decide what you will do with that information. Once you consider that water (let alone the cotton itself and everything else involved in the production of that single t-shirt) is animate, everything changes.

That water flows through all life just as does breath. It touches every surface, is in every crease, fold and form. Without it we die and yet en masse we squander it without a second thought for its sacred worth. It can no longer be an option to buy an item of clothing to wear just once or twice when you know that just one kilogram of cotton can take up to 22,500 litres of (sacred, living) water to produce[38]. As each of us become more aware of the livingness of everything, and start to ask questions about every element of our domestic lives, then surely mass change will come. We must demand it. As each of us steps up and takes responsibility, sharing what we know, encouraging others to wake up to the animate nature of Gaia, this Earth, hope is born.

The trajectory in which as a society we are currently headed, is far from positive. As I write this (spring 2018) the English Conservative government have recently announced their plans to impose a single use plastic ban by 2042! By then, without an absolutely fundamental change in how humankind conduct themselves, it will be too late. Most life will be lost and the conditions for human life, if still possible, will be challenging to say the least.

The missing link for most people, I am convinced, is compassion. And that is lacking due to the misunderstanding around the animate nature of Gaia. The fact that plants and animals, rivers and stones, insects and apes are all intelligent, making decisions and able to feel. Once that comes in to mass consciousness, mistreating any species would be like mistreating a child, how could you? How could anyone?

Worryingly, acknowledgement of livingness still seems to be missing in the baseline of so many who even work in the same field as myself. When I speak of the animism within which we are embedded I have noticed a lack of recognition on so many faces. I have witnessed flower essence workers literally destroy whole patches of the flower they are working with, shamanic groups carelessly fling stones out of a sacred circle, healers chop down "annoying" bits of foliage before they begin a ceremony. This is really worrying. There is still a huge disconnect, and if people supposedly working within the realms of spirit are failing to recognise it, we really are in trouble.

You can change that. You can stand up with what you now know and be heard, be seen. We are our only hope. Think of all the relatives who are sacrificing so that you can live your life; the trees and plants, the soil and water. Your responsibility after receiving this gift, this sacrifice, is to live well and with respect for all your relations.

9. A Collaborative Future

Once we have tasted this wildness, we begin to hunger for a food long denied us, and the more we eat of it the more we will awaken.

Stephen Harrod Buhner

Before we can truly heal our rift with the wild we must remember Gaia as a whole undamaged entity and remember all we have done, take personal responsibility, and accept exactly where we are now, no denial. To restore our own wildness, we must feed it with wild immersion and interspecies communication, plant whispering. We can then reintegrate into the wider Gaian community. With the practice of interspecies communication we begin to restore and retrieve the abilities and skills we were born with, our true and wild potential. The skills and abilities that were trained out of us as we grew, so that we could take our place in this domesticated and tame world. As we refurbish ourselves with these skill sets and rediscover the animate nature of the world, we go beyond being observers and admirers, instead finding ourselves fully embedded at all times. Even when not in wild surroundings, as long as there's a bird, a plant, or a stone nearby, that we can commune with, we still have a thread connecting us to the wild that lies outside of ourselves. It is likely that each bird, plant and stone is as isolated in an urban blandscape as each of us is, and so *that being* will benefit just as much as *you* from that contact, dialogue and touch on the wild heart.

There is, in some camps, a tendency to look at native hunter gatherer societies with rose tinted spectacles. To imagine a time when we lived in perfect balance with all our relations. But this would mainly be looking back as there are barely a handful of such communities worldwide hanging on to their traditional ways of life. With the exception of a few tribes in the Amazon, pretty much every tribe everywhere else has been touched and disempowered by its contact with the modern world. Bruce Parry demonstrated this perfectly in his docu-film, Tawai[39]. Although these people, our human relations, our ancestors, lived with a sacred recognition of all their relations, their communities slowly began to be eroded due to contact with modern society.

So we need to create a new, more resilient society that can stand and look modernity in the eye and yet have its toes firmly grounded in the bountiful Earth. The past, peoples of the past, can give us clues and ideas, but they are not the solution. The world has changed and just as the culture of my ancient nature dwelling ancestors eventually failed, it now appears that the culture of most native hunter gathering societies is failing too. We need a new way for us, for the new people, for Younger Brother.

We need a new way in everything we do, including the way we work with land. With wilderness becoming increasingly hard to find, the need for honouring and respecting the whole of Gaia has never been more pertinent. To feed, nurture, and encourage the wild in your locale to grow and strengthen, you may well need to be physically proactive. Perhaps you will choose to join with friends, find some land and plant trees, for example. But all such activities I would approach with caution. Stop and ask the land, ask the plants. Communicate. What does the land wish for? Who does it wish to have living there?

This is the same with all physical rewilding of the landscape. Don't simply fall into the trap of imposing something on the land because somebody says that is what the landscape used to look like, that they are the plants that once were rooted and the animals that once roamed there. Replacing what once was lost in a sense is still seeing wider nature as a machine. A mechanised thing where the replacement of this cog here and that chain there will make it function efficiently and effectively again. Ask if that is what the land needs. And listen for the response. As things currently stand, reintroducing long lost inhabitants, four-leggeds or swimmers, flyers or rooted ones, may not necessarily be the answer. Sometimes as humans the best we can do is take a step back, let go, and see what the new landscape yearns to be.

This is exactly what happened in the area surrounding Chernobyl, so horrifically destroyed by the nuclear disaster in 1986. Humans stepped back from the landscape to avoid exposure to the high levels of radiation in the aftermath. With no human intervention the area has, according to some reports, become a verdant wilderness; rich and ripe in the shadow of post-industrial decay[40]. So much so, that in Belarus, the Polesie State Radioecological Reserve, is now running nature-watching tours in what the park claims to be "Europe's largest experiment in re-wilding." Given a chance Earth can heal, even though it may end up different to the original form.

Joining The Dots

Currently as a collective we are failing to make essential connections, as a result disconnect runs right through society and touches everything. It is time to make the connections in every corner of our lives. If the food we eat is not organic, or is heavily processed and packaged, it will damage our personal health. The impact on the land and its non-human inhabitants caused by chemicals used in conventional farming and the proliferation of single use plastic wrapping, is very clear. Both destroy the health of the land *and* our own health. Everything is connected. What is bad for us, is bad for the planet. Once again we find *there is no separation*.

Consider this; people are still looking for a cure for cancer, when so many (albeit certainly not all) cancers are know to be triggered and caused by lifestyle and environmental factors, such as the toxins we are exposed to. Prevention, for all but hereditary cancers, surely is to live the wild life we were predestined to live. That in itself is the cure. Just as it is the cure for depression, anxiety, allergies and so many other conditions. It could be as simple as returning to eating natural foods, spending time outside, walking barefoot, and removing plastics and other chemicals from our homes and locale. And yet, as we instead treat these illnesses and conditions with pharmaceuticals, it becomes a vicious cycle. As we ingest chemical medications there are "side effects", these are also the effects of the medications, just the ones we *don't* want. To treat the so called side effects we then take further medications. In the process of generating these medications, more pollution is created, more plants are synthesised and butchered to be used as resources, more ancient sunlight is being sucked from beneath our feet. And so we kill more of our wild world to treat symptoms caused by the death of our wild world and our artificial isolation from it. Is it just me, or is this plain nuts??

Consumption and over consumption in its many forms, alongside use of pharmaceuticals to "treat" the conditions that our collective lifestyles have caused, have become the standard coping mechanisms. All of which lead to greater economic disparity and more ecological destruction in the form of waste, pollution, deforestation, etc.

We cannot, in no uncertain terms, meet the latest IPCC (Intergovernmental Panel on Climate Change) recommendations by continuing to live as we have been[41]. Consuming as we do. All of our lives have to change. We each have to step up and make that change. We cannot wait for government and multinationals, they *will* follow.

Maybe when our never ending appetite for "stuff" declines, our hours in the office will be cut. Gifting us more time in which to foster wild connections. Maybe we will let our gym memberships lapse and enter the wild gym, moving in the landscape, nurturing and gathering medicines and foods. If this approximates what you dream of, then work towards it. Reject single use plastic wrapped exotic foods. Reject the chemical medications of big pharma. Reject spray tans and sun beds for the colouring gifted by the sun from spending time outside. Walk, whether to the fresh produce market rather than driving to the store, or to your kids school.

You may not at this point feel you have the time to gather your food, to walk, to communicate directly with the more-than-human, but find the time, make it happen. I know I am probably talking to the converted here, but still, we each need to continue to connect those dots and make change after change in the way we lead our daily lives.

> *Poets wrote odes to nature, even as nature vanished before their eyes.*
> **Elizabeth Gilbert**

To protect ourselves and wider nature from further damage our whole paradigm must shift. As soon as we stop feeding the current system of over consumption the negative feedback loops will slow. The solution and cure is recognising the animate nature of Gaia. Not just knowing the web of life exists but actually making the connection mentally to treat it all as alive, intelligent and sentient. This is the pregnant point. The break through moment. And when the hundredth monkey does that, the way we collectively live will change, very rapidly.

Plant whispering, or more accurately understanding viscerally the sacred nature of all of the more-than-human realms, is absolutely essential for personal and planetary rewilding. Neither can actually happen in an effectual way without it. Consider that, for example, in pursuit of personal rewilding you will be spending time in the great outdoors. You will be hiking, wild camping, you will be foraging. If you are not operating with absolute understanding of the sacredness and sacrosanct nature of all life, then your presence and activities, although making *you* feel good, could be causing greater stress, damage and degradation to the landscape and populations that inhabit it. Many of us have walked in the desert or the tundra, we walk in spectacular places to feel that awe, that in-breath of wilderness. But in places such as these it can take decades to establish a tiny patch of plant or bacteria that is perhaps not even visible to the naked eye and yet damaged by a single footprint. Moss that took decades to form, can easily be disturbed and damaged by a clumsily placed foot or hand. Simply moving stones (without asking permission or replacing after) to build a fire pit, can upset microscopic communities. Throwing organic peels and cores in an area where they do not grow, and will take months to degrade, is nothing more than littering.

There are too many of us and too few wild places for it to absorb everyone if we all felt inclined to vacate the towns and cities each weekend and forage for our supper or our medicines. If we all decided to collect old "dead" wood to warm ourselves by. If we all tramped on the same track. Anyone who does walk or trek on upland tracks already knows how paths erode with use. As soon as you raise the level of consciousness and understand that even by undertaking such personal rewilding activities you are having a potentially detrimental impact, you *have* to act differently. You begin to notice and communicate and then suddenly you are no longer human, alone, brave and wild, conquering nature. You are a wild human of the woods, working in concert with the other life forms that you encounter. Treading, gathering and moving respectfully. It becomes a whole other thing. One that hopefully will have huge impact and allow us all to be outside but without causing more damage. Instead, moving with understanding, love and respect, so that we actually help benefit and improve conditions.

The hope for our collective future lies in you. In all the people who are re-learning the lost art of plant whispering. In all who stand barefoot in awe and gratitude each morning. In those who make a sacred contract with Gaia to make things better, to live well, in respect and balance with all life. It lies within those who carry love in their hearts, not just love for humankind, but for all our relations.

Personal rewilding does not mean going "back" to an idyllic, bucolic world where we lived amongst the trees, dressed in nothing but beads and feathers, hunting and gathering all our meals and living in a basic jungle lean-to. But it is a return, a return to a place of balance, and that requires a change of mind. A return to a former paradigm. One where all species matter, all species count. Our state of perceived exile from the wild simply evaporates as we reconnect with our own wild core and thus the wild Gaian soul that is this animate Earth. I know this is a huge leap in a world where people discriminate against other humans based on the shade and tone of their skin, their accent, their eye colour. If we cannot even accept our human brothers and sisters how will it ever be possible that we do so with brothers and sisters that fly and crawl, that are rooted and that swim? But if we do not, I fear that it will not be long for us, our time as part of Gaia, existing "on" this planet will soon pass.

Consciousness Revolution

> *Let yourself be silently drawn by the strange pull of what you really love. It will not lead you astray.*
>
> **Rumi**

As we are waking up to the fact that we have been misled, that there *is* spirit in "things", that our world *is* animate and sentient, our conscious mindset is changing. This is a societal shape shift, a consciousness revolution. The plants are helping us, telling us to wake up. All the information is out there, we just have to become adept at not only tuning into it, but also acting on it.

Life is as we dream it, as we perceive it to be. We have to change the dream generated by consensus reality. The one of greed, and lack, and brutality; to one of compassion, inclusivity, and enough. No, more than that, abundance. If you don't like the dream, change it. Take appropriate action *every day* to manifest the dreams you have, to bring in the change you want to see in the world, nobody else is going to do it. We all have to participate, it is our duty. You are not alone on this path, more and more people are joining from their own unique wild path and direction. We all have different ways of changing the world, so do what you love, have fun, otherwise no one will pay attention anyway.

It takes just *one* person to believe in a new dream, to then spread it, to share it clearly, for group perception to change.

Live It

> *The telling is crucial. We must own our true stories. In doing so, we begin again to belong to the world in the way only we can. The door to soul opens.*
>
> **Bill Plotkin**

Once you have breached the perceived species divide and you feel yourself to be woven in, with the lines of communication open; use your whole body, all of your senses, all of your dimensions, to notice, to feel, and to respond. Embody the wisdom of the plants and what they have gifted you with, what snippets of information they divulged to assist your quest, your life journey. This is Gaian soul medicine. Let the wild whisperings that run through you sing their song so that all your threads, golden and otherwise vibrate in harmony. Your unique resonance contributing to the wild awakening song, gaining, rippling, spreading.

Plant whispering is not what I do at weekends, or in my spare time, it is not even what I do as a job. In fact it is not what I *do* at all. It is who I am.

One of my greatest lessons has been to stand up and be seen. Throughout my adult life, various plants and fungi called to me in different ways and asked me, very specifically, to share this knowledge; to call people to a more integrated existence of perpetual communication with other life forms. It has become that the plants work through me; and I work for them. Perhaps that in itself leads me to conclude that anyone, once initiated into the art of plant whispering, has a responsibility to both live it and share it. Secrets have got us nowhere; this way of being needs to be out there for everyone.

To live the wild life of a plant whisperer, connections and communications must flow through your veins, you must let them infuse into everything that you do. You may be an herbalist, a chef, a gardener, an urban planner. You may be a mum or a dad, a dog walker. The way that you live will touch and trigger those around you, influence them, even in imperceptible, invisible ways, but it will. If you keep the art alive in all that you do, then even without conscious effort you will be both living and sharing it.

If you work with clients in the healing arts, this work will help you improve your practice. Also, if for example, you work in human resources, or are a garden designer, you will be better and clearer in what you do, because you will know more than is actually being said, or asked of you. Whatever it is that you do, this work will help you do it more cleanly and clearly. Even when communicating with people where there is no common language, you become better at understanding the meaning that is being conveyed. You will have the same communication skills as young children do. Children who although they share no common language can play together all day on a tourist filled beach. This is nothing special, anyone who has observed young children playing with those who speak a different language will know that at that age, anyone can do it. In learning the art of plant whispering one reclaims that skill set (if you didn't manage to keep it alive all along).

Personal rewilding and the path of plant whisperer, are both a life journey; a life dedication. Neither can be taught or learnt in 3 months, not even on a year long retreat. You have to live it and be it. For that you must allow the wider aspects of Gaia to lead you. The most important point is the noticing; awareness of communications at all times. And persistence. Persistence in practising the art and in finding your own way to live it.

It is important not to be territorial with your art, with your new skills and medicine for the world. We are at a time in the history of Gaia that more than ever before we need to see huge and fundamental change within the human community. For that we all play our part, and getting the more-than-human accepted as conscious, is key.

There is indigenous medicine in each of us. We are all of the Earth and of the stars, each an inseparable part of Gaia. Plants can help us find our personal medicine and compassion for all beings, humans included. Compassion is what the rest of Gaia needs from us right now. When we respect each difference we will experience *everything* in a different way, because then it becomes sacred. Spread the word, the plant love, the responsibility to Earth, to Gaia; to all those that do not yet remember.

It can no longer be each person for themselves. We have a huge trauma, the original one (separation from our wildness), to heal collectively. Without doing so our addictive, abusive and dissociative behaviours will continue to play out until the end of times for humanity. So, it is not just that you *could* share this; you *must*, as a matter of survival. And not even so much for humanity – in a sense we deserve what we get – but for all our relations...

Your medicine for the world, what you came here to do, does not have to be grandiose; it could be as simple as being your authentic self. You have to drop any attachment to outcome and simply do what it is that you need to do in the world. Will it restore hope for humanity? Does it matter? You have to do your best anyway whether hope will be restored or not...

It's never too late to be what you might have been.
George Eliot

Wider Implications

In remembering the language of the ancients, the language that runs through our DNA and that of all life on this planet, you will learn much about yourself. That is inevitable. You cannot listen to the whispers of the trees and rivers, of the boulders and bees, and remain unmoved. This is exactly the heart-opening stuff that in our domesticated isolated lives we had closed ourselves to and cut ourselves off from. So allowing yourself to feel, feel into not only the wild that surrounds you, but the wild within, you will discover soul truths. You alone cannot "save" the world, you cannot save Gaia. But if you are willing to pay attention to the communications you are party to, if you are willing to pay attention to the great stirrings that generates within yourself; then you will find yourself belonging more fully within the wild Gaian community. You will know your home more wholly amongst mosses and lichens than in the company of micro-chips and plastic chairs. The further you take it, the more insights you will have into the unique gifts that you personally can offer the world, the things that make you you; and how you can use them to serve Gaia. Being brave enough to face the true you is the greatest gift you can give yourself and the world. If you live your life with your heart not your head, facing and exploring all facets of both yourself and the wider world; not just the pretty, the nice bits, but the scary and sometimes ugly truths too, then you will be living the life you came here to live. Doing the work Gaia had lined up for you all along, and as a result, you will be giving the most valuable gift to Gaia; your true essence, no shields, pure you. That in itself will change the world, save your bit of it. And the more of us who take on this wild, twisted, beautiful challenge, the more integrated our kind will be with all our relations, and the greater will be the chance for wildness and life itself to thrive.

This work, both personal rewilding and the art of interspecies communication, is about compassion. It's about empathy. It's about collaboration; not competition. It's about sharing what you know. Not about keeping it to yourself for personal gain; that's misuse of power. That is how we got into this mess...

The way I see us now, those of us who are fully participatory in this animate Gaia, is like a network of invisible yet present points of light. Each of us going into our communities, both local in person and international online ones, and sharing this work each in our own unique and beautiful way. Each persons medicine for the world is unique and different but equally needed and equally valid. Each way is different, yet each light is joined to all others. We have all been taught by different teachers; be they plants, landscapes, soils, humans. It goes without saying that it is not just me and my way! We each have to come to this work in our own way, and carve our own personal off-road magical path through the wildness of the world. We need to encourage the diversity in medicine and allow our individual light to feed and encourage each other. Let each person engage with their own truth, their own medicine. This is a central principle of livingness, respecting diversity and the voice of the individual. So that we form an awake and aware global network.

Our separation from wider nature is the sickness of humanity, reconnection is the healing process. The realisation of our connection is fundamental. We are each an expression of the whole; you are the universe itself. The moment you start to heal yourself, love yourself, you are also doing it to the planet. The universe will feed you. Trust, and let it feed you; so that you can take all of this further, it is a feedback loop. Create it as you wish it to be... We all have the power to initiate change.

There is no magic wand. There is no hope unless we experience that complete paradigm shift, followed up with generation upon generation working in remedial care to restore Gaia to something we barely even dare dream. Currently, we are on a runaway train heading downhill straight into a cliff face. We need to collectively ditch the magical thinking and really take a long hard look at where we are at, and what we have left to work with. At some point someone is going to have to exercise some restraint in how they live, and say "no, no more. This ends with me".

This is no time to be shy, to hide your skills, your art. We have literally billions of people to convince that this original way of being with the more-than-human aspects of Gaia is not only relevant but essential if we are to divert the current trend of mass ecocide. We need to regain our place amongst all beings in a living moving dance of micro-adjustments and work alongside all our relations, for the betterment of all life.

Let's get some momentum behind this wild movement, let's get it mainstream! An impossible task? No way! Think of veganism. Back in the 1980's anyone mentioning the word vegan was considered a freak. Even five years ago it was challenging to eat out as a vegan and you would expect plenty of ribbing from peers about your quirky nut milk drinking ways. But not now. Every restaurant has a vegan option, every supermarket has a section devoted to vegans. Within a few short years everyone now knows what a vegan is, and not only that, no one laughs and jokes at vegans any more, instead they are asking questions. And trends are tending towards everyone cutting back at least a little on their consumption of animal products.

The rumblings have begun, acknowledgement of the animate nature of this Earth is on the rise. It is already here and happening. It *is* possible to get everyone on this planet awake and aware; whispering to Oak and Stream, Pebble and Peregrine. And the world at that point is how *I* dream it.

It's all about falling in love with plants deeply. With plants, with Gaia. That's it. That's the bottom line.

We are a growing community and together we must spark a renaissance in this way of living amongst all our relations – in free-flowing communication with them. This is such important work at this desperate hour on this planet. I offer my deepest gratitude and love to all that choose to open back up to the richness that is to live with an open heart and a living communication with the sentient world.

The time will come when humanity does not stop to think or even break their stride while they communicate with the more-than-human world. A time when we listen to all our relations and our wisdom and knowledge blends. When we fit better in the wild Gaian matrix and no longer block the flow of energy and information, but get fed and nourished by it.

It is time to rend the veil, to override the ennui of our modern bereft lifestyles, our lonely, meaningless lives, to be done with days and hours, long lonely nights of wishful thinking – the time is now. Not only is it time to acknowledge that "we are the ones we have been waiting for"; but also, and perhaps, more pertinent would be to say that *you* are the one *you* have been waiting for. There is no knight on a white horse who will come and endow meaning into your life, or who will save our collective home from ecocide, there is only you. *But*, don't think for a nanosecond that this is a lonely road with all that responsibility on your head alone, because the wild path is one of inclusivity. Where you are not just a single isolated human but a manifestation of Gaia and all that encapsulates: you are a representation of all your relations and as such are intrinsically connected on an innate level with all life. There is only you and yet you are never alone – this is the beautiful wild Gaian paradox.

When you look upon the world with wild soul ignited and enlivened, you look upon it with a thousand eyes – all open. As you have found the key to hundreds of different perspectives in hundreds of different realms. You have a firm base for your encounters and a diversity of perspectives to work from. You become more free, more flexible and thus stronger and more resilient. So much to call upon and fall back upon when encountering the complexities, the surprises, the knowns, the ups and downs of life. You gain freedom to follow your urges, to trust your longings and the energy to action them.

Don't let "nature" be something that you are not. Claim it. You are it. Let it wildly flow through you and be you. Never forget personal rewilding and plant whispering is not solely about what you gain, but what the wider planet gains.

It takes courage to claim the mistakes you have made, the damage you personally have wrought. First you need the courage to step out of denial and see it for what it is. You need courage to step out of your dissociated state and to actually feel what has been done; what it means and what the implications are. And it takes courage once more to act, to change things. But the plants are with you, they have your back. They want to help you in this process, their lives depend on it too.

We are not alone in wanting to fix our relationship to wild and fix the damage to Gaia. The mountains, rivers, creatures and birds are all with us, there to help and guide us in whatever ways they can. Why do you think the plants are standing up – jumping up and down, waving, sending strong envoys like Ayahuasca, San Pedro and Cacao across the planet to assist in the cause "wake the humans up before it's too late for all of us!"? We are not alone. It is not humans trying to save their inanimate home – it is the whole of Gaia standing up, asking humans to stop. Offering their wisdom and medicine, whatever it takes to start turning things back around.

The pace of change is encouraging. Ten years ago when I tried to describe what I do, that I talk to trees, I used to get the "you've taken too much LSD" look. The thing is at some point in our collective history, most likely pre-agriculture, we used to live in a continuum. There was no line drawn to separate the lives of human and non-human. So perhaps when our ancestors drew an antelope on the wall of their cave before hunting, they were drawing in that part of themselves. There was no separation, the people would have had to have been taught the concept of separation and they would have had a very hard time understanding the concept. Yet for us the opposite is the case. We have been brought up in a paradigm where all is separate and to think of all life as a continuum, where all life is simply a part of ourselves and thus can be communicated with, is just as alien a concept as the opposite was for our ancestors.

But as I said, things are changing. What I and my peers struggled to learn because it was a completely new concept, is now more accessible, more easy to accept immediately, because it is more in the common arena. We need to keep that pace of change up. When I talk about my relationships with plants these days people don't give me that look any more, not at all. People are interested and eager to share their experiences, they relish talking about it and do so with passion in their eyes, with a hunger that has been awakened. So in part our job is to elevate the subject. Keep it being spoken of and not just limited to the circumstances of entheogen experiences, but conversations of real and deep connections existing at all times with all species; no special circumstances, elixir ingestions or prerequisites required. This lonely world is humanities creation, humanities illusion. Perceiving a world that is alive with shared energies, shared relationships, is a big jump but it's not impossible. It is where we came from and where we need to go, if we are to continue life on this planet. By choosing the path of plant whisperer you are choosing a sacred path, one that is heading towards a total paradigm shift for all of humanity.

It is really important to own your unique relationship, your own unique story, with each plant. When we do so, something opens within us and also in the wider world, we begin to truly belong again. We have always belonged, but now we really begin to feel it, to know it. The doorway to one's own soul opens as does the door to Universal wisdom, the Gaian hologram.

It can be painful, messy and ugly, but it is also beautiful, as we collectively find ways to shape shift into a people who can have hope. A people who can and do have compassion for other species. Who can and do communicate with those other species and who do feel a responsibility of care. Who proactively want change and are working towards it.

To have a beloved first you must have someone that you love. To belong, first you must long for something. So ask yourself, what is it that you long for? A community? Somewhere that you fit perfectly? A place where you feel nurtured, loved, heard? A place that is vibrant and alive? Relations, friends, allies, lovers that respect and care for you as you do for them? A place where teachers and learned ones share their wisdom with you? If that approximates what you long for, then through practising the art of plant whispering, or indeed any inter-species communication, you will truly find a place that you belong.

Trees are not supposed to grow in solitude, but in community. We cut the woodlands. Now they, like us, stand alone. Honour them, talk to them, love them. Like us they operate in less than optimal conditions. Let us stand together with the trees. Support them.

When you know that trees can talk, you suddenly know that they can tell you their story. And so when you furnish your home think about that. A wooden spoon has a story and a life, a very different one to a plastic spoon. Fill your home with characters, with life. With story. The story you choose to surround yourself with and live amongst is your choice, so choose wisely. You can read the story of that tree and of its archetype with your hands as they touch that spoon. You can read the story also of the hands that made it, artisan or machine. You can read the story of anyone else who has loved that thing. And you, you can add to its story, by layering on your feelings, your gratitude, for the tree that gave its life for your spoon, lay on your gratitude for the artisan whose hands carefully worked with the beauty and grain of that wood. You can add gratitude for how well it does its task (stirring your dinner) and as you do so, all of that also goes into the food that you eat. As you expand this way of being further and further out, into your furniture, bedding, clothing, every living moment of your life becomes a love story. And you will feel it (as will your guests and visitors), every time you open your front door. Your home becomes a temple of love, compassion and respect. Of gratitude for all those who gave their lives so that you can live in the manner that you do...

This is reclaiming a magical life, living every day like Cinderella or Snow White, where all the plants and animals are communicating with you constantly. You don't need to take Mushrooms or Ayahuasca, you don't need synthesised Ergot to talk to trees. You can live like this all day every day, it just requires that initial paradigm shift and suddenly you find yourself inhabiting an alternate dimension. Parallel to the one where you used to exist but more coloured in, more complete. In fact what you were searching for all along; deep connection, full life, magical happenings...

> *A world where – even amidst such devastating loss of cultures, languages, wild lands and species – magic and mystery still occupy the borderlands of civilisation, waiting patiently for us to remember that we don't know everything about the nature of so-called reality, or even about our imaginative capacity to create other possibilities, other ways of being human.*
>
> **Geneen Marie Haugen**

When you step into a place where wider nature reigns and when you then switch off from your technology and human made distractions. When you let go of humanity and the world of humanity as your focus. It is then that you can feel it clearly. The vibrant pulse of a world and a life much bigger and greater than that which we have created for ourselves. It is in those moments that anxiety melts away and pure feelings arise. And so, the more you do this it follows that the more you then inhabit this world. It becomes your domain. The place where you gather your strength, clarity and insights. Where you unwaveringly know. Once you are plant whisperer this can be any place where a plant resides. It need not be the Serengeti or Alaska. It can be your back yard. It need not be in the presence of ancient Giant Redwoods, it can be in the presence of your beloved Dahlias. When it can be this close to home you can live it every day. You can be surrounded by beauty and extraordinariness in the most normal of places.

In A Nutshell

Any attempts at rewilding our world would benefit greatly if we humans were to rewild ourselves. After all it is the actions of humankind that have led to the taming, domesticating and de-wilding of Earth, there is no question. So, within ourselves we need to identify the one thing that will change everything else. The underlying root of the beliefs and habits we have adopted that have allowed us to damage our home to the extent that we are not just endangering all other lives, but our own as well. I believe this root is our illusion of separation. The belief that we are somehow separate from all other life on this planet. That we are the important ones, the only ones with soul and purpose, the only ones with meaning in our lives. If we overcome that illusion, absolutely everything will change, and for that we must begin to know ourselves as nature. To remember that we are nature, nothing more, nothing less. We cannot force other humans to accept this, but we can make the change ourselves, with the hope that as we gain momentum as a collective, eventually it will once again be part of mass consciousness that we are connected to all forms and manifestations of life, even the apparently inanimate, all of it. There is no separation.

There is no separation. When you break down what we perceive to be life through our narrow logic-based viewpoint, beyond the material realm and discover what we and everything else is made from, we discover energy. We discover a vast field or grid of energy. Particles and or waves, both at the same time, and nothing else. We are each of us, points on this energetic continuum, as is everything else, all of those other physical manifestations that we consider to be separate. But once you see it in this way you absolutely realise there is and can be no separation. We each touch everything else, just as everything else touches us. Our lives entwined. All made of the same stuff. It then becomes apparent that every perturbation on that energetic field affects the whole.

Our illusion of separation runs deep, way back in human history at least to the earliest days of agriculture. At some point we lost awareness of the connectivity of life and began to stand alone. It hasn't worked out that well for us. It is becoming increasingly apparent on a daily basis how immense the crisis we have initiated as a result of our perceived separation actually is.

To reach back in and reconnect with the rest of life on this planet is our one opportunity to remember who we truly are. Where we fit. That we are not alone. That other beings are sentient. In making those connections, we are guided by the other points of light on the grid, the other living beings, to become more whole. To live lives that are more congruent, that allow *all* life to thrive. It is a big lesson and we need to act fast if we are going to slow our own destruction. Even if we cannot do that, what we can do is live better, more fulfilling lives. How this manifests in the physical world, as we perceive it, is actually taking steps back to our wild roots. Acknowledging and working in cooperation with the rest of the natural world, not waging a destructive war against it. We are led to walk barefoot and eat plants, spend time away from screens and cars and four walls, and breathe deeply in the full knowledge of what that living breath actually is. We are drawn to drink wild waters and acknowledge the journey that water has made.

This life leads us to find allies, wise elders, teachers, lovers, relations, equals everywhere we look. We fall in love with ourselves, with life, with wider nature – there is no separation.

Every day that passes without rebuilding our respect and connections with more-than-human nature is one where the resilience of life on this planet is undermined further. Where we lose wisdom, points of view, experience.

Personal rewilding, through the process of interspecies communication, will change everything for all lives, for Gaia herself. Plants are stepping forward to assist us, to remind us, to show us. By accepting their offerings and gifts we enter sacred relationship with all life. And although I do not know what the future holds for us, I do know that facing it with strong allies in the more-than-human realms, will allow us to change individually and be better equipped to be a positive part of the changes that are now occurring globally.

Epilogue

> *The sadness aches in my bones. Sadness of lost forest that I never knew, lost connection, lost love. Is this what drives me? The dream of hope and reconciliation, of revival, of reawakening, of breaking this current dream, this vale of sadness with the joy of new love, the revival of lost communications. The spreading of forest anew. I can hear the voices of the ancient ones, still echoing in this ancient land, in the last vestiges of remaining forest, isolated elders, ancient trees, in the desert lands of our creation. My bones heave with grief as tears spill down my face in an endless outpouring, washing and cleaning ready for the new, the more, the revival. We have to sing it, let it rise up and hear the voices, let it flow and grow anew, there is no one else. We are the ones we've been waiting for.*

I stand in the deep forest watching the ebb and flow of mist curling and rising around the trees in the pearly lunar luminescence. I hear and realise truths in a language without words. I am beginning to understand in my bones, in the deep knowing of my soul...

This book is about the magic and mystery of the universe. We all have access to it, we are all part of it. To live without recognition of that is to live in the shadow. To remember how to access it is to remind our cells how to read the text of the world, and how to incorporate the sense of peace and deep wisdom touching that truth instils. To read that text is to unravel the meaning of life and our place within it. And through it regain a peaceful purpose, a deep knowing that each one of us is needed, and loved, and not alone.

Don't believe anything I say. Go to the source, go to the plants, and find out for yourself.

The Beginning...

Notes

2. Rewilding And Why We Need It

1. https://www.theguardian.com/environment/2017/dec/21/losing-the-wilderness-a-tenth-has-gone-since-1992-and-gone-for-good *Losing the wilderness: a 10th has gone since 1992 – and gone for good*. Susan Chenery. December 21, 2017.
2. https://assets.publishing.service.gov.uk/government/uploads/system/uploads/attachment_data/file/208436/auk-2012-25jun13.pdf *Agriculture in the United Kingdom 2012*.
3. https://www.bbc.co.uk/news/uk-18623096 *The Great Myth of Urban Britain*. Mark Easton. June 28, 2012.
4. https://www.forestresearch.gov.uk/tools-and-resources/statistics/statistics-by-topic/woodland-statistics/ *Woodland Statistics. The Forestry Commission*. June 14, 2018.
5. https://www.theguardian.com/environment/2018/jun/17/where-have-insects-gone-climate-change-population-decline?CMP=share_btn_tw *Where have all our insects gone?* Robin McKie. June 17, 2018.
6. https://www.huffingtonpost.com/2010/08/17/un-environment-programme-_n_684562.html *UN Environment Programme: 200 species extinct every day, unlike anything since dinosaurs disappeared 65 million years ago*. John Vidal. May 25, 2011.
7. As Matt Mellen noted in his inspiring article published by Plant Based News. *Why Do Humans Ignore The Intelligence Of Animals?* October 11, 2017. https://www.plantbasednews.org/post/humans-ignore-intelligence-animals
8. BBC Horizon – *Allergies, Modern Life And Me*. First aired August 27, 2014 – Professor Syed Hassan Ashad, University of Southampton.
9. https://www.asthma.org.uk/about/media/facts-and-statistics/ *Asthma facts and statistics*.
10. https://www.telegraph.co.uk/news/health/children/10130653/Antibiotics-linked-to-eczema-risk-in-children.html *Antibiotics linked to eczema risk in children*. Nick Collins. June 20, 2013.
11. http://www.who.int/mental_health/prevention/suicide/suicideprevent/en/ *WHO mental health; suicide data*, 2016.
12. William J. Ripple and Robert L. Beschta, *Trophic cascades in Yellowstone: the first 15 years after wolf reintroduction*. 2012.
13. https://www.scotsman.com/news/environment/tayside-farmers-shooting-german-beavers-1-3958204 *Tayside farmers shooting German beavers*. Kirsty Steward. November 25, 2015.

3. Personal Rewilding

[14] If you are looking for specific reports to back this up, I recommend reading *Last Child in the Woods* and *The Nature Principle* both by Richard Louv, as he discusses many such reports, statistics and findings.

[15] https://www.theguardian.com/world/2017/mar/16/new-zealand-river-granted-same-legal-rights-as-human-being *New Zealand River Granted Same Legal Rights As Human Being.* Eleanor Aigne Roy. The Guardian. March 2017.

[16] https://amp.theguardian.com/australia-news/2018/apr/01/its-only-natural-the-push-to-give-rivers-mountains-and-forests-legal-rights?CMP=share_btn_tw&__twitter_impression=true&fbclid=IwAR3TF8mGp6xCqWs_hc5XUoWAqR84XS3f8IDR9yJKutzORKe9GWINCjiFzfI *It's only natural: the push to give rivers, mountains and forests legal rights.* Jane Gleeson-White. The Guardian. April 1, 2018.

[17] Harari, Yuval Noah. Sapiens. *A Brief History of Humankind.* (this edition) London: Harvill Secker, 2014. pp90-100.

[18] For a much more in depth explanation of this read Franckh, Pierre. *The DNA Field and the Law of Resonance: Creating Reality Through Conscious Thought.* Rochester, Vermont: Destiny Books, 2014. pp17-21.

[19] Mueller, Martin Lee. *Being Salmon Being Human.* White River Junction, VT: Chelsea Green Publishing, 2017. p188

[20] This article is a must read for an in depth description of the benefit Salmon give to their wider ecosystem and the reciprocal nature of it all. http://www.adfg.alaska.gov/index.cfm?adfg=wildlifenews.view_article&articles_id=407 *Why Fish Need Trees And Trees Need Fish.* Anne Post. Alaska Fish & Wildlife News. November, 2008.

[21] As far as I am aware this phrase was first coined as part of a Hopi elders prophecy http://www.awakin.org/read/view.php?tid=702

[22] From a social media meme – author unknown.

4. Interspecies Communication

[23] https://www.nbcnews.com/news/world/bees-are-dying-alarming-rate-amsterdam-may-have-answer-n897856 *Bees are dying at an alarming rate. Amsterdam may have the answer.* Linda Givetash. NBC News. September 7, 2018.

[24] Wohlleben, Peter. *The Inner Life of Animals.* London: Vintage, 2018. p247

[25] https://www.theguardian.com/books/2015/jan/13/oxford-junior-dictionary-replacement-natural-words *Oxford Junior Dictionary's replacement of "natural" words sparks outcry.* Alison Flood. January 13, 2015.

[26] Collins Concise English Dictionary. Glasgow, HarperCollins Publishers, 3rd edition, 1992.

[27] Lovelock, James. *The Revenge Of Gaia.* London, England: Penguin Books Ltd., 2006. pp18-19.

[28] Wohlleben, Peter. *The Hidden Life of Trees*. Vancover, Canada: Greystone Books Ltd., 2015. p223.
[29] Wohlleben, Peter. *The Hidden Life of Trees*. Vancover, Canada: Greystone Books Ltd., 2015. pp7-9.
[30] https://www.heartmath.org/research/science-of-the-heart/intuition-research/
[31] *The Physiological Effects Of Shinrin-Yoku (taking in the forest atmosphere or forest bathing): Evidence From 24 Field Experiments In Forests Across Japan*. Bum Jin Park, Yuko Tsunetsugu, Tamami Kasetani, Takahide Kagawa, Yoshifumi Miyazaki. Environmental Health and Preventative Medicine, 2009. https://environhealthprevmed.biomedcentral.com/articles/10.1007/s12199-009-0086-9

5. The Art of Plant Whispering

[32] The word psychedelic comes from the ancient Greek. Psykhē meaning soul, mind, spirit and dēlos meaning clear, manifest. First coined by Humphry Osmond in correspondence with Aldous Huxley in describing the effects of Mescaline.
[33] For a great explanation of the basic concepts of quantum physics, in layman's terms, I recommend watching the 2006 release *What The Bleep: Down The Rabbit Hole*. Revolver Entertainment. This is a set of 5 DVD's which includes practical experiments, interviews, clips from the film *What The Bleep Do We Know* (2004) and even cartoons, to help explain things simply.

6. Practical Ways Of Opening Up to The Wisdom Of Plants

[34] Tompkins, Peter and Christopher Bird *The Secret Life of Plants*. 1973. Reprint, New York, NY: Harper Perennial, 2002. The whole of chapter 10 (pp145-162) discusses the effects of sounds on plant growth.
[35] https://www.businessinsider.com/magic-mushrooms-change-brain-connections-2014-10?r=US&IR=T *How Tripping On Mushrooms Changes The Brain*. Eric Brodwin. Business Insider. October 29, 2014.
[36] https://beckleyfoundation.org/ayahuasca-stimulates-the-birth-of-new-brain-cells/ *Ayahuasca Stimulates the Birth of New Brain Cells*. Jordi Riba. Beckley Foundation.

8. Plant Whisperer

[37] https://www.triplepundit.com/2013/02/water-make-shirts-impact-environment/ *It Takes 2700 Liters of Water to Make a T-shirt*. Julie Malone. February 6, 2013.
[38] https://www.theguardian.com/sustainable-business/2015/mar/20/cost-cotton-water-challenged-india-world-water-day *World Water Day: the cost of cotton in water-challenged India*. Stephen Leahy. March 20, 2015.

9. A Collaborative Future

[39] https://www.tawai.earth/

[40] http://www.bbc.co.uk/earth/story/20160421-the-chernobyl-exclusion-zone-is-arguably-a-nature-reserve *The Chernobyl exclusion zone is arguably a nature reserve.* Colin Barras. April 22, 2016.

[41] IPCC Special Report: *Global Warming of 1.5°C.* October, 2018. https://www.ipcc.ch/sr15/

Recommended Reading

Just a small selection of really inspiring books to help you take you new learnings further...

Abram, David. *Becoming Animal.* New York, NY: Vintage Books, 2011.
Blackie, Sharon. *If Women Rose Rooted.* September Publishing, 2016.
Buhner, Stephen Harrod. *The Fasting Path.* New York, NY: Avery, 2003.
Buhner, Stephen Harrod. *The Lost Language Of Plants.* White River Junction, VT: Chelsea Green Publishing Company, 2002.
Buhner, Stephen Harrod. *The Secret Teachings Of Plants.* Rochester, VT: Bear & Co., 2004.
Corby, Rachel. *Rewild Yourself: Becoming Nature.* Stroud, UK: Amanita Forrest Press, 2015.
Franckh, Pierre. *The DNA Field and the Law of Resonance: Creating Reality Through Conscious Thought.* Rochester, Vermont: Destiny Books, 2014.
Glendinning, Chellis. *My Name Is Chellis & I'm In Recovery From Western Civilisation.* Boston, Mass: Shambhala Publications Inc., 1994.
Harari, Yuval Noah. *Sapiens. A Brief History of Humankind.* (this edition) London: Harvill Secker, 2014.
Hughes, Nathaniel & Owen, Fiona. *Intuitive Herbalism.* Quintessence Press, 2014.
Hughes, Nathaniel & Owen, Fiona. *Weeds In The Heart.* Quintessence Press, 2016.
Monbiot, George. *Feral.* London: Penguin Books, 2013.
Mueller, Martin Lee. *Being Salmon Being Human.* White River Junction, VT: Chelsea Green Publishing, 2017.
Plotkin, Bill. *Soulcraft.* Novato, California: New World Library, 2003.
Wohlleben, Peter. *The Hidden Life of Trees.* Vancover, Canada: Greystone Books Ltd., 2015.
Wolfe, David. *The Sunfood Diet Success System.* San Diego, CA: Maul Brothers Publishing, 1999.

About The Author

Rachel is a plant whisperer, nature dreamer, biophile. Rachel first discovered the deep soul medicine of wild during the 1980's, whilst hiking among the mountains of Wales. Her first love affair with a plant followed not long after, in a wild Scottish valley. At the time she was researching the ecological niche different plants preferred as part of her degree dissertation. Since that time she has followed the call of the plants and the path that they have laid before her.

Under the direction of her plant allies Rachel completed a course in sustainable land use, an apprenticeship in sacred plant medicine and qualified as a plant spirit medicine practitioner. She has a great passion for cultivating her own plant foods and medicines.

Rachel loves to share her knowledge and encourage others to learn of native medicines through wild medicine foraging walks. She also encourages people to reconnect with their wild sensate body, and their belonging amongst wider nature, through forest bathing sessions.

Rachel has been guiding people to rediscover the art of plant whispering since 2006, when she ran her first workshop. Rachel currently mentors people from around the world online, and runs retreats, apprenticeships and 1-2-1 sessions in the UK and Europe, covering both plant whispering and personal rewilding.

Rachel lives in Stroud, UK, with her husband and many beloved plants.

For events and happenings visit Rachel's website www.wildgaiansoul.com or follow Rachel on Twitter/ Facebook/ Instagram: @mugwortdreamer

Other Books By Rachel Corby
The Medicine Garden
20 Amazing Plants & Their Practical Uses
Rewild Yourself: Becoming Nature

Printed in Great Britain
by Amazon